HELP YOUR KIDS WITH

MUSiC

HELP YOUR KIDS WITH

MUSiC

A UNIQUE STEP-BY-STEP VISUAL GUIDE

DK UK
Senior Editors Carron Brown, Chris Hawkes, Jenny Sich
Project Editor Lizzie Davey
Editor Kaiya Shang
US Editors Jill Hamilton, Margaret Parrish, Allison Singer
Senior Designer Sheila Collins
Designer Mabel Chan
Managing Editor Linda Esposito
Category Publisher Andrew Macintyre
Managing Art Editor Philip Letsu
Senior Producer, Pre-production Ben Marcus
Producer Christine Ni
Jackets Assistant Editor Claire Gell
Jacket Design Development Manager Sophia MTT
Associate Publishing Director Liz Wheeler
Publishing Director Jonathan Metcalf
Art Director Karen Self

DK DELHI
Project Editors Suefa Lee, Neha Pande
Project Art Editors Amit Malhotra, Parul Gambhir
Editor Sonia Yooshing
Art Editors Sanjay Chauhan, Vanya Mittal
Jacket Designer Suhita Dharamjit
Jacket Managing Editor Saloni Talwar
DTP Designers Harish Aggarwal, Sachin Gupta
Managing Editor Rohan Sinha
Managing Art Editor Sudakshina Basu
Pre-production Manager Balwant Singh

CD TEAM
CD Producers Kaiya Shang, Alex Valizadeh
Musicians Brian Chui, Amy Donaldson, Freya Gillon, Rosanna
Goodall, Alec Harmon, Will Henderson, Bethan Irving, Oscar Ikeda,
Cameron Johnson, Christopher Karwacinski, Alanna Macfarlane,
Paul Rosenberg, Ian Sankey, Alex Valizadeh, Simon Williams

First American Edition, 2015
Published in the United States by DK Publishing
345 Hudson Street, New York, New York 10014

A catalog record for this book is available from the
Library of Congress.
ISBN: 978-1-4654-3604-7

DK books are available at special discounts when purchased in bulk for sales
promotions, premiums, fund-raising, or educational use. For details, contact: DK
Publishing Special Markets, 345 Hudson Street, New York, New York 10014
SpecialSales@dk.com

Printed and bound in China

A WORLD OF IDEAS:
SEE ALL THERE IS TO KNOW

www.dk.com

CAROL VORDERMAN M.A. (Cantab), MBE is one of Britain's best-loved TV hosts and is renowned for her skills in mathematics, and her enthusiasm and encouragement for education. She hosts numerous shows on the BBC, ITV, and Channel 4, from light entertainment to scientific programs. From hosting Channel 4's *Countdown* for 26 years to becoming the second best-selling female nonfiction author of the noughties in the UK, Carol demonstartes a passion for education in all she does. Carol was a founding trustee of NESTA, is a patron of the Cambridge Science Festival, a member of the Royal Institution, a member of an advisory education panel for engineering, and a holder of many honorary degrees from universities around Britain.

COAUTHORS

PETER NICKOL is a music book editor, music typesetter, and composer. He is a member of SfEP (Society for Editors and Proofreaders) and teaches for them a one-day course on editing and proofreading music. He has written *Learning to Read Music* and cowritten *Pop Music: The Text Book*. His composing has taken up an increasing part of his time since the 1990s. Five of his compositions were shortlisted by the Society for Promotion of New Music, and in 2014 "Commuter" won the composition competition for the Big Bend Community Orchestra (Tallahassie, Florida, USA). For audio clips, visit: https://soundcloud.com/pnickol/tracks.

PETER QUANTRILL has written about music since graduating from the University of Cambridge in 1995. His reviews, interviews, articles, and features have appeared in *Gramophone*, *Opera* Magazine, *The Strad*, *The Wagner Journal*, and many other publications. For 10 years he commissioned and managed the editorial content of releases by EMI Classics, Warner Classics, Sony Classical, and other labels. He has made broadcasts for BBC Radio 3's *CD Review* and written program notes for the Salzburg Festival and Sir Paul McCartney, among others. He is a regular contributor to amati.com, *Sinfini Classical*, and *The Arts Desk*.

LAURA SANDFORD has several years' experience in the classical music industry, commissioning and editing CD and DVD booklets and notes for leading record labels such as Decca, Warner Classics, Sony Classical, and Opus Arte. Laura has taught children piano and music theory, and regularly participates in music educational outreach programs in London and southeast of England. In her spare time, Laura sings in two choirs and plays clarinet in various bands and chamber ensembles.

ANN MARIE STANLEY, Ph.D., has been on the music education faculty of the Eastman School of Music at the University of Rochester, in New York since 2007. Ann Marie is widely known for her in-depth qualitative research, engaging writing, and interactive teacher workshops—all of which center around ways to make music teaching and learning for elementary-school-aged children more musical, creative, and collaborative. She has written numerous journal articles and book chapters, and has made international presentations on music teaching. Before receiving her Ph.D. from the University of Michigan, Ann Marie taught general music, gave instrumental lessons, and conducted a children's choir for seven years in northern California.

SUE STURROCK is former Director of Communications at the Royal College of Music, London, England. She has contributed to many books about music, broadcast on BBC Radio, and written for *The Times*, *Classical Music*, *Music Teacher*, and other publications. Originally an orchestral oboist, Susan has taught, lectured, and coached in schools, universities, and conservatories internationally.

CONSULTANT

CLAIRE LANGFORD, BA, LGSM, PGCE, has been teaching music in UK secondary schools for 20 years since receiving her teaching degree from Homerton College, Cambridge, UK. She is currently a Lead Practitioner (AST) and Head of Music at Fort Pitt Grammar School in Kent, UK. Claire is also the secondary school representative for the "Dynamics" Music Hub, supporting teachers to raise standards and enjoyment of music education in Medway.

Foreword

Music is a powerful, memorable presence throughout our lives; it allows us to access, express, or alter our deepest feelings—whether joyful, peaceful, energetic, nostalgic, sorrowful, or angry. Music bonds us to others, and lets us intimately experience our own unique, artistic creativity. Music is one of the most personal ways we have of making sense of our world.

Music is invaluable in the lives of children. Students who learn and make music get to practice all sorts of skills: choosing interpretations, making inventive decisions, solving problems, breaking down difficult issues into manageable subsections, practicing perseverance, and being creative. A musical education helps young people see themselves as artistic beings.

Too often, musical learning is considered a special endeavor reserved for the innately talented. In truth, musical knowledge is not a mysterious gift bestowed upon a lucky few with high musical aptitude. Rather, learning music relies upon understanding and successfully using the systems musicians have created through the years to organize and notate sound. These musical conventions, both aural and written, are best learned in a sequential, orderly way. *Help Your Kids With Music* is just that: a thoughtful, systematic approach to understanding the building blocks of music.

Parents and students with little prior knowledge will benefit from the logical way elements of music are organized in this book. The book progresses methodically explaining the key concepts of music—pitch, rhythm, intervals and keys, melody, harmony, form, instruments, and styles—through clear, easy-to-grasp graphics and text. Detailed annotations of musical examples illustrate how theoretical concepts are used in the real-world practice of composers and performers. Precise definitions of terminology enable readers to use the book as a handy reference guide.

The approach to musicianship presented in this book is organized in a thoughtful way that will allow parents and children working together to "crack the code" of music, and achieve a deeper understanding of this art that is so important to so many of us.

ANN MARIE STANLEY, PH.D.

Assistant Professor of Music Education, Eastman School of Music

Thomas Tallis (c.1505–1585), **Giuseppe Ottavio Pitoni** (1657–1743), **Alessandro Scarlatti** (1660–1725), **Antonio Lotti** (1667–1740), **Johann Sebastian Bach** (1685–1750), **Giovanni Battista Pergolesi** (1710–1736), **Domenico Alberti** (1710–1740), **Johann Stamitz** (1717–1757), **Franz Pokorny** (1729–1794), **Joseph Haydn** (1732–1809), **Wolfgang Amadeus Mozart** (1756–1791), **Ludwig van Beethoven** (1770–1827), **Franz Schubert** (1797–1828), **Heinrich Heine** (1797–1856), **Felix Mendelssohn** (1809–1847), **Frédéric Chopin** (1810–1849), **Franz Liszt** (1811–1886), **Richard Wagner** (1813–1883), **Johannes Brahms** (1833–1897), **Nikolai Rimsky-Korsakov** (1844–1908), **Edward Elgar** (1857–1934), **Gustav Mahler** (1860–1911), **Claude Debussy** (1862–1918), **Scott Joplin** (c.1868–1917), **Ralph Vaughan Williams** (1872–1958), **Arnold Schönberg** (1874–1951), **Olivier Messiaen** (1908–1992), **Dizzy Gillespie** (1917–1993), **Leonard Bernstein** (1918–1990), **Miles Davis** (1926–1991), **Elvis Presley** (1935–1977), **John Lennon** (1940–1980), **Paul Simon** (b.1941), **Paul McCartney** (b.1942), **Eric Clapton** (b.1945), **Michael Jackson** (1958–2009), **Mariah Carey** (b.1970

Contents

Look for this sign, which gives a track number for the CD. Listen to and experience extracts of music featured in the book.

What is music?

We create music by organizing sounds. All around the world people make music to accompany their lives—singing, playing musical instruments, finding rhythms, melodies, and combinations of sounds.

The origins of music

Music began with singing, with percussive sounds using wood, stone, and animal skins, and with flutes made from bamboo or other suitable plants. We began by imitating natural sounds—birdsong especially—just as the earliest painters drew the animals they saw.

▷ **Lyre**
Among the first string instruments to be developed, lyres were popular in Egypt and Mesopotamia, and later in ancient Greece.

▷ **Chinese pellet drum**
A pellet drum has two heads, and two pellets, or hard beads, each connected to the drum by a cord. The beads strike the drum alternately when it twists back and forth.

The sounds around us

Many sounds such as wind, rain, and thunder occur naturally. Others are made by animals and birds, or by us when we breathe, laugh, or cry. There are accidental sounds, the by-products of work, the sounds of machines, of footsteps on a pavement, or the sound of marching soldiers. Musicians often draw on such sounds for inspiration, imitating them with voices or instruments.

◁ **Creating music**
We create music by organizing sounds in different ways to make melody, harmony, and rhythm. There are always new ways of combining and shaping sounds.

MELODY
Melody concerns pitch— how high or low the notes are. A melody is formed when a sequence of notes of varying pitch is played or sung.

HARMONY
Harmony is what we get when different notes (notes of different pitch) are produced at the same time. Different combinations of pitches can be consonant (harmonious) or dissonant.

RHYTHM
Melody and rhythm are what we hear as the music moves forward in time. Rhythm concerns the duration of notes, and the way in which they are played or sung in relation to a regular beat or pulse.

Writing music

Sounds have pitch—higher or lower. They also have duration—longer or shorter. When music is written, pitch is represented vertically (high or low) and time is represented horizontally, setting out the notes (long or short, fast or slow) from left to right, with different symbols showing rhythm and tempo.

◁ **Music symbols**
The difference between the symbols tells us about their duration, or time value. We will learn about pitch, key, structure, and so on with the use of other symbols.

▷ **Staff**
The staff is formed of five thin, parallel lines. It is used to show the pitch of different notes.

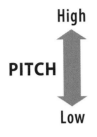

High

PITCH

Low

TIME

Unpitched sounds

Most musical sounds have a definite pitch, but some percussion sounds are unpitched, for instance drums, cymbals, and woodblocks. They make a characteristic sound rather than having a definite pitch. Some percussion instruments come in sets, ranging from larger (lower pitch) to smaller (higher pitch). Examples of such instruments are shown below.

Temple blocks are traditionally shaped like a dragon's mouth.

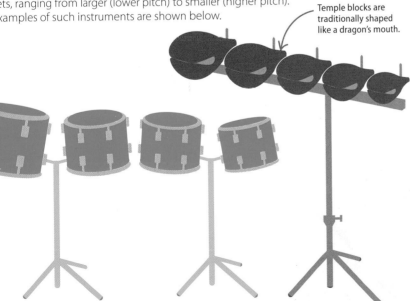

△ **Tom-tom drum**
Tom-toms are cylindrical drums that are mounted on stands; the smaller drums are higher pitched. Drummers often play a flourish from high to low.

△ **Temple block**
Temple blocks resonate with a wooden crack and usually come in a set of five.

Live music-making

A tambourine, with its complex mixture of metallic bell-sounds along with the hand striking the wooden shell, makes a vivid addition to any percussion group or rhythm section. Instruments are distinguished by their timbre, or tone color. This, along with the melody, harmony, and rhythm, makes a big contribution to music—what it expresses and how we experience it.

Pitch

High and low

When we play notes on an instrument, one at a time, or sing a few notes, we can distinguish one note from another by their pitch—some notes are higher, and some are lower.

How music sounds are made

Musical sounds are vibrations in the air. When the vibrations are regular, we can hear exact pitches. We hear high notes when the vibrations are fast, and lower notes when the vibrations are slower.

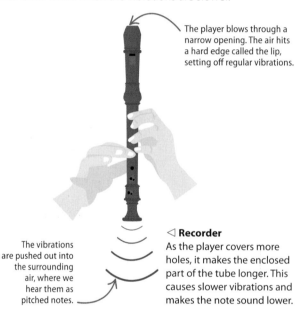

The player blows through a narrow opening. The air hits a hard edge called the lip, setting off regular vibrations.

The vibrations are pushed out into the surrounding air, where we hear them as pitched notes.

◁ **Recorder**
As the player covers more holes, it makes the enclosed part of the tube longer. This causes slower vibrations and makes the note sound lower.

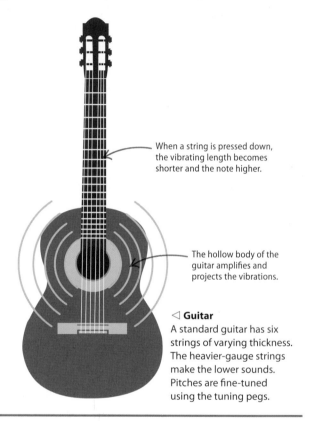

When a string is pressed down, the vibrating length becomes shorter and the note higher.

The hollow body of the guitar amplifies and projects the vibrations.

◁ **Guitar**
A standard guitar has six strings of varying thickness. The heavier-gauge strings make the lower sounds. Pitches are fine-tuned using the tuning pegs.

High and low sounds

Smaller objects generally vibrate faster and make higher sounds. On a piano or harp, the shorter strings make the high notes. In families of instruments, such as saxophones or the violin family, the smaller instruments play the higher notes. Tuned percussion instruments, such as the xylophone, have a set of bars graded from large (low notes) to small (high notes).

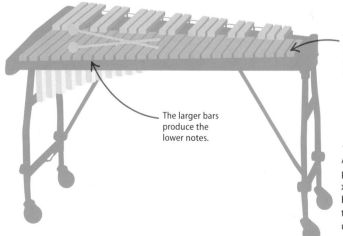

The xylophone keys are hard and polished, producing a short, clear-pitched note when struck.

The larger bars produce the lower notes.

◁ **Xylophone**
A member of the tuned percussion family, xylophones have wooden bars and resonating tubes that help pick up the vibrations and amplify them.

Notes and octaves

Notes are named using seven letters of the alphabet from A to G. After G, the sequence starts again with A, as shown in the diagram below. The distance from one A to the next A, or one B to the next B, is called an octave (from the Latin *octavus*, eighth). This sequence of note names from A to G repeats through the audible range of around ten octaves.

▷ **Note names**
This diagram shows the note names over a range of two octaves. A piano has a range of about seven octaves, and the human ear can detect around ten octaves from the lowest notes to the highest.

These two As are two octaves apart.

Two octaves

One octave

The distance from one A to the next A is one octave.

◁ **Octaves**
Any two notes that are an octave apart have a very similar quality, making them sound almost like the same note, even though one is higher than the other. We hear this similarity through any series of notes with the same letter name. Try getting someone to play scales up and down the white notes on a piano, and then ask them to pick out the notes with the same letter name.

Playing **octaves with one hand** is a characteristic of **ragtime piano** playing and many **other styles**.

Why octaves are special

There is a scientific reason why two notes an octave apart sound similar, even though one is higher-pitched than the other. This is because the higher note vibrates exactly twice as fast as the lower one.

▷ **Sound waves**
This diagram represents two sound waves. The upper one is vibrating twice as fast as the lower one, so the sound we hear from it is one octave higher.

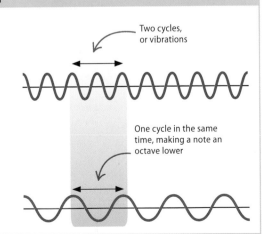

Two cycles, or vibrations

One cycle in the same time, making a note an octave lower

The piano keyboard

To understand note names and octaves, it is helpful to look at a piano keyboard. The pattern of white keys and black keys explains a lot about how pitch is organized.

The piano keyboard

The distinctive pattern of black keys—grouped alternately in twos and threes—marks out the octaves. Each octave has seven white keys—A B C D E F G—and five black keys. A full-sized keyboard usually has around seven octaves. The central C on the keyboard is called Middle C, and this is a fixed point of reference, which is important when music is written down in notation.

REAL WORLD

Grand piano

The piano is the most versatile of instruments, and many string, brass, and wind players like to learn it as a second instrument. Unlike most wind and string instruments, it can play several notes at the same time—for instance a melody plus chordal accompaniment.

The black keys occur in twos and threes. This pattern marks out the octaves, and enables us to locate the white keys. 🔊 1

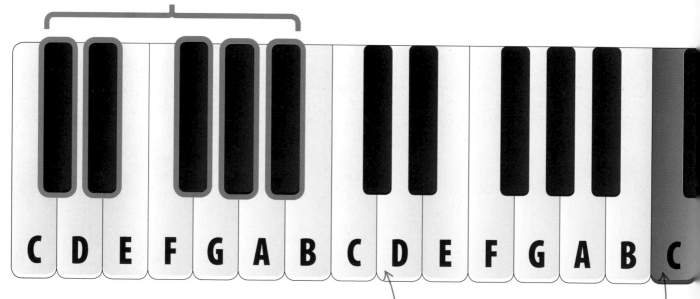

△ **The piano**
With its unique layout, the piano is a useful instrument for learning music theory. The relationships between the notes, especially the white and black keys, is made clear.

The white key between the two black keys grouped in twos is always D. C is always the white key just below these two black keys.

🔊 2 The C nearest the middle of a full-size keyboard is called Middle C.

LOOKING CLOSER

Note names in other languages

The note names A to G are not used everywhere. German note names are slightly different from English ones, and include an H—the composer J. S. Bach used the letters of his name B A C H as a musical theme. Some countries, such as France, use "do re mi" for C D E, while for many people "do" is movable; the do-re-mi scale can start on any note.

English B♭ = German B

English B = German H

◁ **Note names in German**
German-speaking musicians use two different note names. B in German is B♭ (the black key just below B) in English, and H in German is B in English.

▷ **French, Italian, and Spanish**
French, Italian, and Spanish musicians use "do re mi fa sol la si" in place of "C D E F G A B."

| do | re | mi | fa | sol | la | si |

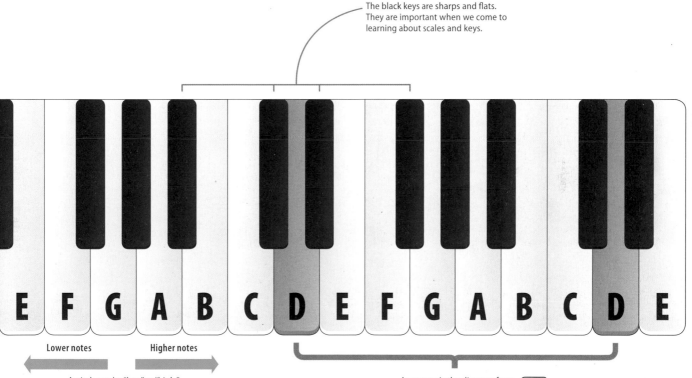

The black keys are sharps and flats. They are important when we come to learning about scales and keys.

E F G A B C D E F G A B C D E

Lower notes   Higher notes

A pitch can be "low" or "high." On a piano keyboard, this works from left to right—the highest notes are at the right-hand end of the keyboard and the lowest notes are at the left-hand end.

An octave is the distance from one note to the next one with the same letter name. These two Ds are one octave apart.

 3

Notes on the staff

Writing music, like writing words, evolved as a way of recording or fixing musical ideas or compositions. It enabled these ideas to be passed from one generation to another, or carried from one place to another.

The staff

When we write down a piece of music, or "notate" it, we use a staff consisting of five parallel lines. Notes are written on the staff, placing them higher or lower according to their pitch. The staff is the basic background element in nearly all music notation.

△ **High and low on the staff**
Higher-pitched notes go toward the top of the staff, while lower-pitched notes are placed toward the bottom.

Using staff lines and spaces

Notes are placed on the lines, or in the spaces between them. Below you can see notes written on each of the five lines of the staff (on the left), and in each of the four spaces (on the right). The staff in itself does not define the pitch of a written note; a clef is also needed.

▽ **Careful placing of notes**
When writing music by hand, always be careful to make it clear whether the note head is on the line or in a space.

Evolution of the staff

Music was written by monks to help remember the melodies that accompanied religious texts. Early notation showed the shape of a melody—how the notes rise and fall—using marks placed above or below a single horizontal line. A more detailed picture of the rise and fall of a melody could be shown with more than one staff line. Early examples of written music used a four-line staff, but the five-line staff became standardized around 1500.

Single-line staves, or staves with **two, three, or four lines,** still have their uses. **Percussion lines** are often **written** on a **one-line staff**, because the information is **rhythmic rather than melodic**.

Stems and note heads

Most notes in the top half of the staff have downstems, and notes in the bottom half have upstems, but there are many exceptions to this, for instance when two lines of music are written on the same staff.

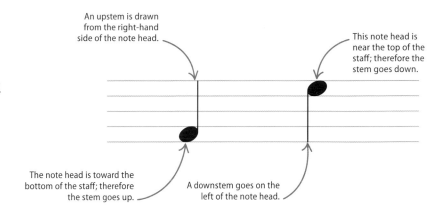

An upstem is drawn from the right-hand side of the note head.

This note head is near the top of the staff; therefore the stem goes down.

The note head is toward the bottom of the staff; therefore the stem goes up.

A downstem goes on the left of the note head.

Practicing writing notes
You can buy books of blank manuscript paper, useful for practicing writing notes and other musical elements such as clefs.

△ **Note with upstem**
Draw the notehead carefully in the space, or on the line, as desired. Then, for a low note like this one, add an upstem, starting on the right-hand edge of the note head.

△ **Note on the middle line**
By convention, a note on the middle line has a downstem. Draw the note head first, then a downstem starting on the left-hand edge.

Ledger lines

With its five lines and four spaces, the staff covers just a little over an octave. However, it can be extended, upward or downward, by adding short lines called ledger lines. Notes can be placed on these lines, or in the spaces, in exactly the same way as on the staff.

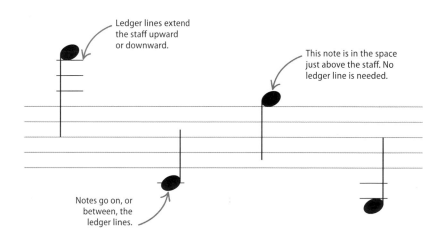

Ledger lines extend the staff upward or downward.

This note is in the space just above the staff. No ledger line is needed.

Notes go on, or between, the ledger lines.

▷ **How many ledger lines can you add?**
Theoretically, there is no limit to the number of ledger lines that can be added, but in practice they can become difficult to read if there are more than about four ledger lines.

Clefs

A clef is normally written at the start—the left-hand end—of every staff on the page. It fixes the pitches of the lines and spaces.

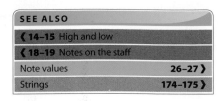
SEE ALSO

⟨ **14–15** High and low
⟨ **18–19** Notes on the staff
Note values   **26–27** ⟩
Strings   **174–175** ⟩

What is a clef?

Clefs are some of the most important signs used to write music. Music notation uses clefs with staves to show what pitch a composer wants in the music. The two most common clefs are the treble and the bass clefs. A third, the C clef, is less common, but is used by particular instruments.

◁ **Treble clef**
The shape of the treble clef has become symbolic of music in general. It evolved from the letter G, because it marks the position of the note G on the staff.

◁ **Bass clef**
The bass clef is often seen and used in sheet music. It evolved from the letter F, as its purpose was to mark the position of the note F on the staff.

The treble clef

The most common clef is the treble clef, also known as the G clef. The treble clef is widely used by singers and for playing many instruments. It is the usual clef used for writing down a tune.

◁ **The G clef**
The center of the treble clef encloses the second line up—the G note, curling around it. This fixes that line as the G above Middle C.

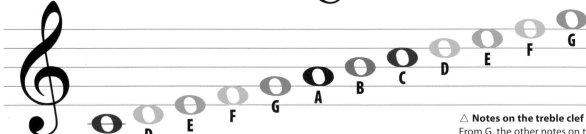

△ **Notes on the treble clef**
From G, the other notes on the staff can be worked out by going forward or backward through the musical alphabet.

The bass clef

The second most common clef is the bass clef, which is also known as an F clef. The bass clef is used by many low-pitched instruments, including cello, bassoon, timpani, and bass guitar, and also by bass singers.

◁ **The F clef**
The note on the second line down is the F below Middle C. The bass clef is placed on the staff with two dots on either side of this line, fixing that line as the F below Middle C.

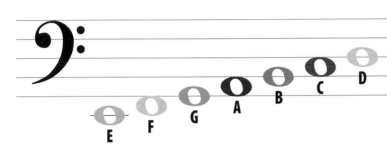

△ **Notes on the bass clef**
Once F is fixed, the other notes on the staff can be worked out by going forward or backward through the musical alphabet.

Both clefs together

The treble and bass clefs are often paired. The combination of these two clefs is very common and useful, because it covers the ranges of most voices and many instruments.

▷ **Writing Middle C**
Middle C is written on the first ledger line below the staff with the treble clef. Or it is written on the first ledger line above the staff with the bass clef.

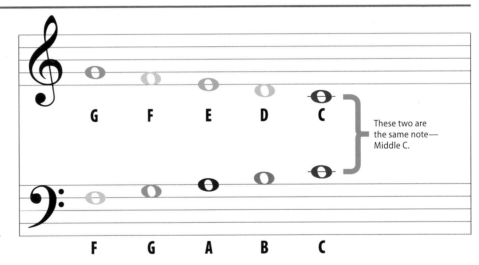

These two are the same note—Middle C.

LOOKING CLOSER

C clefs

The third type of clef is a C clef. Its center, where the two curves meet, points to Middle C. A movable clef, it sometimes points to the middle line of the staff, where it is called an alto clef. When it points to the second line down it is called a tenor clef. The line that it points to is always Middle C.

△ **The alto clef**
This clef fixes Middle C on the central line of the staff. It is regularly used by viola players, as it suits the range of their lower strings.

△ **The tenor clef**
This clef fixes Middle C on the second line down. It is sometimes used by cello, bassoon, or trombone players, when they are playing their higher notes.

Rhythm

Beats and measures

Most music has a regular beat or pulse, like a ticking clock, that propels it forward in time. A conductor stands in front of an orchestra to show the beat and keep everyone together.

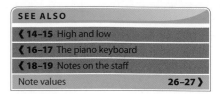
Beats

Beats are music's heartbeat. Underlying each piece of music is a regular beat or pulse, irrespective of whether it is fast or slow, or whether we can hear it or not. We can only feel it; it is the background to the music.

 4

▽ **A regular beat**
The red triangles represent a regular beat or pulse. They are not the actual music, but we need to feel the beat even before we start playing.

▲　▲　▲　▲　▲　▲　▲　▲　▲　▲　▲　▲

Meter

When a regular pattern of accents is imposed on the pulse, so that some beats are stronger than others, it is called a meter. The meter gives the beat a character, depending on how many weak beats come between each strong beat. The beats can be marked off in groups of 2, 3, or 4.

 5

◁ **In 2s**
Try repeating the numbers in a regular pattern, like a march, **1**, 2, **1**, 2, emphasizing the 1s.

1　2　**1**　2　**1**　2　**1**　2　**1**　2　**1**　2

◁ **In 3s**
Now shift to 3-time, repeating the numbers **1**, 2, 3, **1**, 2, 3 **1**, 2, 3, still emphasizing the 1s.

1　2　3　**1**　2　3　**1**　2　3　**1**　2　3

◁ **In 4s**
These beats are grouped in 4s: one of the most common musical meters, especially in pop music.

1　2　3　4　**1**　2　3　4　**1**　2　3　4

Can you hear the beat?

The beat is not always audible, through long notes for instance, but it continues as a regular measure of time. Performers nearly always keep counting, or feeling, the beat in their head, even through slow music, or long notes, or when they aren't playing.

1 2 1 2

△ **Counting beats**
Musicians feel the pulse, the steady flow of beats. Most of the time they count beats without thinking about it.

Measures and bar lines

The meter—the grouping of beats into a regular pattern of strong and weak beats—is marked off in measures. Measures and bar lines help performers keep track of where they are, and ensure that they keep playing together. The first beat in each measure is a strong beat. Musicians, particularly in orchestras, spend a lot of time counting beats and, if there's a long gap when they don't play, counting measures, so that they "come in" (start playing) at the right moment.

▽ **Bar lines**
Bar lines are drawn through the staff so that music can be read one measure at a time.

Bar lines separate one measure from another, and are an essential visual aid to reading music.

This is one measure

This is the next measure

REAL WORLD

The conductor shows the beat

The most important role of a conductor is to set the beat and tempo of the composition. Conductors use patterns associated with the different meters, which are widely understood by singers and instrumentalists. The first beat of each measure is normally indicated by a downbeat. In slow-moving music, the conductor may show the beat although no new notes are being played.

Differences in musical terminology between the US and Britain: Americans use **"measure"** for "bar" and **"measure number"** for "bar number." **"Bar line,"** however, means the same in both countries.

Note values

The time value of a note is relative to that of other notes. Rhythms are created when patterns of longer or shorter notes are played or sung against the background of the steady pulse and meter.

Time values of notes

Here are the five most common note values. Notice how they are drawn—whether the note head is filled in, if there is a note stem, or if there is a tail or flag (see p.28) attached to the stem. You could practice writing these on a sheet of music paper, taking care to put the note head clearly on a line or in a space.

△ **Whole note**
This is a long note, equal to four quarter notes. The note head is not filled in and there is no stem.

△ **Half note**
A half note has half the time value of a whole note, and twice the value of a quarter note.

△ **Quarter note**
A very common time value, a quarter note is often the note value chosen for the beat.

△ **Eighth note**
Equal to half a quarter note, an eighth note is distinguished by its tail or flag.

△ **Sixteenth note**
A sixteenth note is short, half as long as an eighth. It has two tails or flags joined to the stem.

Tempo

Note values are not measured in an absolute way. A quarter note may last a long time if the tempo is slow, or a short time if the tempo is fast. "Tempo" is the word used to describe the speed of the music. The same rhythm may be played fast or slow, depending on the tempo.

△ **Tempo indication**
This rhythm could be played both fast or slow. Until we add a tempo indication (see p.44), we cannot tell simply from the way this is written.

LOOKING CLOSER

Other note values

Apart from the common note values shown above, you may also come across longer notes such as a double whole note or shorter ones such as a thirty-second note, or even a sixty-fourth.

△ **Double whole note**
Twice as long as a whole note, this is rarely encountered.

△ **Thirty-second note**
A thirty-second note is a short note, half as long as a sixteenth.

△ **Sixty-fourth note**
A sixty-fourth note is even shorter—half as long as a thirty-second.

Relative, not absolute

Always remember that note values are not measured in seconds, they are measured in relation to each other. A quarter note is always half as long as a half note, and a sixteenth note is always half as long as a eighth note. A half note is always twice as long as a quarter note, and a whole note is always twice as long as a half note.

 6 ▽ **Note values**
The chart below shows how the note values relate to each other. Each column represents one quarter note, so the whole note stretches across four quarter notes.

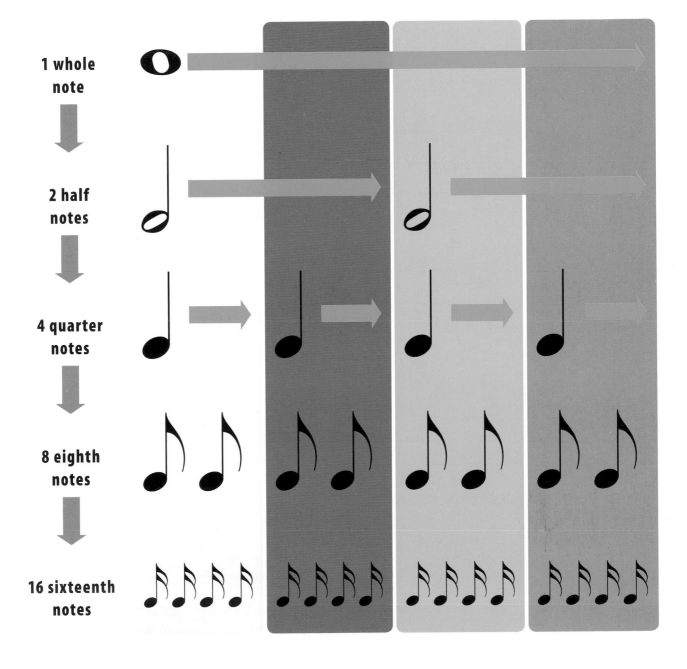

1 whole note

2 half notes

4 quarter notes

8 eighth notes

16 sixteenth notes

Beams and dots

Beams and dots are two ways of making rhythms easier to read. Beams join groups of eighth or sixteenth notes. Dots, placed after the note head, extend the duration of the note by half again.

SEE ALSO

❰ **18–19** Notes on the staff

❰ **26–27** Note values

Time signatures   **30–31** ❱

Stems and tails

The straight line attached to a quarter note head is called a stem. Upstems are written on the right-hand side of the note head, and downstems are written on the left of the note head. The curved line attached to an eighth note stem is called a tail or flag. Tails are always on the right-hand side of the stem, whether it's an upstem or a downstem.

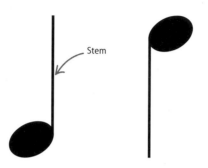

△ **Quarter note**
A note with a stem but no tail is called a quarter note. Downstems are on the left, upstems are on the right.

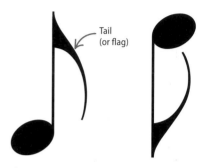

△ **Eighth note**
A note with one tail is called an eighth. Two tails make it a sixteenth. The tail always goes on the right of the stem.

Beams

Two or more consecutive eighth notes can be joined together with a thick line called a beam, which replaces the individual tails. Sixteenth or thirty-second notes can also be joined in the same way. Beams are used to make the rhythm and beat structure as clear and easy to read as possible.

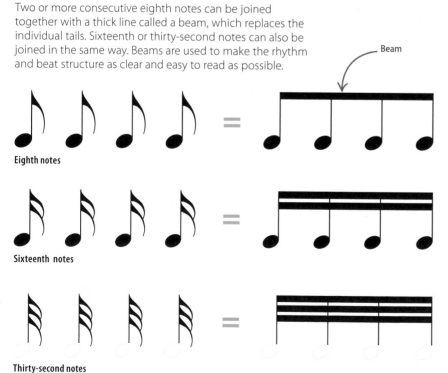

Eighth notes

Sixteenth notes

Thirty-second notes

REAL WORLD

Handwriting eighths

When writing an eighths by hand, it is acceptable to use a straight line for the tail. The important thing when writing music by hand is to make it clear. The notehead should be either on the line or in a space. When writing a group of notes, ensure that there is good spacing between them.

Dotted notes

When a note is followed by a dot, it makes the note 1½ times longer. The dotted quarter note shown below is 1½ times longer than a quarter. In the same way, a dotted eighth note is 1½ times longer than an eighth, and a dotted half is 1½ times longer than a half.

Double-dotted notes

Double-dotted notes also exist. The second dot adds another ¼ of the original note value, so that a double-dotted quarter note is 1¾ as long as a quarter.

▽ **Dotted half**
Half a half note is a quarter note. Therefore, a dotted half has the same time value as three quarter notes.

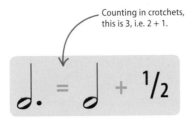

Counting in crotchets, this is 3, i.e. 2 + 1.

▽ **Double-dotted eighth note**
Double-dotted notes are much less common than dotted notes. Double-dotted eighth notes are sometimes combined with a thirty-second note.

Writing dotted notes

Dots are placed after the note head, to the right. This is easy if the note head is in one of the spaces of the staff, but what if it's on a line? The dot would be harder to see, so instead it goes in the space above.

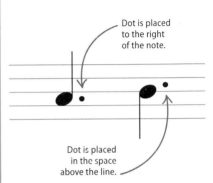

Dot is placed to the right of the note.

Dot is placed in the space above the line.

△ **Placing the dot**
Shown here are two dotted quarter notes, one in a space and the other on a line. The second note is on a line, so its dot is placed in the space above.

Note value sums

Different combinations of note values "add up" to make the same total. Just as in math, you can find the lowest common denominator to check the sum. For instance, the lowest common denominator in the first example is an eighth note.

△ **1**
Two dotted quarter notes have the same total time value as one dotted half note. Counting in eighth notes, this is 3 + 3 = 6.

△ **2**
In quarter notes, this is 1½ + 1½ + 1 = 4. Or in eighths, 3 + 3 + 2 = 8. This rhythm is often used in popular music.

△ **3**
The dotted rhythm—dotted eighth note and thirty-second together—is very common. Each unit here lasts one quarter note.

△ **4**
Double-dotted eighth notes are sometimes paired with thirty-second notes to make a jerky rhythm.

Time signatures

At the beginning of a piece of music, we mark the meter using a time signature. It tells us the number of beats in each measure and the time value of each beat.

Naming the meter

When we talk about the meter in a piece of music, we say, for instance, "two-four," with the top number first. If we are writing text, we can write "2/4," but we must remember that it is not a fraction.

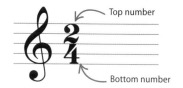

Top number

Bottom number

◁ **Time signature**
There is a top and a bottom number, but a time signature is not a fraction.

The top number

This shows how many beats there are in each measure. It tells us how to count as we read or play the music. Similarly, it tells a conductor how to beat time.

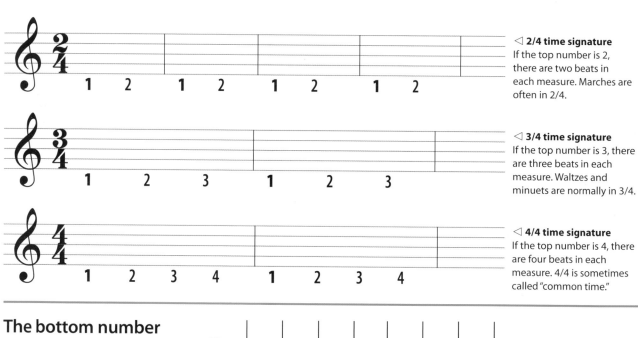

◁ **2/4 time signature**
If the top number is 2, there are two beats in each measure. Marches are often in 2/4.

◁ **3/4 time signature**
If the top number is 3, there are three beats in each measure. Waltzes and minuets are normally in 3/4.

◁ **4/4 time signature**
If the top number is 4, there are four beats in each measure. 4/4 is sometimes called "common time."

The bottom number

The bottom number describes which note value is used for the beat. When the bottom number is 4, as in these examples, it means the beat is a quarter note. The quarter note is the most common note value for a beat.

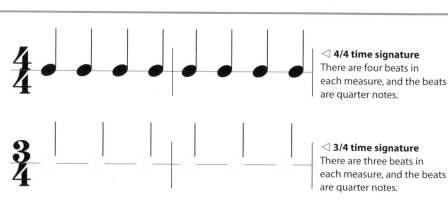

◁ **4/4 time signature**
There are four beats in each measure, and the beats are quarter notes.

◁ **3/4 time signature**
There are three beats in each measure, and the beats are quarter notes.

Beats are not always quarter notes

The most common time signature is 4/4, followed by 3/4 and 2/4, but the beat does not always have to be a quarter note. It could be a half note (in which case the bottom number would be 2), an eighth note (the bottom number is 8), or a sixteenth note (the bottom number is 16).

△ **2/2 time signature**
Each measure has two beats, and the beats are half notes.

△ **3/2 time signature**
Each measure has three beats, and the beats are half notes.

△ **3/8 time signature**
Each measure has three beats, and the beats are eighth notes.

△ **3/16 time signature**
Each measure has three beats, and the beats are sixteenth notes.

Common and cut time

The C time signature symbol, often called "common time," is exactly the same as 4/4. Another symbol you might see is the C symbol with a line through it. This is the same as 2/2 and is often called "cut time."

◁ **Common time, or 4/4**
The C is just another way of writing 4/4. There are four quarter notes in each measure.

◁ **Cut time, or 2/2**
This is another way of writing 2/2. There are two half notes in each measure.

Unusual time signatures

A versatile time signature, 4/4 is very common in pop music. But there is no rule against having an unusual top number, and a composer may choose this if he wants a different rhythmic feel. "Mars" from *The Planets* by Gustav Holst is a famous example of a piece in 5/4.

◁ **5/4 time signature**
There are five beats in each measure, and the beats are quarter notes.

◁ **7/8 time signature**
There are seven beats in each measure, and the beats are eighth notes.

Waltz

Musicians are not the only people who need to know about meter and time signatures. Dancers also count beats and measures. Different types of dance are distinguished by their meter, and by their typical rhythms. Waltzes are in 3/4 or 3/8, tangos in 2/4, and both use characteristic rhythmic patterns.

Compound time

Compound time refers to the meters where the beat is subdivided into three parts instead of the more usual two. For this to be possible, the beat is always a dotted note, such as a dotted quarter note.

SEE ALSO

❮ **26–27** Note values

❮ **28–29** Beams and dots

❮ **30–31** Time signatures

Grouping notes **36–37** ❯

Dotted quarter notes

Compound time signatures are an exception to the rule about the bottom number. For instance, in 6/8 there are six eighth notes in the measure, but the beat isn't an eighth note, it's a dotted quarter note worth three eighth notes with two beats in each measure. Similarly, 9/8 time has three dotted quarter notes in each measure, and 12/8 has four.

▷ **6/8, 9/8, 12/8**
These three time signatures are all compound time meters, with each beat being a dotted quarter note.

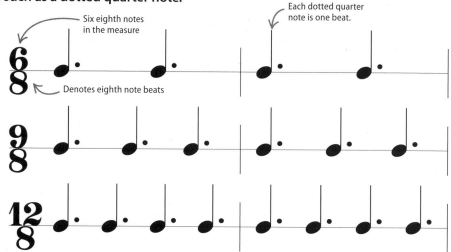

Six eighth notes in the measure

Denotes eighth note beats

Each dotted quarter note is one beat.

Simple time, compound time

The meters 2/4, 3/4, and 4/4 are examples of simple time. The beat can be subdivided into two—each quarter note divides into two eighth notes. 6/8, 9/8, and 12/8 are compound time signatures. Each beat in these time signatures is divided into three. It is helpful to compare 3/4 with 6/8, because they have the same number of eighth notes in each measure, but the note value of the beat and the way it subdivides are different.

 7

◁ **Simple time**
This example shows the beats and subdivisions in 3/4 time. There are three beats per measure, each subdividing into two eighth notes.

◁ **Compound time**
Shown here are the beats and subdivisions in 6/8 time. There are two beats per measure, each subdividing into three eighth notes.

Other compound time signatures

Other dotted note values can also be used for the beat. In 3/2, there are three half note beats per measure (simple time), but 6/4 is a compound time signature—the beat is a dotted half note, and there are two beats in each measure. Compound time signatures normally have 6, 9, or 12 as the top number (multiples of three).

△ **3/2**
In 3/2, there are three half notes per measure (simple time). Each half note subdivides into two quarter notes.

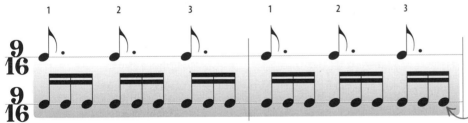

△ **6/4**
In 6/4, the beat is a dotted half note and there are two beats in each measure. Each dotted half note subdivides into three quarter notes.

One in a measure

Some fast music, typically in 2/4, 3/4, or 3/8, is too fast for a conductor to beat all the quarter notes or eighth notes. In those instances, musicians talk about the music having a "one in a measure" feel—the conductor beats one beat per measure. The second movement of Beethoven's *Ninth Symphony*, marked "Molto vivace," is a good example.

◁ **9/16**
A 9/16 meter might be used for fast dancelike music, with three beats to the measure—each beat being a dotted eighth note.

In 9/16, each beat subdivides into three sixteenth notes.

Irregular beat-groupings

Simple time signatures can be subdivided in irregular ways. A typical example has a 4/4 meter divided into a 3 + 3 + 2 pattern (where the numbers count as eighth notes), instead of the standard four quarter note beats. This sort of meter is widespread in African Caribbean and Latin American music.

 8

▽ **Calypso rhythm**
The 3 + 3 + 2 pattern is particularly associated with calypso, but can be heard in folk and popular music from many parts of the world.

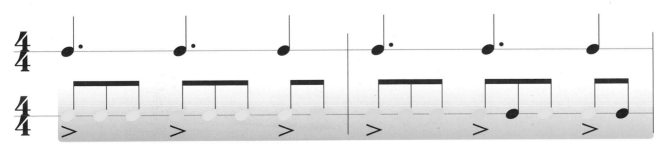

Rests and ties

Rests and ties are two essential elements in music notation. Rests are used to notate silences within the music. Ties join two or more notes together to form a longer note.

SEE ALSO
❰ **24–25** Beats and measures
❰ **26–27** Note values
❰ **28–29** Beams and dots
❰ **30–31** Time signatures

Gaps in the music

Rests assign a time value to silences—gaps in the music during which a player or singer does not produce any sound. They work just like notes and have the same time values. When playing or writing music, the rests are just as important as the notes.

▽ **Rests**
The flowchart below shows rests and how their time values relate to each other. It corresponds to the chart of note time values (see page 27).

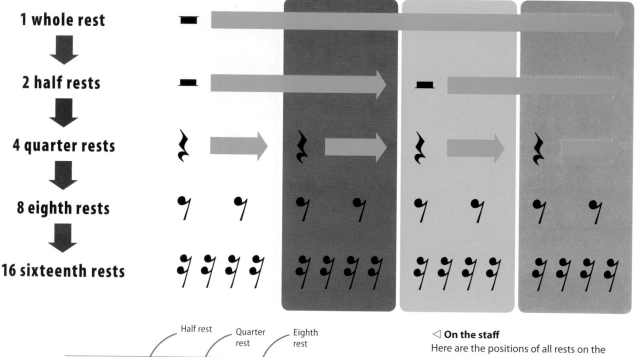

1 whole rest

2 half rests

4 quarter rests

8 eighth rests

16 sixteenth rests

Half rest

Quarter rest

Eighth rest

Whole rest

Sixteenth rest

◁ **On the staff**
Here are the positions of all rests on the staff. A half rest sits on a staff line, usually the third line from the bottom. A whole rest hangs from a staff line, usually the second line down.

Whole measure rests

The symbol for the whole rest is also used as a whole measure rest in any time signature. Whole measure rests are centered within the measure, not placed at the left-hand end.

◁ **Whole measure rests in action**
This example has a 3/16 time signature. The rest indicates silence for the whole measure, regardless of the meter.

Notes and rests together

Most music is a mixture of notes and rests. The examples below show how they might be combined in different time signatures. Note how the rests and notes always add up to the correct time value indicated by the time signature.

◁ **Notes and rests in action**
Look at these examples and try to hear the rhythm in your head—imagining how the rests contribute to the musical effect. For wind players or singers, the music needs to allow them spaces to breathe. Rests are a common way of achieving this.

Dotted rests

Just like notes, rests of all time values can also be dotted, making them one-and-a-half times as long. Two examples, a dotted quarter rest and a dotted eighth rest, are shown here.

△ **Dotted quarter rest**
The dotted quarter rest has a time value of $1^1/_2$ quarter notes, the same as a quarter note plus a eighth note.

△ **Dotted eighth rest**
The time value of a dotted eighth rest is $1^1/_2$ eighth notes, the same as an eighth note plus a sixteenth note.

Ties

Two notes can be joined by a tie to make a single, longer note. Joining notes serves various purposes—a composer may want a note that cannot be represented by a single time value, or a very long note that goes across several measures. Sometimes the rhythm is easier to read using a tie than it is by having a single note that crosses a beat.

◁ **A single longer note**
The half note is tied to the eighth note, making a single longer note. Its time value cannot be represented by a single note, so a tie is used.

◁ **Across a bar line**
Ties are often used to join notes across a bar line. The notes and rests within a measure must never exceed the time value of the measure.

◁ **Adding tied notes**
Several tied notes can be added together to achieve the desired length of a note.

Grouping notes

The way a rhythm is written should reflect the meter, making the beat structure clear and easy to read. The arrangement of rests, beams, and ties all contribute to the clear notation of rhythms.

Showing the beat

Generally, notes and rests are grouped to show the separate beats. This depends first on the time signature, and then on the details of the note values within each measure. It should be so clear that the performer doesn't notice how it is done.

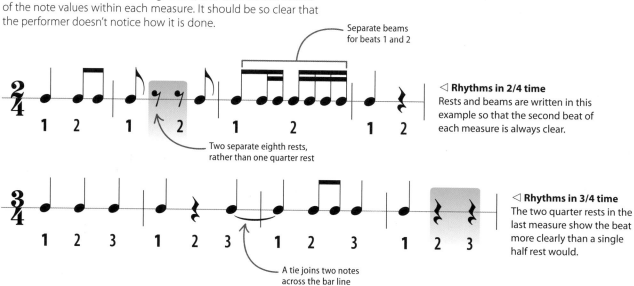

Separate beams for beats 1 and 2

▷ **Rhythms in 2/4 time**
Rests and beams are written in this example so that the second beat of each measure is always clear.

Two separate eighth rests, rather than one quarter rest

▷ **Rhythms in 3/4 time**
The two quarter rests in the last measure show the beat more clearly than a single half rest would.

A tie joins two notes across the bar line

Beaming across the beat

In 2/4 time, four even eighth notes can be beamed across the beat, or six eighth notes in 3/4 time. If the rhythms become more complicated, it is best to separate the beats. Dotted rhythm pairs—a dotted eighth note followed by a sixteenth note—stand out clearly if beamed separately.

▷ **2/4 time**
In the second measure, the eighth notes are even and can be beamed together.

▷ **3/4 time**
In this example, with its regular rhythm, the eighth notes can be beamed together.

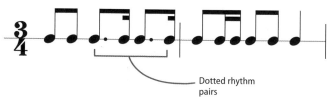

Dotted rhythm pairs

▷ **3/4 time**
Here, the rhythms are more complicated. It is clearer if the beats are shown separately.

Beaming in 4/4

In 4/4, the third beat is stronger than the second or fourth. Even eighth notes can be beamed across the first or second half of the measure, but not across the middle, so that the third beat remains clear for performers, even at a brief glance.

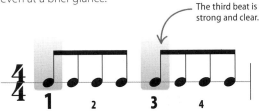

The third beat is strong and clear.

△ **Even eighth notes in 4/4 time**
This is a common arrangement, with the eighth notes beamed in two groups of four, provided they are even. More varied rhythms—for instance dotted rhythms—may be clearer with each beat beamed separately.

Rests in 4/4

As with notes, it is best to avoid having a rest that crosses the middle of a 4/4 measure. Two separate rests can be used instead, as in the example below. A performer, who will be subconsciously counting the beat, will grasp the rhythm at a glance.

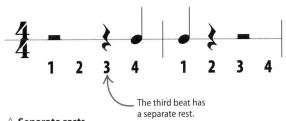

The third beat has a separate rest.

△ **Separate rests**
This example shows how rests are used to make the 4/4 meter clear, with the third beat always visible.

Compound time

In compound time, the beats should always be clear. They should not be crossed by a note, beam, or rest—except for long notes that last for two whole beats or more. The examples below show how this works in practice.

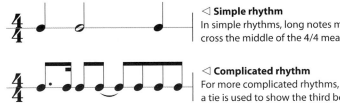

◁ **6/8 time**
In this example, the beat, with its subdivisions into three eighth notes, is very clear.

▽ **12/8 time**
This example is more complicated, so the rests are arranged to show the beats clearly.

This dotted half rest covers beats 1 and 2.

You can beam across a rest within the beat.

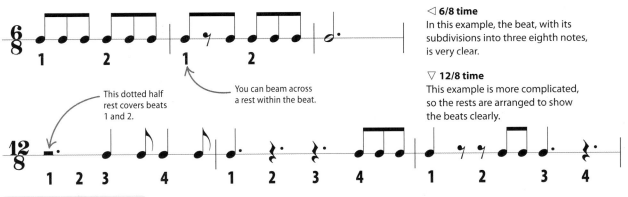

Using ties within the measure

With tied notes, the same principles apply as for beams and rests. The notation should be made as clear as possible for a performer. In 4/4, the third beat should usually be visible, although with very simple rhythms this may not be necessary.

◁ **Simple rhythm**
In simple rhythms, long notes may cross the middle of the 4/4 measure.

◁ **Complicated rhythm**
For more complicated rhythms, a tie is used to show the third beat.

Triplets and tuplets

In music notation, triplet means three notes in the time of two. Tuplet is a generic term meaning x notes in the time of y, where x and y are two numbers.

Triplets

Triplets and tuplets enable us to write rhythms that do not fit the meter in a regular way. A triplet is a group of three notes in the time of two. It is indicated by writing a 3 over or under the group of notes.

▷ **3 in the time of 2**
Triplet rhythms are quite common. They usually occur where most of the note values are regular divisions or subdivisions into two.

Long notes

Regular sudivisions

Triplet group

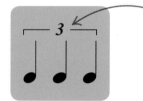

The 3 is usually written on the stem side of the notes.

△ **How to write a triplet quarter note group**
For quarter notes, or any notes without a beam, the 3 is combined with a bracket to show which notes are in the triplet.

△ **How to write a triplet eighth note group**
For a group of beamed eighth notes or sixteenth notes, the bracket is generally not needed. The 3 is usually written next to the beam.

Triplets in action

Here are two examples of triplets in action—a simple upward scale, notated first using eight notes, then using quarter notes. Try to sing it, or imagine the rhythm in your head, keeping the beats regular so that you can hear the effect of the triplet rhythm.

1   2   3   4

△ **Triplet eighth notes**
Shown here is a group of triplet eighth notes on the third beat. They are played, or sung, in the time of two ordinary eighth notes.

 9

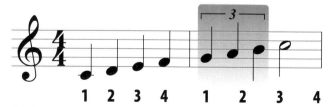

1   2   3   4   1   2   3   4

△ **Triplet quarter notes**
In the second measure, the three triplet quarter notes cross the second beat, with the bracket indicating which quarter notes form the triplet group.

Triplet rhythms

One of the most familiar examples of triplet rhythms is in "Amazing Grace," shown here. You can also hear triplets at the start of Beethoven's "Moonlight" piano sonata. "These Foolish Things," by Eric Maschwitz and Jack Strachey, also has triplets, especially in the chorus with the title words. Another good example is in "Turn, Turn, Turn" by Pete Seeger.

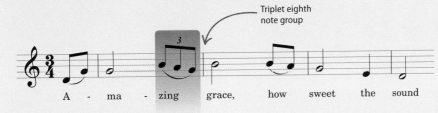

Triplet eighth note group

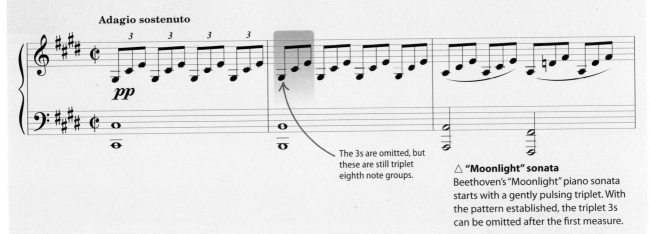

Adagio sostenuto

The 3s are omitted, but these are still triplet eighth note groups.

◁ **"Amazing Grace"**
Old songs are not always sung or notated in the same way. Some hymn books omit the note A in the triplet eighth note group, and just notate straight eighth notes for the notes B and G.

△ **"Moonlight" sonata**
Beethoven's "Moonlight" piano sonata starts with a gently pulsing triplet. With the pattern established, the triplet 3s can be omitted after the first measure.

Duplets

Duplets are two notes in the time of three, which is an exception to the usual practice, whereby tuplet notes are faster than their regular equivalents. Duplets are much less common than triplets, but may occur in compound time.

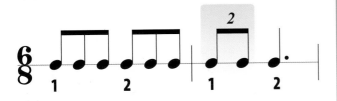

△ **Duplets in compound time**
This is a typical use of a duplet. Here two eighth notes are written in the time of three, within a 6/8 meter.

Other groupings

Quintuplets are five notes played in the time of four. Other rhythms in which irregular numbers of notes are fitted within the beat are also possible—for instance seven in the time of four, or nine in the time of eight. All of these examples are given the general heading "tuplets."

Quintuplet sixteenth notes

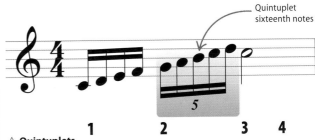

△ **Quintuplets**
Shown here is a group of quintuplet sixteenth notes. The five notes are played in the time of four.

Syncopation and swing

SEE ALSO
❮ **30–31** Time signatures
❮ **36–37** Grouping notes
❮ **38–39** Triplets and tuplets

Syncopated rhythms tend to cross the beat, or are accented in a way that contradicts the beat. Syncopated music often uses ties or rests on the main beats, creating a more energetic kind of rhythm.

Ragtime

A classic example of a syncopated style, ragtime is typically written in a steady 2/4 or 4/4 time, but with many melody notes held across the beat, which is marked emphatically in the bass line. It became popular in the early 20th century, especially through the compositions of Scott Joplin (c.1868–1917).

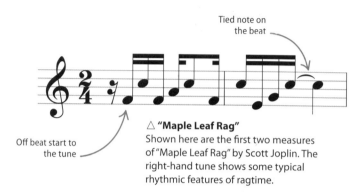

Tied note on the beat

Off beat start to the tune

△ **"Maple Leaf Rag"**
Shown here are the first two measures of "Maple Leaf Rag" by Scott Joplin. The right-hand tune shows some typical rhythmic features of ragtime.

Calypso

Calypso is another style that often syncopates across the beat. Calypso songs usually use an irregular division of the 4/4 beat, a 3 + 3 + 2 division of the eight eighth notes. Originally from West Africa, this type of rhythm is widespread in Caribbean and Latin-American music.

▽ **Irregular division**
The stressed notes in this example are in a 3 + 3 + 2 rhythm cut across the normal beat accents of a straight 4/4 meter.

Measuring in eighth notes, this is 3 + 3 + 2

▽ **"Linstead Market"**
This Jamaican folk song features syncopated rhythms, typical of Caribbean music. The tied notes in the first and third measures cross the third beat, making a 3 + 3 + 2 rhythm.

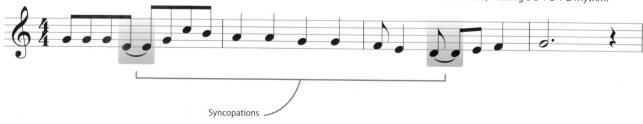

Syncopations

Changing time signature

Sometimes composers like to swap between different rhythms and meters. Complex modern music may have many changes of time signature. The example below switches from 6/8 to 3/4. Both these time signatures have six eighth notes per measure, but the beats and emphases are different.

▽ **"America"**
"America" from *West Side Story* by Leonard Bernstein has this type of rhythm. The change of meter adds energy and excitement.

This tells the performer that eighth notes continue at the same tempo.

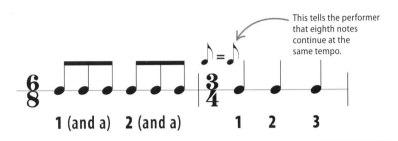

Polyrhythms

Sometimes different rhythms and meters are played at the same time by different instruments. Some styles of West African traditional drum music use polyrhythms that combine several layers of drum patterns, each played by a different type of drum.

Ghanaian drum

Free rhythms

Written without either a time signature or bar lines, free rhythms rely on note values, spacing, and any symbols or text instructions to explain what is required. If a composer wants an unconventional rhythmic (or nonrhythmic) effect, he or she must devise a clear way of describing it to the performer.

Pitches are no longer defined here. The performer follows the general upward direction.

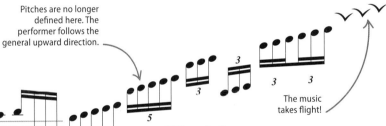

The music takes flight!

There is no meter, but the performer has note values for guidance.

▽ **Free rhythm**
The performer is asked to exercise increasing levels of imagination, first rhythmically then melodically as well. The music becomes both faster and freer.

Swing

Swing rhythms are written in simple time, but played "with a swing", as if in triplets or compound time. Each pair of eighth notes is played with a longer first note and a shorter second note. This way of playing can be indicated simply by putting "Swing" at the start, with the tempo, or by using the notational key shown on the right.

◁ **Swing instruction**
This instruction can be written at the start of a piece, above the staff. It tells the player to use a swing rhythm.

▷ **Performing swing**
This example shows a 4/4 bar of eighth notes as written, then as played in a swing rhythm.

Swing

Written as

Performed as

Beginnings and endings

Not all melodies begin on the first beat of the measure. In fact, many begin on the last beat. Some examples of these are shown here.

SEE ALSO

❮ 24–25 Beats and measures

Writing your own melody   112–113 ❯

Repeats   154–155 ❯

The conductor   186–187 ❯

Upbeats

An upbeat is the last beat of the measure, especially at the beginning of a piece (or section of a piece). The name describes how a conductor indicates that beat—with an upward movement, in preparation for a clear downward gesture (the downbeat) at the start of the next measure. Many tunes begin on an upbeat, including the hymn "Amazing Grace," "Hey Jude" by the Beatles, and the three examples shown below.

▽ **"Auld Lang Syne"**
"Auld Lang Syne" is a famous tune that starts on an upbeat, the fourth beat of the measure.

▽ **"My Bonnie Lies Over the Ocean"**
The words of a song may determine if the music has an upbeat—if they lead from an unstressed syllable to a stressed one, for example.

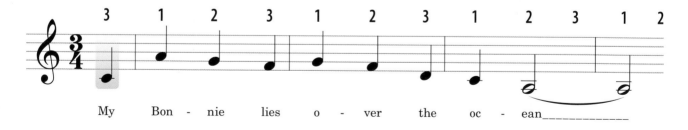

My   Bon - nie   lies   o - ver   the   oc - ean_____

The upbeat leads into the strong first beat of the next measure.

◁ **Chopin's Prelude No. 4**
An instrumental tune may also begin with an upbeat, as seen in the opening of Chopin's Prelude No. 4.

Opening incomplete measures

Here are examples of melodies in which the initial incomplete measure is either less than a whole beat (as in "Papageno's Song") or more than a whole beat (as in "When the Saints Go Marching In"). They are not exactly upbeats, but the feel is similar, leading into the strong first beat of the next measure.

◁ **"When the Saints Go Marching In"**
This famous jazz tune can be notated in different ways—most often in 2/2, as shown here, with the melody beginning halfway through the first beat.

◁ **Papageno's Song from** *The Magic Flute*
In this tune by Mozart, introducing the bird-catcher Papageno, the first two sixteenth notes are the second half of the upbeat.

Measure numbers

Upbeats are not counted when numbering measures; measures are counted from the first full measure in a piece. Here is the opening of the "Passion Chorale," a Lutheran hymn tune used by Bach in the *St. Matthew Passion* and other works, showing the measure numbers.

▽ **"Passion Chorale"**
As shown in this opening from Bach's "Passion Chorale," measure numbers always start from the first full measure.

Endings

Many pieces that start with an upbeat also end with a balancing, incomplete measure, so that there is a standard number of measures. The "Passion Chorale" begins on an upbeat, as shown above, and ends with a dotted half note that balances the opening.

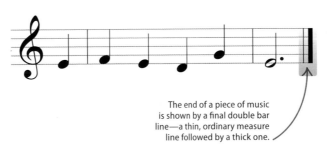

The end of a piece of music is shown by a final double bar line—a thin, ordinary measure line followed by a thick one.

◁ **"Passion Chorale"**
To balance an opening incomplete measure with a closing incomplete measure, as shown here, is common, but not an absolute rule.

Tempo

The speed at which music is played, or asked to be played, is known as tempo. There are two main ways of indicating the tempo on a score—by using descriptive words, or using a metronome mark.

SEE ALSO

❮ 26–27 Note values
❮ 30–31 Time signatures
Musical expression   104–105 ❯
What is the score?   194–195 ❯

A rhythm may be fast or slow

If we look at a rhythm, as shown below, the note values in themselves do not say anything about the tempo. The rhythm could be played fast or slow, or somewhere in between. We need more information to know what tempo to use.

▽ **Note values are relative**
The information we get from note values concerns their duration in relation to each other. The underlying quarter note beat in this example may be fast or slow.

Indicating tempo

The tempo indicates how fast, or slow, the music should go and is usually marked at the beginning of a piece, above the time signature, and at any place in the music where the tempo changes. One really simple, though imprecise, way is to use words as a direct instruction to the player, as shown below.

▽ **Using words**
Words can be used to indicate the desired tempo. One may use English words like "fast" or "very fast," or their Italian equivalents such as "allegro" or "presto."

Fast   Faster   Very fast

GLOSSARY

Words for tempo

It is perfectly normal for composers to use their own language, for instance English, to indicate the tempo. However, it is conventional in music to use Italian terms that musicians understand. Shown here are some of these common terms, though there are plenty more. It is helpful for performers to have a small music dictionary to explain any obscure terms they encounter.

Presto
Allegro
Moderato
Andante
Adagio
Lento

fast
slow

△ **Italian tempo terms**
Here are six of the most common terms, arranged from the fastest at the top to the slowest at the bottom.

Accelerando
Più mosso
Stringendo (pressing on)
Ritenuto (holding back)
Ritardando
Rallentando

getting faster
getting slower

△ **Gradual changes**
These terms are sometimes followed by a row of dashes, showing how far in the music they apply.

MORE TEMPO WORDS AND THEIR MEANINGS	
Term	**Meaning**
A tempo	as before (for instance, following ritenuto)
Tempo primo	original tempo
Rubato	varying the tempo in a controlled way

MODIFYING WORDS AND THEIR MEANINGS	
Term	**Meaning**
Poco	a little
Molto	very
Più	more
Poco a poco	gradually

TEMPO WORDS WITH EXPRESSIVE MEANINGS	
Term	**Meaning**
Allegretto	fairly fast, but often implying "lightly"
Grave	slow and solemn
Largo	slow, broad
Allargando	slower, broader
Vivace	fast, very lively, spirited

◁ **Modifying words**
These are widely used alongside other tempo words—for instance, "Più allegro."

△ **Tempo plus expression**
Some tempo words may express something about the spirit of the music as well as how fast it should be played.

Metronome marks

How fast is "fast" or "allegro"? A more precise way of indicating the tempo is by specifying the number of beats per minute. These indications are called "metronome marks." They are written at the start of a score, above the time signature, and can also be added at other places where the tempo changes (like text instructions).

This indicates that there are 60 quarter-note beats per minute.

△ **Metronome mark position**
Metronome marks are written above the time signature, where they are most needed.

△ **Metronome marks with text**
Metronome marks are often combined with other forms of tempo indication, such as text instructions.

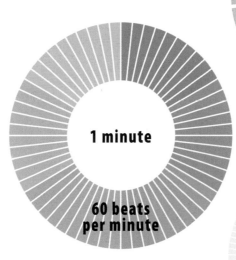

1 minute
60 beats per minute

1 minute
30 beats per minute

1 minute
120 beats per minute

△ **Beats per minute**
"Beats per minute" (BPM or bpm) is a term with a similar meaning to a metronome mark. It is not encountered on classical scores, but is widely used in the world of pop music, especially electronic dance music.

Intervals, scales, and keys

Sharps and flats

Sharps and flats are used to indicate a raised or lowered note. Sharps raise a note to the note immediately above it on the keyboard. Flats lower a note to the note immediately below it.

SEE ALSO

‹ **16–17** The piano keyboard

‹ **18–19** Notes on the staff

Half steps	52–53 ›
Whole steps	54–55 ›
Keys	64–67 ›
Accidentals	72–73 ›

What are sharps and flats?

Sharps and flats are symbols that indicate when a note is raised or lowered by a half step to the note immediately above or below it on the keyboard. Notes that are not sharp or flat are called naturals. Sharps raise naturals by one half step, and flats lower naturals by one half step.

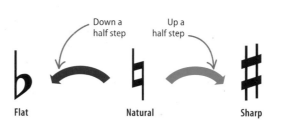

Down a half step

Up a half step

Flat

Natural

Sharp

◁ **Symbols**
These are the symbols for flats, naturals, and sharps. Naturals move down a half step to become flats or up a half step to become sharps.

Look at the black keys

A black key on the keyboard can be called either sharp or flat. If a white key moves up a half step to a note, that note is written as a sharp. If it moves a half step down, the note is written as a flat.

🔊 10

▽ **Sharps and flats on black keys**
The black keys are sharps or flats depending on whether the white keys are below or above them.

This note is called D♯ because it is one half step up from D, but it can also be called E♭ because it is one half step down from E.

G moves up a half step to become G♯.

B moves down a half step to become B♭.

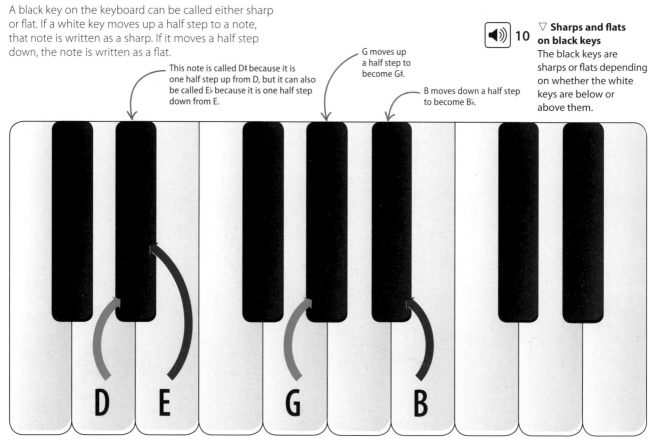

D E G B

What about white keys?

The white keys immediately next to each other on the keyboard, without black keys in between, can also be called sharps or flats. A white key that is a half step down from another white key is that note's flat, and a white key that is a half step up from another white key is that note's sharp.

This note is usually called E, but because it is one half step down from F, it can also be called F♭.

This note is usually called C, but because it is one half step up from B, it can also be called B♯.

▽ **Sharps and flats on white keys**
The white keys on the keyboard have different names. They can be known as naturals, sharps, or flats.

11

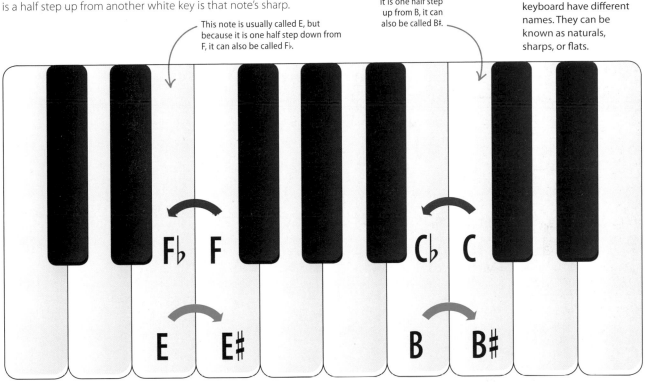

On the staff

When sharps and flats are written on the staff, the symbol for the sharp or flat is written just before the note that is sharpened or flattened. The symbol is written on exactly the same line or space of the staff as the note itself.

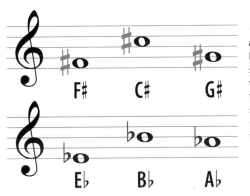

F♯ C♯ G♯

E♭ B♭ A♭

◁ **Writing sharps and flats**
In music notation, the sharp or flat symbol is written just before the note, on the same space or line as the note, while they are written after the letter name in text.

Naturals

A natural cancels a sharp or a flat. The symbol for a natural is only written next to a note if the note was previously sharp or flat. It makes the note return to being a natural.

Previously sharp or flat note is sharp.

Note becomes natural again.

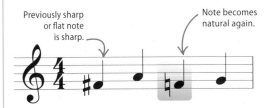

△ **Canceling sharps and flats**
Here F♯ is canceled by a natural symbol, becoming F♮. Flats can be canceled by naturals in the same way.

⟫ Double sharps and double flats

Double sharps raise naturals by two half steps and double flats lower naturals by two half steps. Double sharps and double flats are not found in music as often as single sharps and flats, but they do feature in some of the scales and keys that will be introduced in this chapter.

◁ **Double flat**
This is the symbol for a double flat, which is written immediately before the note that is doubly flattened on the staff.

◁ **Double sharp**
This is the symbol for a double sharp, which is written immediately before the note that is doubly sharpened on the staff.

▷ **Moving a half step**
Naturals move up one half step to become sharps, and up another half step to become double sharps. They move down one half step to become flats, and down another half step to become double flats.

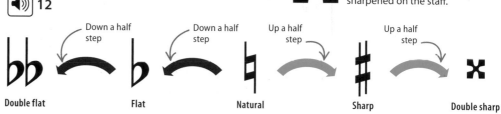

🔊 12

| Down a half step | Down a half step | Up a half step | Up a half step |

Double flat   **Flat**   **Natural**   **Sharp**   **Double sharp**

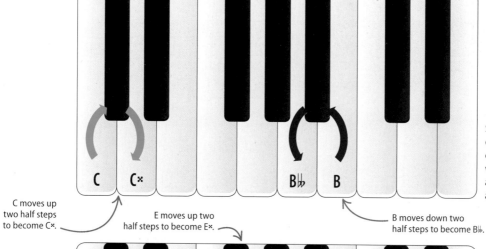

◁ **C and B keys**
Starting from C♮ and B♮ on the keyboard, these examples show how a white key can be written as a double sharp or as a double flat.

C moves up two half steps to become C𝄪.

E moves up two half steps to become E𝄪.

B moves down two half steps to become B𝄫.

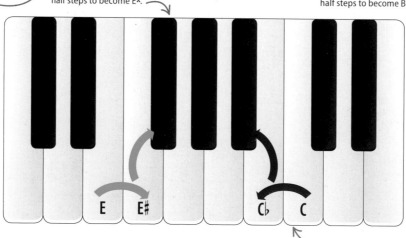

◁ **E and C keys**
Starting from E♮ and C♮ on the keyboard, these examples show how a black key can be written as a double sharp or as a double flat.

C moves down two half steps to become C𝄫.

One sound, many names

Sharps, flats, naturals, double sharps, and double flats mean
that the same key on the keyboard can be given several different
names, and can be written in various positions on the staff.
Here are a few examples:

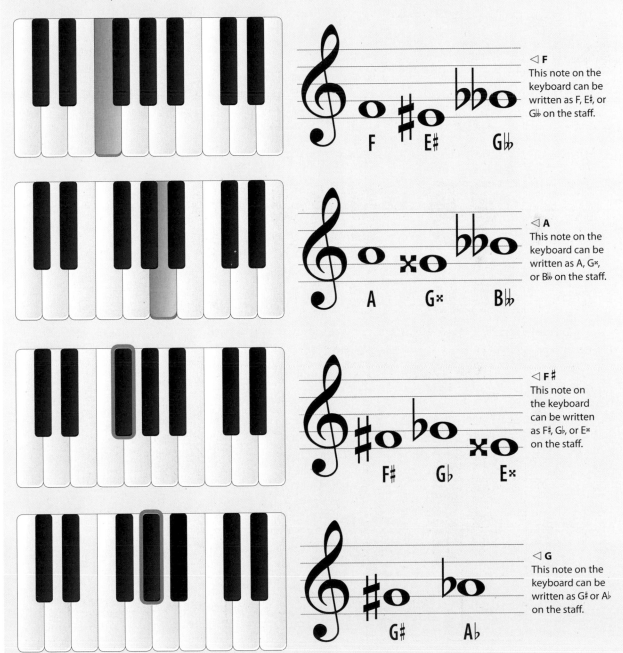

◁ **F**
This note on the
keyboard can be
written as F, E♯, or
G♭♭ on the staff.

◁ **A**
This note on the
keyboard can be
written as A, G×,
or B♭♭ on the staff.

◁ **F♯**
This note on
the keyboard
can be written
as F♯, G♭, or E×
on the staff.

◁ **G**
This note on the
keyboard can be
written as G♯ or A♭
on the staff.

Half steps

A half step is the musical term for the interval
or gap between notes that are immediately
next to each other on the keyboard.

SEE ALSO

❮ **48–51** Sharps and flats

Whole steps **54–55** ❯

Major scales **60–61** ❯

What are half steps?

A half step means "half a whole step" and represents a half
step on the keyboard. If a note moves up a half step on the
keyboard, it moves to the note immediately above it.
Depending on the starting note, the note one half step
above could be a black key or a white key.

▽ **Half step**
Below are some examples of half steps—
involving only white keys (E to F), a white key
moving to a black key (A to B♭) on
the keyboard, and a black key moving
to a white key (D♭ to D♮).

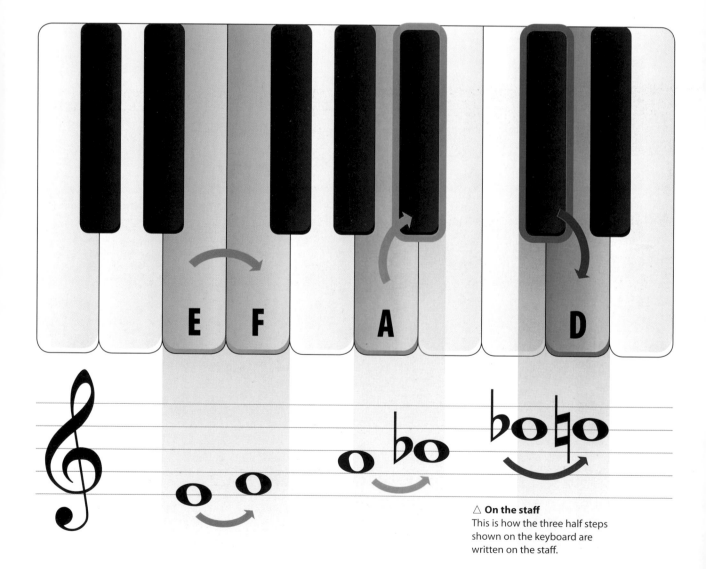

△ **On the staff**
This is how the three half steps
shown on the keyboard are
written on the staff.

Examples of half steps

Here are some more examples of half steps on the keyboard and on the staff, including a mixture of black keys, white keys, sharps, flats, and naturals.

 13

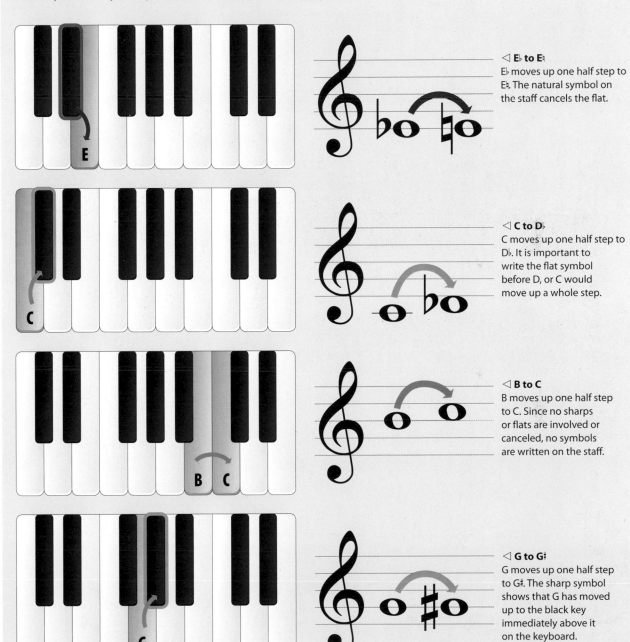

◁ **E♭ to E♮:**
E♭ moves up one half step to E♮. The natural symbol on the staff cancels the flat.

◁ **C to D♭:**
C moves up one half step to D♭. It is important to write the flat symbol before D, or C would move up a whole step.

◁ **B to C:**
B moves up one half step to C. Since no sharps or flats are involved or canceled, no symbols are written on the staff.

◁ **G to G♯:**
G moves up one half step to G♯. The sharp symbol shows that G has moved up to the black key immediately above it on the keyboard.

Whole steps

A whole step is the equivalent of two half steps in music. While a half step will go just to the adjacent key, whether black or white, a whole step always skips a note. Two notes a whole step apart always have one note between them on the keyboard.

SEE ALSO

❮ **48–51** Sharps and flats

❮ **52–53** Half steps

Major scales **60–61** ❯

Whole steps on the keyboard

If a note moves up a whole step, it skips over the note immediately above it to the next note on the keyboard. The note one half step above could be a black key or a white key, depending on the starting note.

Because the white keys B and C are a half step apart, B moves up a whole step to the black key C♯.

▷ **Whole step**
C and D are a whole step apart because they have a black key (C♯ or D♭) between them. F♯ and G♯ have a white key (G) between them. B and C♯ have C♮ between them.

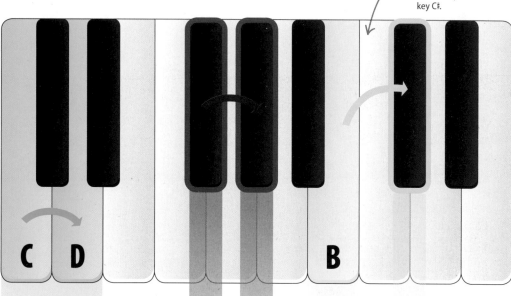

▽ **On the staff**
This is how the three whole steps shown on the keyboard are written on the staff.

Examples of whole steps

Below are some more examples of whole steps on the keyboard and on the staff, including a mixture of black keys, white keys, sharps, and flats.

 14

◁ **E to F♯**
E skips over F♮ and moves up one whole step to F♯.

◁ **G to A**
G skips over G♯ (or A♭) and moves up one whole step to A.

◁ **D♭ to E♭**
D♭ skips over D♮ and moves up one whole step to E♭.

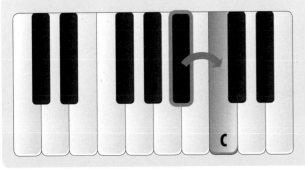

◁ **B♭ to C**
B♭ skips over B♮ and moves up one whole step to C.

Intervals

An interval is the musical term for the distance between two notes on the keyboard and on the staff. Intervals are defined by their number and quality.

SEE ALSO

Major scales	60–61 〉
Consonance and dissonance	120–121 〉

Simple intervals of the major scale

The simple intervals of the major scale are called unison, second, third, fourth, fifth, sixth, seventh, and octave. The number of the interval is determined by the number of notes between the starting note and the top note, including the starting note and top note itself.

The interval from C to G spans five notes, so it is called a fifth.

▽ **C major scale**
The keyboard below shows the intervals between Middle C and the other notes of the C major scale. Going up the scale, the intervals rise from unison, through second, third, fourth, fifth, sixth, and seventh, to one octave.

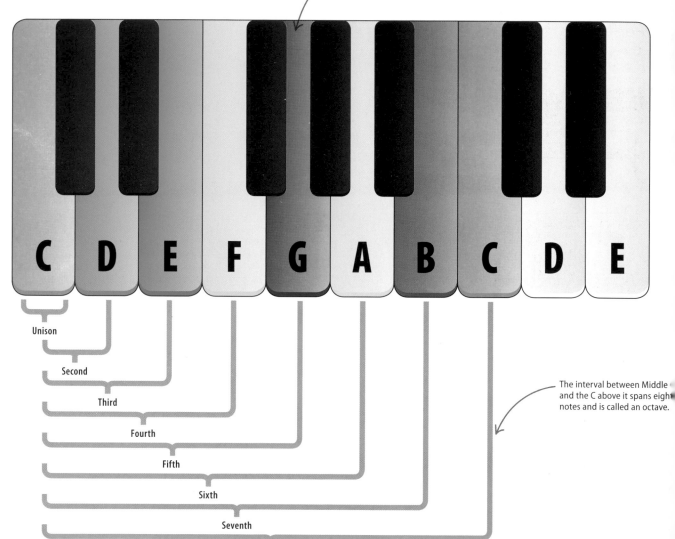

The interval between Middle C and the C above it spans eight notes and is called an octave.

Unison
Second
Third
Fourth
Fifth
Sixth
Seventh
Octave (eight notes)

Intervals on the staff

Here are the intervals of the C major scale written on the staff, when both notes are played at the same time. The bottom note of the interval is always Middle C, but the top note rises up the scale as the number of the interval increases.

 15 ▽ **C major scale on the staff**
As the intervals increase from unison up to one octave, the top note of the interval rises through the eight notes of the C major scale on the staff.

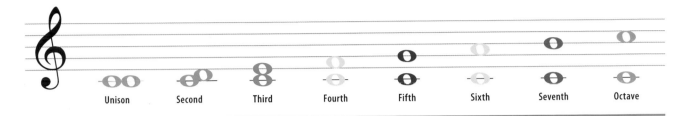

| Unison | Second | Third | Fourth | Fifth | Sixth | Seventh | Octave |

Perfect intervals and major intervals

As well as being defined by their number, intervals are also defined by their quality—whether they are major, minor, perfect, augmented, or diminished. Some of the intervals of the major scale are called major intervals, and some are called perfect intervals.

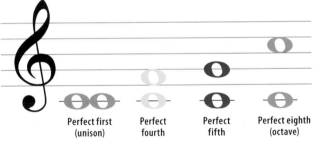

Perfect first (unison) Perfect fourth Perfect fifth Perfect eighth (octave)

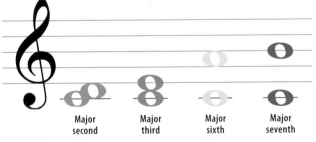

Major second Major third Major sixth Major seventh

△ **Perfect intervals**
The staff above shows the intervals of the major scale that are called perfect intervals. These are perfect unison, perfect fourth, perfect fifth, and perfect octave.

△ **Major intervals**
The staff above shows the intervals of the major scale that are called major intervals. These are major second, major third, major sixth, and major seventh.

LOOKING CLOSER

Octaves

An octave is the standard musical term for the interval of an eighth. Octaves are important intervals because they are the distance between the starting note and the top note of a scale.

▷ **One octave**
Going up the C major scale, the eight notes of the scale are shown on the staff. The interval between the top note and bottom note is one octave.

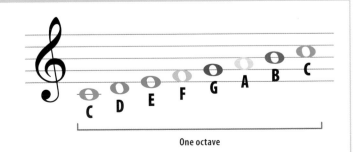

C D E F G A B C

One octave

») Minor, augmented, and diminished intervals

In addition to major and perfect intervals, the other qualities of intervals are minor, augmented, and diminished. Perfect intervals can only become augmented or diminished, but major intervals can become minor, augmented, or diminished.

What happens to perfect intervals?

If the top note of a perfect interval moves up a half step, the interval becomes augmented. If the top note moves down a half step, the interval becomes diminished.

▽ **Changing perfect intervals**
This flowchart shows how a perfect interval becomes an augmented interval when the top note moves up a half step, and becomes a diminished interval when the top note moves down a half step.

◁ **Diminished 8ve**
On this staff, the top note of a perfect octave moves down a half step to make the octave diminished.

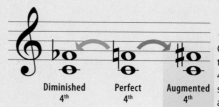

◁ **Augmented 4th**
On this staff, the top note of a perfect 4th moves up a half step to make it an augmented 4th.

What happens to major intervals?

Just like perfect intervals, major intervals become augmented if their top note moves up a half step. However, if the top note of a major interval moves down one half step, it becomes a minor interval. If it moves down two half steps, the interval becomes diminished.

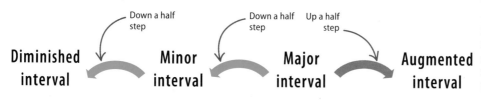

◁ **Changing major intervals**
The top note of a major interval moves up one half step to make it an augmented interval, and moves down one half step to make it a minor interval. The top note moves down two half steps to make it a diminished interval.

△ **Major 2nd**
The top note of a major 2nd moves up a half step to make it an augmented 2nd, and it moves down a half step to make it a minor 2nd. It moves down two half steps to make it a diminished 2nd.

△ **Minor 7th**
If the top note of a major 7th moves down one half step, the interval becomes a minor 7th. An augmented and diminished 7th are also shown on this staff.

Intervals in half steps

It is possible for different intervals to have the same number of half steps between their top and bottom notes. Intervals that span the same number of half steps will have different names (qualities) depending on how they are written on the staff.

▽ **Intervals**
This table shows the number of half steps between all of the different possible simple intervals. Both the size and quality of the intervals determine the number of half steps.

Quality \ Size	Unison	2nd	3rd	4th	5th	6th	7th	Octave (8ve)
Augmented	1	3	5	6	8	10	12	13
Major		2	4			9	11	
Perfect	0			5	7			12
Minor		1	3			8	10	
Diminished	-1	0	2	4	6	7	9	11

No interval

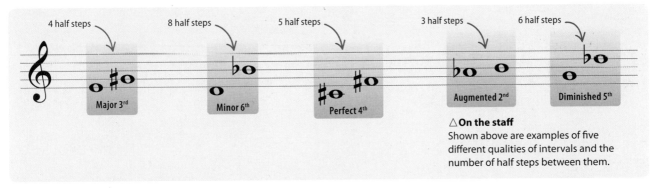

4 half steps — Major 3rd
8 half steps — Minor 6th
5 half steps — Perfect 4th
3 half steps — Augmented 2nd
6 half steps — Diminished 5th

△ **On the staff**
Shown above are examples of five different qualities of intervals and the number of half steps between them.

Compound intervals

Intervals of an augmented octave or less are known as simple intervals. The intervals that are bigger than an augmented octave are known as compound intervals. Compound intervals can be broken down into a perfect octave and a given simple interval.

> Octave + simple interval = compound interval
> (8ve)   (5th)   (12th or compound 5th)

Combination	Interval
Octave + 2nd =	Compound 2nd (9th)
Octave + 3rd =	Compound 3rd (10th)
Octave + 4th =	Compound 4th (11th)
Octave + 5th =	Compound 5th (12th)
Octave + 6th =	Compound 6th (13th)
Octave + 7th =	Compound 7th (14th)
Octave + 8th =	Double octave (15th)

△ **Interval combinations**
Simple intervals are combined with a perfect octave to make compound intervals. The alternative names for these compound intervals are also shown in this table.

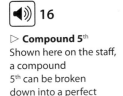 16

▷ **Compound 5th**
Shown here on the staff, a compound 5th can be broken down into a perfect 8ve and a perfect 5th.

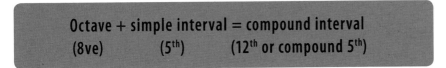

Perfect 5th   Compound 5th

Perfect 8ve

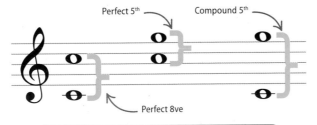

Perfect 8ve + perfect 5th = compound 5th

Major scales

A scale is a series of notes that rise and fall over the range of an octave. Major scales are one of the most important building blocks of music.

SEE ALSO

❮ **52–53** Half steps

❮ **54–55** Whole steps

❮ **56–59** Intervals

Minor scales   **62–63** ❯

What is a scale?

Scales are patterns of notes that rise up and then fall down between two notes that are an octave apart. There are two main types of scale: major and minor. Scales are played as a way of practicing a musical instrument.

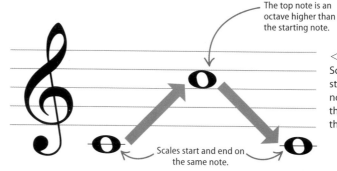

The top note is an octave higher than the starting note.

◁ **Up and down**
Scales go from a starting note up to the note an octave above the starting note, and then back down again.

Scales start and end on the same note.

The major scale

All major scales are broken down into the same pattern of whole steps and half steps. Whatever note a major scale starts on, it will always follow this pattern. The pattern of whole and half steps used on the way up is reflected on the way down—the same notes are played in both directions.

▽ **Whole steps and half steps**
All major scales follow the same pattern on the way up: whole step, whole step, half step, whole step, whole step, whole step, half step. On the way down the pattern is: half step, whole step, whole step, whole step, half step, whole step, whole step.

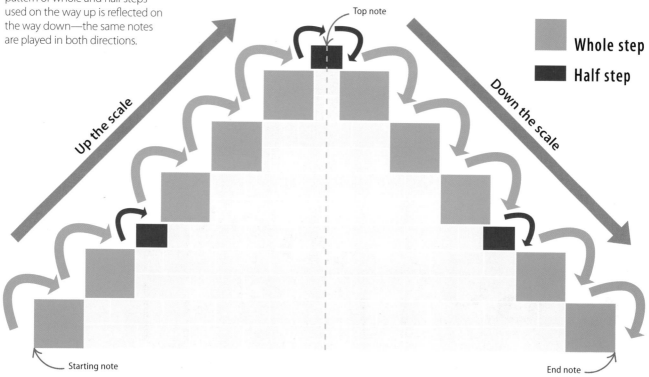

Top note

Up the scale

Down the scale

Whole step

Half step

Starting note

End note

The C major scale

This scale follows the major pattern of whole steps and half steps without having to use any of the black keys of the keyboard—it has no sharps or flats. The whole steps skip over the black keys, while the half steps are between white keys that sit next to each other.

C major scale

Anyone who plays a musical instrument or takes music exams has to learn and practice scales. The C major scale is one of the first scales that a musician will learn on the piano because it has no sharps or flats.

▷ **Practicing scales**
Musicians understand how music works by practicing scales. This improves their technique on an instrument.

 17

▷ **From C to C**
Shown here on the keyboard, and below on the staff, the C major scale rises from Middle C to the C one octave above.

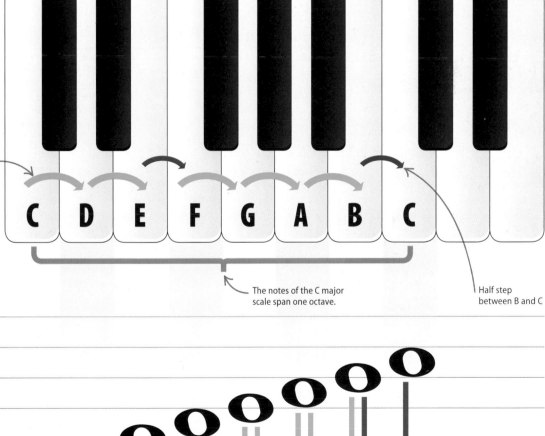

Whole step between C and D

The notes of the C major scale span one octave.

Half step between B and C

Whole step Whole step Half step Whole step Whole step Whole step Half step

Minor scales

Just like a major scale, a minor scale is also a series of notes rising and falling within the range of an octave. But a minor scale takes some of the notes of a major scale and lowers them by a half step.

SEE ALSO
❮ 56–59 Intervals
❮ 60–61 Major scales
Keys   64–67 ❯

From major to minor

There are three main types of minor scales: natural minor, harmonic minor, and melodic minor. The 3rd, 6th, and 7th notes of a major scale can be lowered by a half step in a minor scale that starts on the same note.

▽ **C major and C minor**
In a C minor scale, E (3rd note), A (6th note), and B (7th note) from the C major scale can be lowered by a half step.

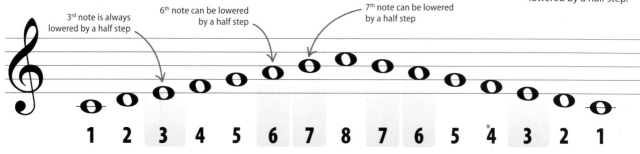

3rd note is always lowered by a half step

6th note can be lowered by a half step

7th note can be lowered by a half step

1 2 3 4 5 6 7 8 7 6 5 4 3 2 1

The natural minor scale

In the natural minor scale, the 3rd, 6th, and 7th notes of the major scale starting on the same note are all lowered by a half step going up and down the scale.

🔊 18

▽ **Pattern of the scale**
This pyramid shows the pattern of the natural minor scales and how it is broken down into whole steps and half steps.

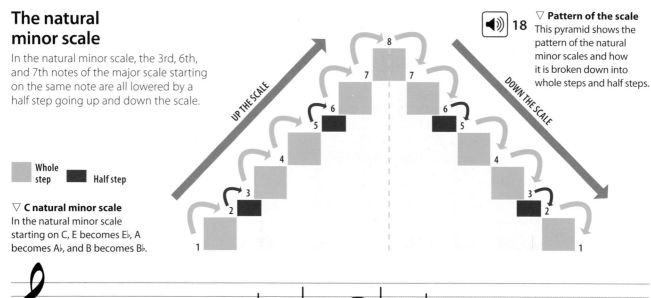

UP THE SCALE

DOWN THE SCALE

▢ Whole step   ▮ Half step

▽ **C natural minor scale**
In the natural minor scale starting on C, E becomes E♭, A becomes A♭, and B becomes B♭.

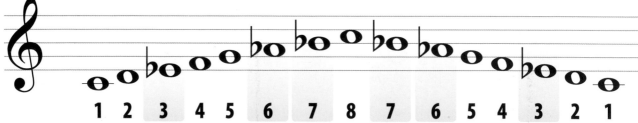

1 2 3 4 5 6 7 8 7 6 5 4 3 2 1

The harmonic minor scale

In the harmonic minor scale, the 3rd and 6th notes are lowered by a half step going up and down the scale. The 7th note is not lowered at all. Unlike other minor scales, the harmonic minor scale has an augmented 2nd—three half steps—between its 6th and 7th notes.

- Whole step
- Augmented 2nd
- Half step

▽ **C harmonic minor scale**
In the harmonic minor scale starting on C, E becomes E♭ and A becomes A♭, but B is still B.

▽ **Pattern of the scale**
This pyramid shows the pattern followed by the harmonic minor scale, going up and down the scale.

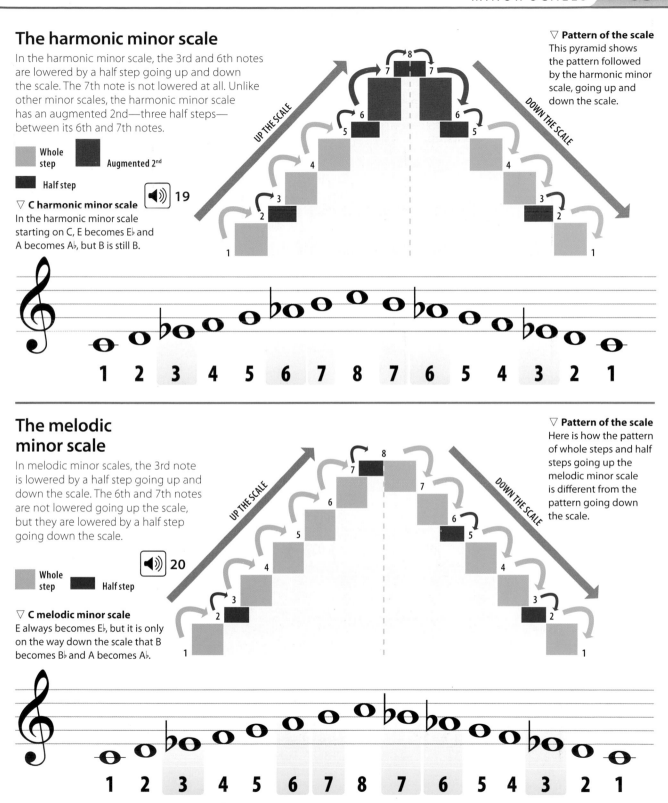

The melodic minor scale

In melodic minor scales, the 3rd note is lowered by a half step going up and down the scale. The 6th and 7th notes are not lowered going up the scale, but they are lowered by a half step going down the scale.

- Whole step
- Half step

▽ **C melodic minor scale**
E always becomes E♭, but it is only on the way down the scale that B becomes B♭ and A becomes A♭.

▽ **Pattern of the scale**
Here is how the pattern of whole steps and half steps going up the melodic minor scale is different from the pattern going down the scale.

Keys

A key is the harmonic, or tonal, center of a piece of music. Keys determine which notes should usually be played as sharps or flats.

What is a key?

A piece in a particular key is based around the notes of that key's corresponding scale. The first note of a scale is known as the keynote, or tonic. For example, in a G major scale, the keynote is G. Music in the key of G major is mainly made up of the notes from a G major scale, so F will usually be sharp.

REAL WORLD

Johann Sebastian Bach

Composers write music in all kinds of different keys, even ones that need lots of sharps and flats. J. S. Bach's *The Well-Tempered Clavier* is a collection of pieces in all 24 of the major and minor keys.

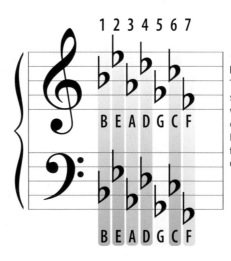

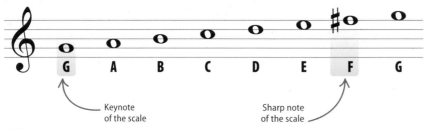

Keynote of the scale

Sharp note of the scale

△ **Key notes**
With music in the key of G major, the keynote is G, and the note F will usually be played as F♯.

What is a key signature?

A piece of music in a particular key will tend to use the same sharps or flats many times. Rather than writing the sharps or flats into the music every time they occur, they can be written at the beginning of the staff as a key signature. Key signatures indicate that notes should always be played as sharps or flats unless they are canceled by naturals.

1 2 3 4 5 6 7

F C G D A E B

F C G D A E B

◁ **Sharps in a key signature**
The sharps in a key signature are always written in this order: F♯ first, then C♯, followed by G♯, D♯, A♯, E♯, and finally B♯.

1 2 3 4 5 6 7

B E A D G C F

B E A D G C F

◁ **Flats in a key signature**
The flats in a key signature are always written in the reverse order from the sharps: B♭ first, then E♭, followed by A♭, D♭, G♭, C♭, and finally F♭.

Key signatures with sharps

The keys shown on the staffs below all have sharps in their key signature, which must be written in the correct order: G major—1 sharp; D major—2 sharps; A major—3 sharps; E major—4 sharps; B major—5 sharps; F# major—6 sharps; and C# major—7 sharps.

▽ **Key signatures on the clefs**
The table below shows how the seven key signatures with sharps are written on different clefs.

	Treble clef	Bass clef	Alto clef	Tenor clef
G major (1 sharp)				
D major (2 sharps)				
A major (3 sharps)				
E major (4 sharps)				
B major (5 sharps)				
F# major (6 sharps)				
C# major (7 sharps)				

»

Key signatures with flats

These are the key signatures with flats. As with sharps, the flats must be written in the correct order: F major—1 flat; B♭ major—2 flats; E♭ major—3 flats; A♭ major—4 flats; D♭ major—5 flats; G♭ major—6 flats; and C♭ major—7 flats.

▽ **Key signatures on the clefs**
The table below shows how the seven key signatures with flats are written on the four different clefs.

	Treble clef	Bass clef	Alto clef	Tenor clef
F major (1 flat)				
B♭ major (2 flats)				
E♭ major (3 flats)				
A♭ major (4 flats)				
D♭ major (5 flats)				
G♭ major (6 flats)				
C♭ major (7 flats)				

How key signatures work

Key signatures are written before time signatures on the staff. Unlike time signatures, which are only written at the beginning of the first line on the staff, key signatures are written at the beginning of every new line. Once a key signature has indicated which notes are to be played as sharps or flats, there is no need to write a sharp or flat sign next to those notes. The exception to this is after an accidental (a sharp or flat outside the key signature) has been used in a bar.

▽ **Key signature with flats**
The music below is in A♭ major. The key signature indicates that the notes B, E, A, and D should be played as flats, so there is no need to write the flat sign next to them.

The key signature shows that B should be played as B♭.

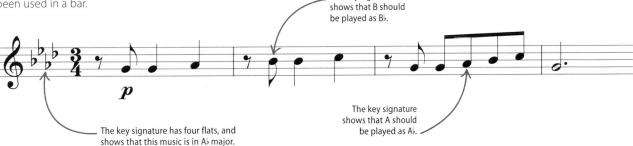

The key signature has four flats, and shows that this music is in A♭ major.

The key signature shows that A should be played as A♭.

▽ **Key signature with a sharp**
The music below is in G major and its key signature indicates that F should be played as F♯, so there is no need to write the sharp sign next to it. However, where other notes are sharp, a sharp sign is needed.

The key signature has one sharp, and shows that this music is in G major.

C♯ is not in the key signature, so the sharp here needs to be written into the music.

The key signature shows that F should be played as F♯.

What about C major?

Because a C major scale has no sharps or flats, the C major key signature has no sharps or flats written in it. If music is in a major key and doesn't have any sharps or flats in its key signature, that means it is in C major.

C major on treble clef

C major on bass clef

C major on alto clef

C major on tenor clef

▷ **On the staff**
This is how the key signature for C major—with no sharps or flats—is written on the treble, bass, alto, and tenor clefs.

If a piece of music does not have a **descriptive title**, its **key** can become an **important part** of its title. A famous example is **Elgar's Cello Concerto in E minor.**

The relative minor

The relative minor is the minor key that is most closely related to a given major key—called the relative major. The relative minor shares a key signature with its relative major key.

SEE ALSO	
❮ **60–61** Major scales	
❮ **62–63** Minor scales	
❮ **64–67** Keys	
The circle of fifths	**70–71** ❯
Harmony	**118–119** ❯

What is the relative minor?

The relationship between the relative major and relative minor can be seen by looking at the notes that their major and natural minor scales use. A natural minor scale is the relative minor to the major scale that uses exactly the same sharps and flats. Shown here are some major scales and their relative natural minor scales.

▽ **No sharps or flats**
Both C major and A natural minor scales have no sharps or flats, so A minor is the relative minor to C major.

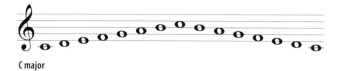

C major

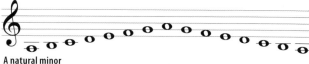

A natural minor

▽ **Two sharps**
Both D major and B natural minor scales have two sharps—F♯ and C♯—so B minor is the relative minor to D major.

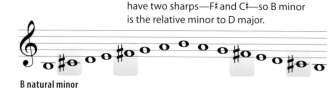

D major

B natural minor

▽ **Four flats**
Both A♭ major and F natural minor scales have four flats—B♭, A♭, E♭, and D♭—so F minor is the relative minor to A♭ major.

A♭ major

F natural minor

Relative major and relative minor

The starting note of a relative minor scale is a minor third below the starting note of its corresponding relative major scale. This means that the keynote of the relative minor is a minor third below the keynote of the relative major.

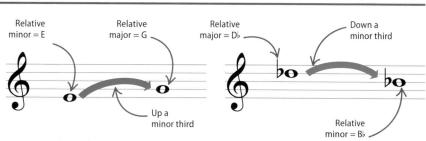

△ **Relative major**
G is a minor third above E, so G major is the relative major to E minor.

△ **Relative minor**
B♭ is a minor third below D♭, so B♭ minor is the relative minor to D♭ major.

Relative minors of major keys

Each major key has a relative minor key. The relative minor to a given major key has exactly the same sharps or flats in its key signature as that major key does.

▽ **Relative minors**
The table below shows all the different possible major keys, and the relative minors to these major keys.

Key signature	Major key	Minor key
B♭, E♭, A♭, D♭, G♭, C♭, F♭	C♭ major	A♭ minor
B♭, E♭, A♭, D♭, G♭, C♭	G♭ major	E♭ minor
B♭, E♭, A♭, D♭, G♭	D♭ major	B♭ minor
B♭, E♭, A♭, D♭	A♭ major	F minor
B♭, E♭, A♭	E♭ major	C minor
B♭, E♭	B♭ major	G minor
B♭	F major	D minor
No sharps or flats	C major	A minor
F♯	G major	E minor
F♯, C♯	D major	B minor
F♯, C♯, G♯	A major	F♯ minor
F♯, C♯, G♯, D♯	E major	C♯ minor
F♯, C♯, G♯, D♯, A♯	B major	G♯ minor
F♯, C♯, G♯, D♯, A♯, E♯	F♯ major	D♯ minor
F♯, C♯, G♯, D♯, A♯, E♯, B♯	C♯ major	A♯ minor

Key signatures for minor keys

The key signature for a minor key is exactly the same as the key signature for its relative major key. This is because the relative major and relative natural minor have exactly the same sharps or flats. Some examples of the key signatures for relative major and relative minor keys are shown below.

B♭ major → G minor

△ **Same key signature**
The key signatures for B♭ major and G minor have the same flats—B♭ and E♭—so they are written in exactly the same way.

E major → C♯ minor

△ **Same key signature**
The key signatures for E major and C♯ minor are written in the same way because they have the same sharps—F♯, C♯, G♯, and D♯.

Minor key signatures in practice

In practice, music in a minor key might use notes from that key's harmonic or melodic minor scales, as well as notes from its natural minor scale. If these notes are different from what is indicated in the key signature, they will need sharps or naturals written next to them wherever they occur in the music.

▽ **G harmonic minor scale**
This melody in G minor uses the notes of the G harmonic minor scale. B♭ and E♭ are in the key signature, but F♯ needs to be written wherever it occurs.

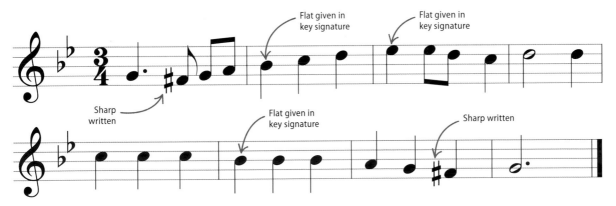

Flat given in key signature

Flat given in key signature

Sharp written

Flat given in key signature

Sharp written

The circle of fifths

The circle of fifths is a diagram that shows the relationship between the various major and minor keys. Understanding this diagram will help you remember how many sharps or flats a key signature has.

How does it work with major keys?

The circle of fifths illustrates the relationship between major keys that are a fifth apart. Starting from C major, as the keynote goes up a fifth, a sharp is added to the key signature of the new key. As the keynote goes down a fifth, a flat is added to the key signature.

▽ **Going up a fifth**
As the keynotes of the major keys shown on the staff below move up a fifth, their key signatures gain another sharp.

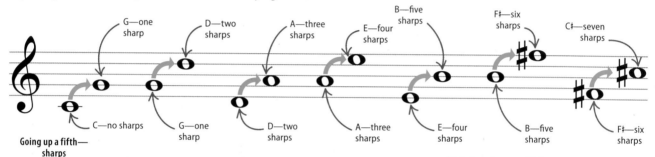

▽ **Going down a fifth**
As the keynotes of the major keys shown on the staff below move down a fifth, their key signatures gain another flat.

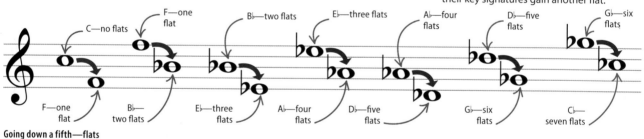

What about minor keys?

Because minor keys share a key signature with their relative major, their key signatures gain a sharp when the keynote goes up a fifth and gain a flat when the keynote goes down a fifth in the same way as major keys.

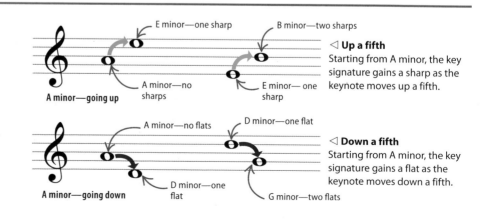

◁ **Up a fifth**
Starting from A minor, the key signature gains a sharp as the keynote moves up a fifth.

◁ **Down a fifth**
Starting from A minor, the key signature gains a flat as the keynote moves down a fifth.

The full circle

The circle of fifths diagram shows the major and minor keys, their corresponding key signatures, and how the key signatures gain or lose a sharp or a flat moving clockwise or counterclockwise through the circle.

▽ **Circle of fifths**
The outer circle shows the major keys, and the inner circle shows the minor keys. The relative major and relative minor keys share a key signature.

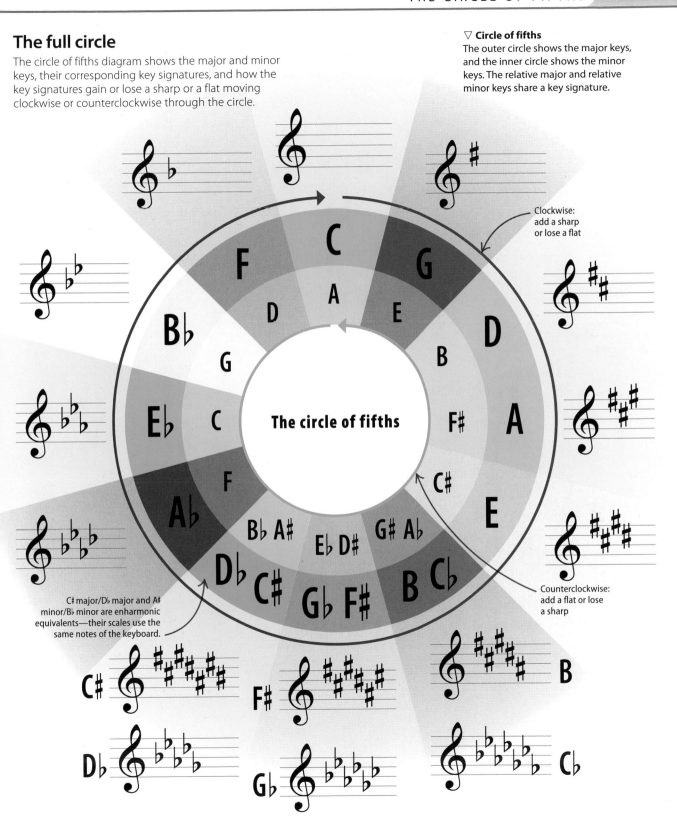

Clockwise: add a sharp or lose a flat

Counterclockwise: add a flat or lose a sharp

C♯ major/D♭ major and A♯ minor/B♭ minor are enharmonic equivalents—their scales use the same notes of the keyboard.

The circle of fifths

Accidentals

Accidentals are notes that are sharp or flat outside a key signature. Depending on the key signature, accidentals may be written as sharps, flats, naturals, double sharps, or double flats.

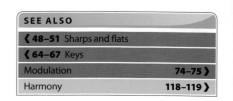

SEE ALSO	
❮ 48–51 Sharps and flats	
❮ 64–67 Keys	
Modulation	74–75 ❯
Harmony	118–119 ❯

Using accidentals

If a sharp, flat, or natural does not belong to the music's key signature, it is an accidental, and the symbol for the accidental must be written before the note on the staff. Double sharps and double flats are always accidentals.

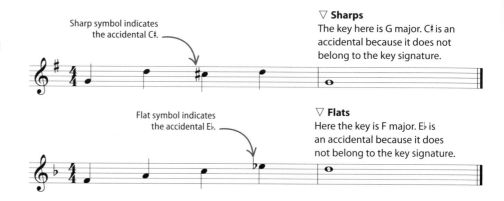

Sharp symbol indicates the accidental C♯.

▽ **Sharps**
The key here is G major. C♯ is an accidental because it does not belong to the key signature.

Flat symbol indicates the accidental E♭.

▽ **Flats**
Here the key is F major. E♭ is an accidental because it does not belong to the key signature.

Canceling accidentals

Accidentals should be canceled if the note that was an accidental earlier returns to being a note that belongs to the key signature within the same measure. This is done by writing a sharp, flat, or natural symbol before the accidental that has been canceled.

Type of accidental	Canceled by the accidental
Sharp	Natural
Flat	Natural
Natural	Sharp or flat
Double sharp	Single sharp
Double flat	Single flat

◁ **Canceling accidentals**
This table shows which accidentals are used to cancel sharps, flats, naturals, double sharps, and double flats.

◁ **Canceling sharps**
The key here is A major. The accidental D♯ is canceled by D♮. Flats are also canceled by naturals.

◁ **Canceling naturals**
Here the key is B♭ major. The accidental E♮ is canceled by E♭. In keys with sharps, naturals are canceled by sharps.

◁ **Canceling double sharps**
The key here is D♯ minor. The accidental C× is canceled by C♯.

◁ **Canceling double flats**
Here the key here is G♭ major. The accidental E♭♭ is canceled by E♭.

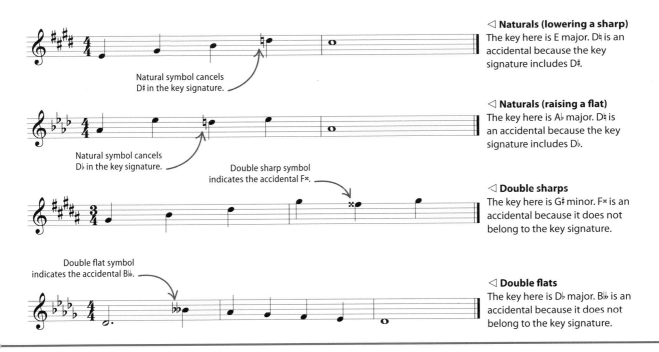

Naturals (lowering a sharp)
The key here is E major. D♮ is an accidental because the key signature includes D♯.

Natural symbol cancels D♯ in the key signature.

Naturals (raising a flat)
The key here is A♭ major. D♮ is an accidental because the key signature includes D♭.

Natural symbol cancels D♭ in the key signature.

Double sharp symbol indicates the accidental F×.

Double sharps
The key here is G♯ minor. F× is an accidental because it does not belong to the key signature.

Double flat symbol indicates the accidental B♭♭.

Double flats
The key here is D♭ major. B♭♭ is an accidental because it does not belong to the key signature.

Bar lines

Unless canceled, accidentals last until the end of the measure in which they are written. Once it is written, there is no need to write it again within the same measure. Bar lines cancel accidentals, unless a note is tied.

▽ **Bar lines**
In the example below, the accidental B♮ lasts until the end of the first measure, but the bar line cancels it in the second measure.

No need to write natural sign again.

B♭—bar line cancels accidental from the previous measure.

Tied notes

If an accidental has a tied note that lasts into the next measure, the bar line does not cancel the accidental. If it is canceled later within the next measure, once it is no longer tied, the canceled accidental needs to be written.

▽ **Tied notes**
The tied accidental F♯ is carried over to the next measure, and there is no need to write it out again.

Still an F♯

Need to show the canceled accidental.

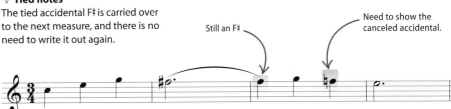

Accidentals in two clefs

When two lines of music are written together (as in piano music), the accidentals that occur in both clefs must be written, even if they occur in the same measure. We cannot assume that if they occur in one clef they will occur in the other too.

▽ **Treble and bass clef**
The accidental C♯ has to be written in both the treble clef and the bass clef.

Modulation

Modulation means moving from one key to another. This can be done either by changing the music's key signature or by adding accidentals to indicate that the music has moved to a different key.

SEE ALSO

❮ **64–67** Keys

❮ **70–71** The circle of fifths

❮ **72–73** Accidentals

Degrees of the scale   **124–125** ❯

Changing the key signature

The music usually has a double bar line if the key signature changes. The new key signature is then written after the double bar line. If sharps or flats in the old key signature are canceled, naturals are usually written before the double bar line, but are written after it if the new key lacks a key signature.

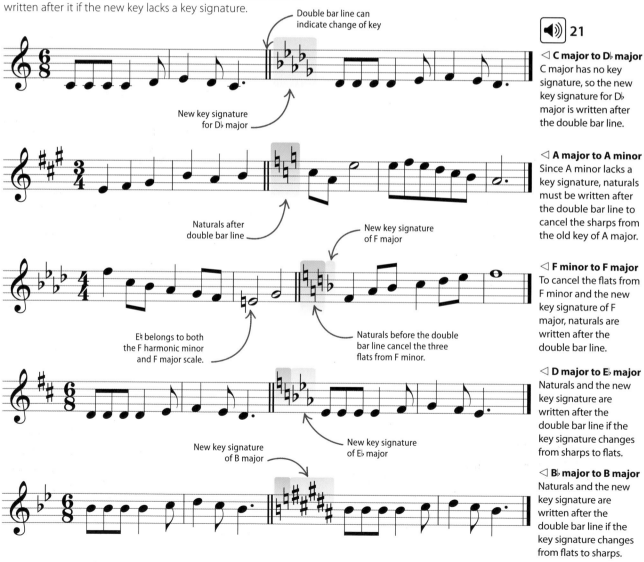

Double bar line can indicate change of key

New key signature for D♭ major

🔊 21

◁ **C major to D♭ major**
C major has no key signature, so the new key signature for D♭ major is written after the double bar line.

Naturals after double bar line

◁ **A major to A minor**
Since A minor lacks a key signature, naturals must be written after the double bar line to cancel the sharps from the old key of A major.

New key signature of F major

E♮ belongs to both the F harmonic minor and F major scale.

Naturals before the double bar line cancel the three flats from F minor.

◁ **F minor to F major**
To cancel the flats from F minor and the new key signature of F major, naturals are written after the double bar line.

New key signature of E♭ major

◁ **D major to E♭ major**
Naturals and the new key signature are written after the double bar line if the key signature changes from sharps to flats.

New key signature of B major

◁ **B♭ major to B major**
Naturals and the new key signature are written after the double bar line if the key signature changes from flats to sharps.

Modulation with accidentals

Modulation may be indicated with accidentals rather than with a new key signature, especially if the modulation is between two closely related keys, and if the music will soon return to its original key. Double bar lines do not occur in such instances.

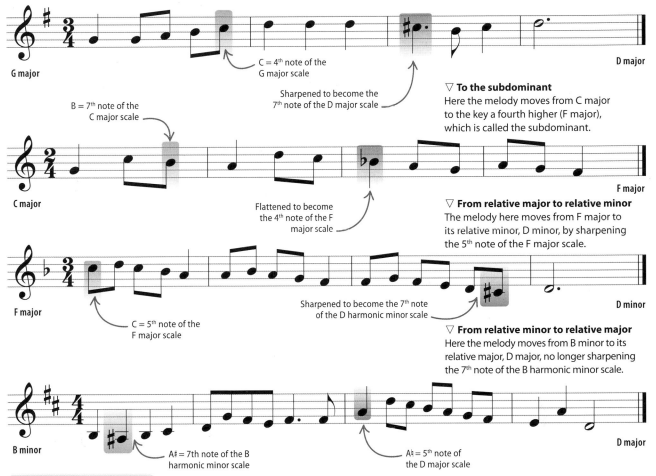

△ **To the dominant**
This melody moves from G major to the key a fifth higher (D major), which is called the dominant.

G major

C = 4th note of the G major scale

Sharpened to become the 7th note of the D major scale

D major

B = 7th note of the C major scale

△ **To the subdominant**
Here the melody moves from C major to the key a fourth higher (F major), which is called the subdominant.

C major

Flattened to become the 4th note of the F major scale

F major

△ **From relative major to relative minor**
The melody here moves from F major to its relative minor, D minor, by sharpening the 5th note of the F major scale.

F major

C = 5th note of the F major scale

Sharpened to become the 7th note of the D harmonic minor scale

D minor

△ **From relative minor to relative major**
Here the melody moves from B minor to its relative major, D major, no longer sharpening the 7th note of the B harmonic minor scale.

B minor

A♯ = 7th note of the B harmonic minor scale

A♮ = 5th note of the D major scale

D major

Ludwig van Beethoven

The German composer Ludwig van Beethoven (1770–1827) is one of the most important figures in the transition between Classical and Romantic music. His use of keys and harmony was very innovative for a composer of his time. A striking example of this is the modulations in "By the Brook" from the *Pastoral Symphony*. The music starts and ends in B♭ major, but modulates to keys such as G major, E♭ major, and C♭ major.

In **American marching band music,** if the march starts in a **major key,** the music often **modulates** to the **subdominant for the trio** section. If it starts in a **minor key,** it often **modulates to the relative major.**

Transposition

Transposition means writing the same music up or down a given interval, and in a different key. This is necessary for certain instruments, which are called transposing instruments.

SEE ALSO

❮ 56–59 Intervals

❮ 64–67 Keys

❮ 72–73 Accidentals

Brass 178–179 ❯

Transposing instruments

If a note is played on a transposing instrument, the note that will sound is a given interval above—or more usually, below—the note that is played and written on the staff. Some of the most common transposing instruments are the clarinet (in B♭ or A), horn, and alto saxophone. Shown here are the notes that sound if the C above Middle C is played on these instruments.

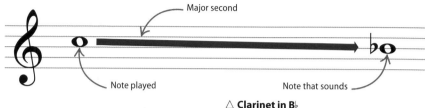

Major second

Note played

Note that sounds

△ **Clarinet in B♭**
The sounding note on a clarinet in B♭ is a major second below the note that is played. Thus, if a C is played on a clarinet in B♭, the note that sounds is B♭.

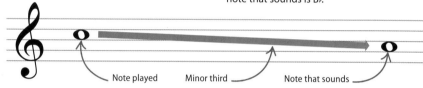

Note played

Minor third

Note that sounds

△ **Clarinet in A**
The note that sounds on a clarinet in A is a minor third below the note that is played. So if a C is played on a clarinet in A, the note that sounds is A.

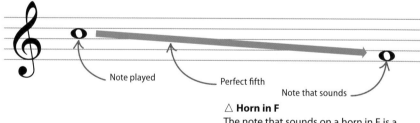

Note played

Perfect fifth

Note that sounds

△ **Horn in F**
The note that sounds on a horn in F is a perfect fifth below the note that is played. Therefore, if a C is played on a horn in F, the sounding note is F.

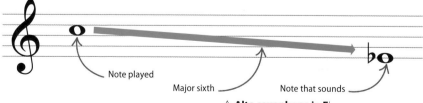

Note played

Major sixth

Note that sounds

△ **Alto saxophone in E♭**
The note that sounds on an alto saxophone in E♭ is a major sixth below the note that is played. So if a C is played on an alto saxophone in E♭, the note that sounds is E♭.

Concert pitch

The pitch at which a note sounds is known as "concert pitch." With transposing instruments, the note that is played or written on the staff is at written pitch, and the note that sounds is at concert pitch. With many instruments, such as the flute, oboe, piano, violin, viola, and cello, the note that is written already sounds at concert pitch. These are known as nontransposing instruments.

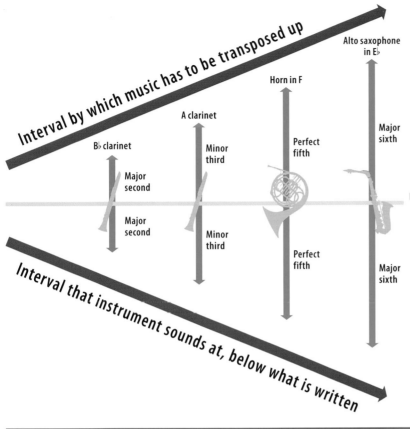

Interval by which music has to be transposed up

Interval that instrument sounds at, below what is written

Alto saxophone in E♭

Horn in F

A clarinet

B♭ clarinet

Major second

Major second

Minor third

Minor third

Perfect fifth

Perfect fifth

Major sixth

Major sixth

Intended pitch

Writing music for transposing instruments

When writing music for a transposing instrument that sounds below concert pitch, the written music has to be transposed above concert pitch. The interval by which the music has to be transposed up mirrors the interval down between the written note and the note that sounds on the transposing instrument.

◁ **Intervals for transposing instruments**
Shown here are the intervals below written pitch for some of the most common transposing instruments. Music for these instruments must be written at the same interval above concert pitch.

How to transpose

The first thing to take into account when transposing is the key. For example, if you are transposing music in G major up a major second, take the keynote, G, and transpose it up a major second to A. The new keynote, A, means the transposed music is in A major.

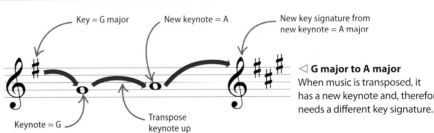

Key = G major

New keynote = A

New key signature from new keynote = A major

Keynote = G

Transpose keynote up

◁ **G major to A major**
When music is transposed, it has a new keynote and, therefore, needs a different key signature.

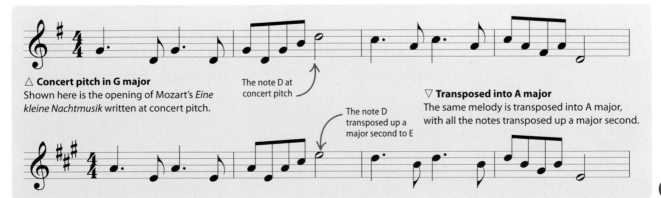

△ **Concert pitch in G major**
Shown here is the opening of Mozart's *Eine kleine Nachtmusik* written at concert pitch.

The note D at concert pitch

The note D transposed up a major second to E

▽ **Transposed into A major**
The same melody is transposed into A major, with all the notes transposed up a major second.

»

» Transposition and accidentals

When transposing a melody that includes accidentals, we must ensure that the accidentals are also transposed. The transposed melody might include the exact same accidentals as the melody at concert pitch, but this is not always the case. It depends on the interval of transposition.

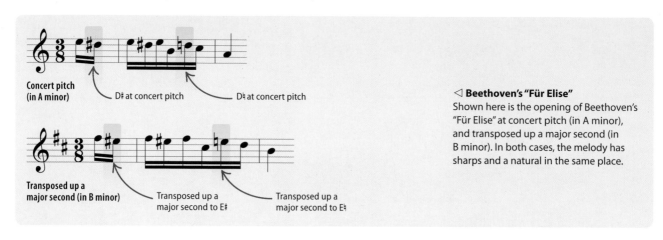

Concert pitch
(in A minor)

D♯ at concert pitch   D♯ at concert pitch

Transposed up a
major second (in B minor)

Transposed up a
major second to E♯

Transposed up a
major second to E♯

◁ **Beethoven's "Für Elise"**
Shown here is the opening of Beethoven's "Für Elise" at concert pitch (in A minor), and transposed up a major second (in B minor). In both cases, the melody has sharps and a natural in the same place.

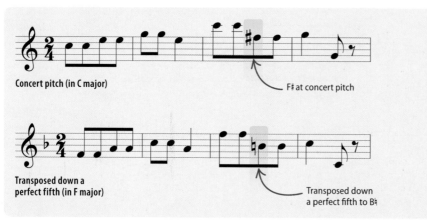

Concert pitch (in C major)

F♯ at concert pitch

Transposed down a
perfect fifth (in F major)

Transposed down
a perfect fifth to B♮

◁ **Haydn's Surprise Symphony**
This extract from Haydn's "Surprise" Symphony at concert pitch (in C major) includes the accidental F♯. Transposed down a perfect fifth, with the melody now in F major, this accidental becomes B♮.

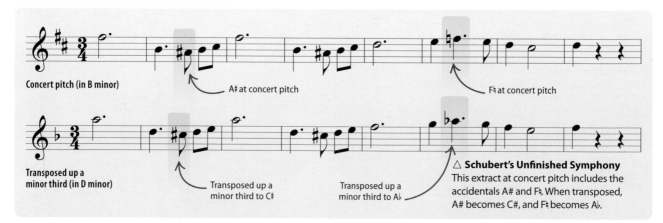

Concert pitch (in B minor)

A♯ at concert pitch

F♮ at concert pitch

Transposed up a
minor third (in D minor)

Transposed up a
minor third to C♯

Transposed up a
minor third to A♭

△ **Schubert's Unfinished Symphony**
This extract at concert pitch includes the accidentals A♯ and F♮. When transposed, A♯ becomes C♯, and F♮ becomes A♭.

Transposition in action

Shown below are extracts from three famous pieces of classical music:
Rossini's *William Tell* Overture, Johann Strauss II's *The Beautiful Blue Danube*,
and Dvořák's "New World" Symphony. These are shown at concert pitch, and
then transposed up a given interval for a particular transposing instrument.

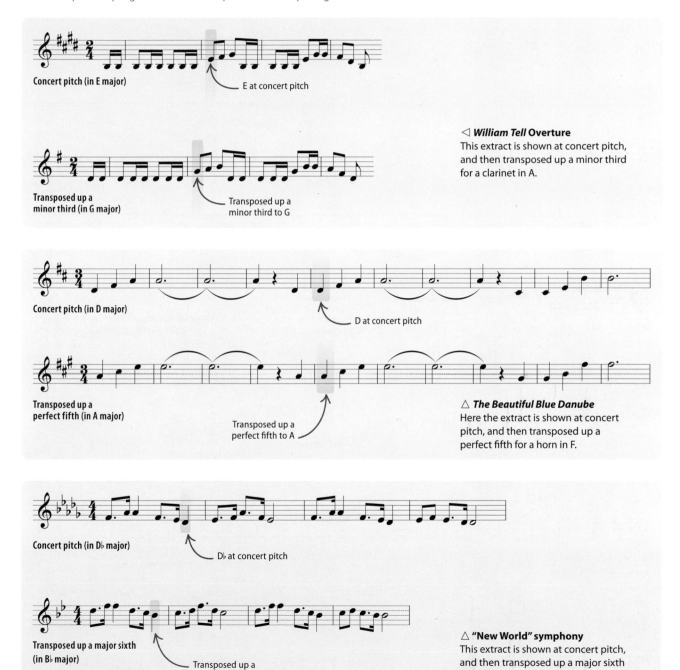

Concert pitch (in E major)

E at concert pitch

Transposed up a
minor third (in G major)

Transposed up a
minor third to G

◁ ***William Tell* Overture**
This extract is shown at concert pitch,
and then transposed up a minor third
for a clarinet in A.

Concert pitch (in D major)

D at concert pitch

Transposed up a
perfect fifth (in A major)

Transposed up a
perfect fifth to A

△ ***The Beautiful Blue Danube***
Here the extract is shown at concert
pitch, and then transposed up a
perfect fifth for a horn in F.

Concert pitch (in D♭ major)

D♭ at concert pitch

Transposed up a major sixth
(in B♭ major)

Transposed up a
major sixth to B♭

△ **"New World" symphony**
This extract is shown at concert pitch,
and then transposed up a major sixth
for an alto saxophone in E♭.

Other scales

In addition to major and minor scales, there are several other types of scales. These scales all cover the range of an octave, but they follow different patterns of intervals from the major and minor scales, and may include more or fewer notes.

Chromatic scales

A chromatic scale includes all the black and white keys of the keyboard, within the range of an octave. Each note of the chromatic scale is a half step apart. This means that the chromatic scale includes 13 notes in all, from top to bottom.

The chromatic scale rises through 12 half steps to reach the top note, which is one octave above the starting note.

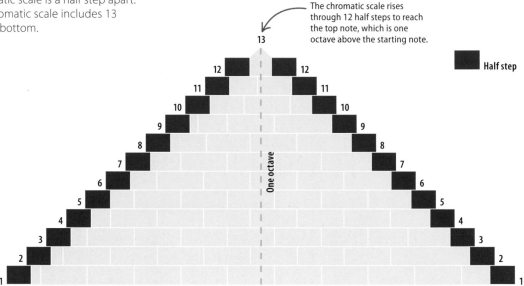

■ Half step

▷ **Chromatic scale**
A chromatic scale spans one octave and includes 13 notes from top to bottom, each of which is one half step apart.

▽ **On the staff**
Here are some examples of chromatic scales on the staff, one starting on C, and the other starting on A♭. Each step in the chromatic scale is one half step.

Chromatic scale starting on C   22

Chromatic scale starting on A♭

Whole step scales

A whole step scale also spans the range of one octave, but each note of the whole step scale is a whole step above or below the next one. This means that this scale includes seven notes in total, from top to bottom. It is broken down into six steps, and does not include any half steps.

REAL WORLD

Claude Debussy (1862–1918)

Claude Debussy is the composer who is most closely associated with Impressionism, a style of music that makes extensive use of colorful harmonies and scales, other than the major and minor scales. Debussy often used whole step scales to make his music evocative and atmospheric.

The whole step scale rises through six whole steps to reach the top note, which is one octave above the starting note.

□ **Whole step**

7

6   6

5   5

4   4

One octave

3   3

2   2

1   1

◁ **Whole step scale**
Shown here is the whole step scale, broken down into six whole steps. Spanning the range of one octave, the whole step scale includes seven notes in all from top to bottom, each of which is one full step apart.

▽ **On the staff**
Shown here are some examples of whole step scales on the staff, one starting on C, and the other starting on E♭. Each one is one whole step from the one before it.

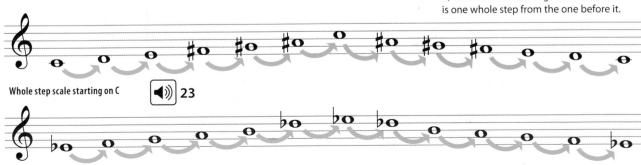

Whole step scale starting on C   🔊 23

Whole step scale starting on E♭

Pentatonic scales

The word "pentatonic" means "five whole steps," and pentatonic scales are built on just five different notes of the scale. They include six notes from top to bottom, but the top and bottom notes count as the same note because they are one octave apart. There are two types of pentatonic scale: major, and minor.

 24

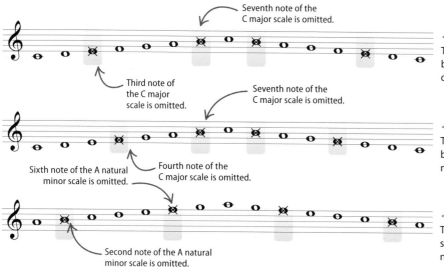

Seventh note of the C major scale is omitted.

◁ **Major pentatonic scale I**
This scale is based on the major scale, but it omits the third and seventh notes of the major scale.

Third note of the C major scale is omitted.

Seventh note of the C major scale is omitted.

◁ **Major pentatonic scale II**
This scale is based on the major scale, but it omits the fourth and seventh notes of the major scale.

Sixth note of the A natural minor scale is omitted.

Fourth note of the C major scale is omitted.

◁ **Minor pentatonic scale**
This scale is based on the natural minor scale, but it omits the second and sixth notes of the natural minor scale.

Second note of the A natural minor scale is omitted.

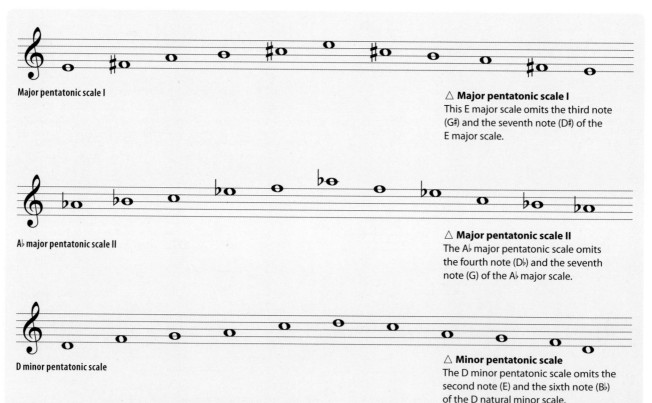

Major pentatonic scale I

△ **Major pentatonic scale I**
This E major scale omits the third note (G♯) and the seventh note (D♯) of the E major scale.

A♭ major pentatonic scale II

△ **Major pentatonic scale II**
The A♭ major pentatonic scale omits the fourth note (D♭) and the seventh note (G) of the A♭ major scale.

D minor pentatonic scale

△ **Minor pentatonic scale**
The D minor pentatonic scale omits the second note (E) and the sixth note (B♭) of the D natural minor scale.

Gamelan music

Gamelan is traditional Indonesian ensemble music that is usually played on tuned percussion instruments, including xylophones and metallophones such as the saron demung shown here. Gamelan music is played together by a group, and prominently features the pentatonic scale.

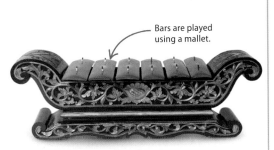

Bars are played using a mallet.

Saron demung

Major and **minor pentatonic scales** can be played using **only** the **black keys** on the **keyboard.**

Blues scales

Used in jazz, blues, and pop music, blues scales are a basis for jazz improvization. They are very similar to minor pentatonic scales, but they include an extra note. This is the third note of the minor pentatonic scale, raised by one half step.

 25

▽ **Blues scale**
The blues scale shown here starts on A. It has all the notes of the A minor pentatonic scale, but also includes a D♯—one half step up from the third note (D) of the A minor pentatonic scale.

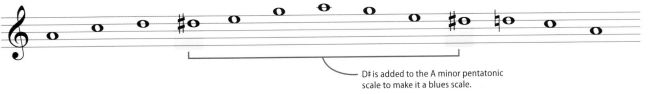

D♯ is added to the A minor pentatonic scale to make it a blues scale.

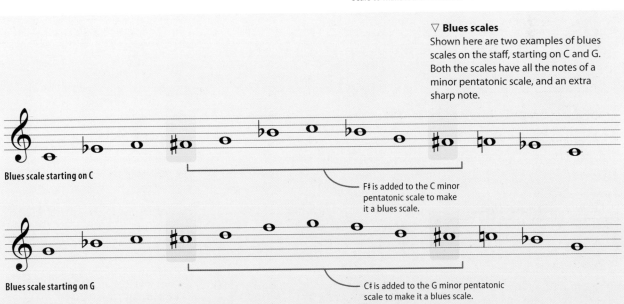

▽ **Blues scales**
Shown here are two examples of blues scales on the staff, starting on C and G. Both the scales have all the notes of a minor pentatonic scale, and an extra sharp note.

Blues scale starting on C

F♯ is added to the C minor pentatonic scale to make it a blues scale.

Blues scale starting on G

C♯ is added to the G minor pentatonic scale to make it a blues scale.

⟫ Diminished scales I

Diminished scales (also called octatonic scales) include a total of nine notes from top to bottom, and follow an alternating pattern of whole steps and half steps. The first type of diminished scale is broken down into the pattern: whole step, half step, whole step, half step, whole step, half step, whole step, half step, going up the scale, and this is mirrored going down the scale as well.

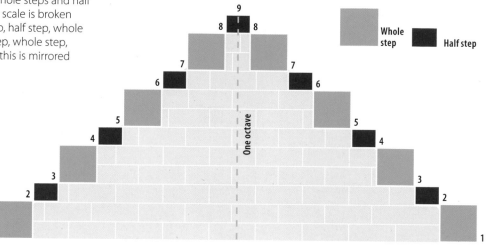

▷ **Beginning with a whole step**
This diminished scale begins with a whole step between its first two notes, and then alternates whole steps with half steps going up and down the scale.

Whole step between C and D, the first two notes of the scale.

Whole step between B and A, following the first half step going down the scale.

Diminished scale starting on C

Half step between B and C at the top of the scale—the pattern of whole steps and half steps going up the scale is mirrored going down the scale.

🔊 26 △ **On the staff**
Shown on the staff is a diminished scale starting on C. The interval between the first two notes is a whole step, the next interval is a half step, and the scale is broken down into alternating whole steps and half steps.

REAL WORLD

Nikolai Rimsky-Korsakov (1844–1908)

Russian composers, such as Nikolai Rimsky-Korsakov, used the diminished scale to make their music sound exotic, and to create a sense of magic and mystery. The diminished scale features prominently in Rimsky-Korsakov's opera *Kashchey the Immortal*, which is based on a Russian fairy tale about an evil wizard.

In his autobiography, **Rimsky-Korsakov** claimed to have **invented** the **diminished scale.** However, it is likely that the **scale dates back** as far as the **7th century,** and was **first used** in **traditional Persian music.**

Diminished scales II

The second type of diminished scale also follows an alternating pattern of whole and half steps, but the interval between its first two notes is a half step. This scale is broken down into the pattern: half step, whole step, half step, whole step, half step, whole step, half step, whole step, going up the scale, and this is mirrored going down the scale.

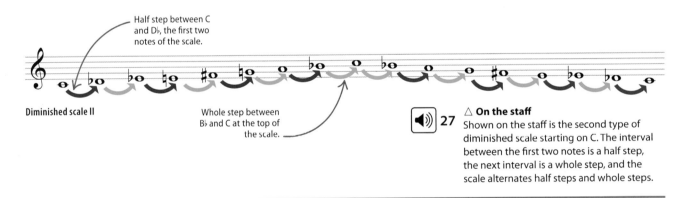

Whole step

Half step

One octave

▷ **Beginning with a half step**
This diminished scale begins with a half step between its first two notes, and then alternates half steps with whole steps going up and down the scale.

Half step between C and D♭, the first two notes of the scale.

Diminished scale II

Whole step between B♭ and C at the top of the scale.

 27

△ **On the staff**
Shown on the staff is the second type of diminished scale starting on C. The interval between the first two notes is a half step, the next interval is a whole step, and the scale alternates half steps and whole steps.

Enigmatic scale

The enigmatic scale is said to have been invented by the Italian composer Giuseppe Verdi, and he used it in "Ave Maria" from his *Four Sacred Pieces*. It is a very unconventional scale that combines the elements of the major, minor, and whole whole step scales.

28

▽ **On the staff**
Shown here is the enigmatic scale starting on C. The striking feature of the enigmatic scale is its fourth note, which is sharp on the way up the scale, but not on the way down.

F♯ going up the scale.

F♮ going down the scale.

Enigmatic scale

Modes

Modes are variants of the major and minor keys, and are based on modal scales. Most modal scales are similar to, but slightly different from, major or natural minor scales.

SEE ALSO

❰ 60–61	Major scales	
❰ 62–63	Minor scales	
Degrees of the scale		124–125 ❱
Folk, world, and roots		202–203 ❱

Modes and the major scale

There are seven main types of mode: Ionian, Dorian, Phrygian, Lydian, Mixolydian, Aeolian, and Locrian. Modal scales use the same notes as the major scale, but each modal scale starts on a different note of the major scale.

▽ **Modes and modal scales**
This table shows the seven modes, and the starting position and note of their modal scales using only the white keys of the keyboard.

Mode	Note of major scale that is starting note of modal scale	Starting note of modal scale using only the white keys
Ionian	1st note (tonic)	C
Dorian	2nd note (supertonic)	D
Phrygian	3rd note (mediant)	E
Lydian	4th note (subdominant)	F
Mixolydian	5th note (dominant)	G
Aeolian	6th note (submediant)	A
Locrian	7th note (leading note)	B

REAL WORLD

Ralph Vaughan Williams

Many folk songs are in Dorian, Lydian, Mixolydian, and Aeolian modes. The composer Ralph Vaughan Williams was a collector of folk songs, and his music features a lot of modal folk tunes. His *English Folk Song Suite*, for example, includes folk melodies in Dorian and Mixolydian modes.

Modal scales

Shown here are the seven main modal scales using only the white keys of the keyboard. If the same modal scale starts on a different note, the pattern of whole steps and half steps must be maintained by using some black keys.

 29

 Whole step   Half step

▽ **Ionian mode**
The Ionian modal scale is exactly the same as the major scale. Music in a major key is, therefore, also in Ionian mode.

▽ **Dorian mode**
The Dorian modal scale is similar to the natural minor scale, but its sixth note is one half step higher.

6th note is one half step higher than in natural minor scale.

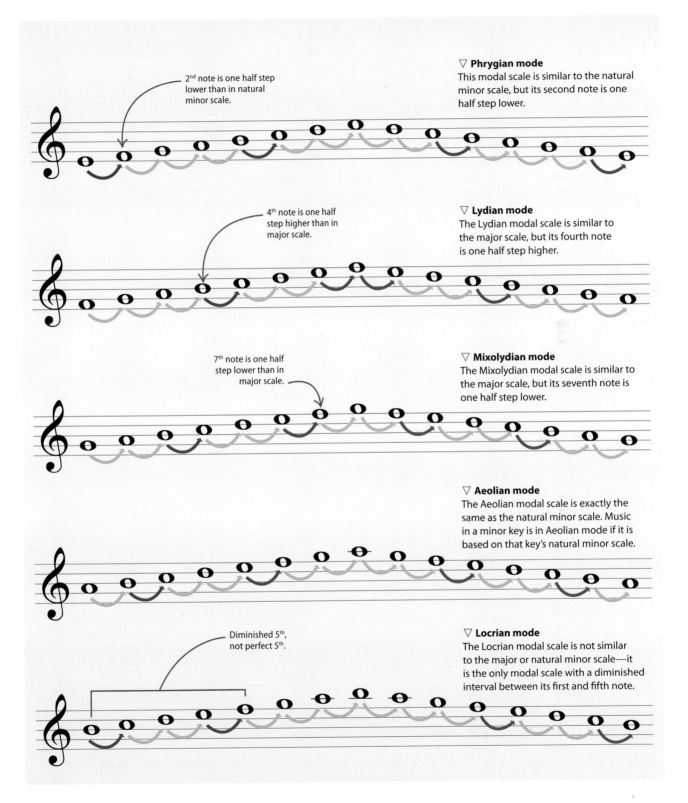

2nd note is one half step lower than in natural minor scale.

▽ **Phrygian mode**
This modal scale is similar to the natural minor scale, but its second note is one half step lower.

4th note is one half step higher than in major scale.

▽ **Lydian mode**
The Lydian modal scale is similar to the major scale, but its fourth note is one half step higher.

7th note is one half step lower than in major scale.

▽ **Mixolydian mode**
The Mixolydian modal scale is similar to the major scale, but its seventh note is one half step lower.

▽ **Aeolian mode**
The Aeolian modal scale is exactly the same as the natural minor scale. Music in a minor key is in Aeolian mode if it is based on that key's natural minor scale.

Diminished 5th, not perfect 5th.

▽ **Locrian mode**
The Locrian modal scale is not similar to the major or natural minor scale—it is the only modal scale with a diminished interval between its first and fifth note.

Tonality and atonality

Music that is in a definite major or minor key, or mode, is known as tonal music. Music that does not have a key signature is known as atonal music.

SEE ALSO	
❰ 64–67 Keys	
❰ 72–73 Accidentals	
❰ 74–75 Modulation	
Harmony	118–119 ❱
Consonance and dissonance	120–121 ❱
Modern period	214–215 ❱

Is it in a key?

Most Western music is tonal, but many 20th- and 21st-century classical works are atonal. To decide whether or not music is in a key, look at the key signature, see if the music is organized around a keynote, and consider what accidentals are featured.

Tonal music	Atonal music
Has a key signature (unless the music is in C major or A minor)	No key signature
Music is organized around the keynote, and usually starts and ends in the key suggested by the key signature	No sense that any one note is more important than the other in the music
Any accidental is likely to be closely related to the key signature	Lots of accidentals that cannot be related back to a key in any logical way

◁ **Comparison**
This table shows the differences between tonal and atonal music. While tonal music has features that identify it with a particular key, atonal music lacks these features.

Tonal music

Shown here is an excerpt from Beethoven's *Pathétique* Piano Sonata—tonal music in the key of A♭ major. It has a key signature, the keynote A♭ features prominently in the music, and the accidentals involve modulations to keys that are closely related to A♭ major.

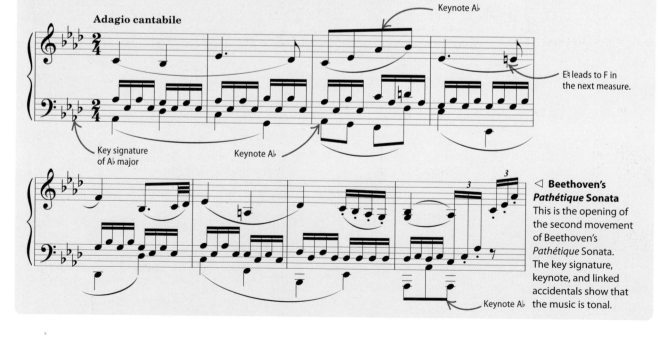

Adagio cantabile

Keynote A♭

E♮ leads to F in the next measure.

Key signature of A♭ major

Keynote A♭

Keynote A♭

◁ **Beethoven's Pathétique Sonata**
This is the opening of the second movement of Beethoven's *Pathétique* Sonata. The key signature, keynote, and linked accidentals show that the music is tonal.

Atonal music

This excerpt from Liszt's *Bagatelle Without Tonality* is atonal, it does not have a key signature, and the notes C and A do not feature prominently enough to show whether the music is in C major or A minor. There are also lots of accidentals, none of which lead the music toward a definite key.

▽ **Liszt's *Bagatelle Without Tonality***
The excerpt below shows that this piece is atonal. There is no key signature or keynote, and the accidentals are not related to any obvious key.

LOOKING CLOSER

Serialism

Some atonal music is composed using a serialist or a 12-tone technique. Serialism involves putting the 12 different notes of the chromatic scale into a chosen order. This is called a tone row. The notes of a serialist piece follow the order of the tone row on which the piece is based.

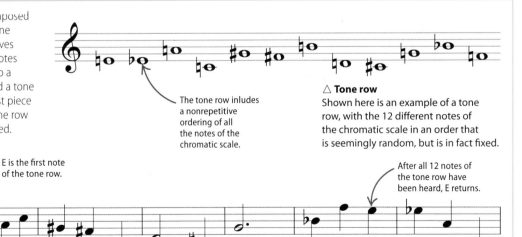

The tone row inludes a nonrepetitive ordering of all the notes of the chromatic scale.

△ **Tone row**
Shown here is an example of a tone row, with the 12 different notes of the chromatic scale in an order that is seemingly random, but is in fact fixed.

E is the first note of the tone row.

After all 12 notes of the tone row have been heard, E returns.

△ **Melody based on tone row**
This melody uses the notes of the tone row shown above, in the exact same order.

Melody

What is a tune?

Tune is another word for melody. When pitch and rhythm combine in a seamless entity, the listener hears both parts as a unit and can easily identify the "tune."

SEE ALSO
❮ **10–11** What is music?
❮ **44–45** Tempo

Familiar tunes

Singable, hummable, or whistleable, familiar tunes are "catchy." This means that they are easy to hear, remember, and repeat. Memorable tunes become familiar ones when they appear over and over in various settings, often with different lyrics or varied instrumentation.

◁ **"Twinkle Twinkle"**
In this well-known tune, both the order of pitches and the rhythmic pattern are familiar and easy to remember.

Rhythm and melody

As the combination of rhythm and melody is linked to the way a listener hears and remembers a tune, separating and examining them separately is often disorienting. Both parts work together to give a melody its individual and distinctive character.

◁ **Rhythmic notation**
Shown here is the rhythmic notation, or pitchless notes, placed along a single horizontal line, for a tune you probably know. You may be able to guess it from the rhythm alone.

◁ **Pitches**
Here are only the pitches for the same melody, with no rhythm, no time signature, bar lines, or note lengths.

△ **Recognize the tune?**
Did you guess the tune from either its distinctive rhythm, or its characteristic melody? It is "Skip to My Lou." Here it is in its entirety.

Wordless tunes

Often tunes are so memorable that even if they have words, the text is less distinctive than the melody itself. If a melody's pitch and rhythm are unforgettable, even humming it without any words at all is rewarding. A good tune is catchy regardless of its words, as in the example shown below.

▽ **"Deck the Halls"**
What is the most unique thing about this tune—the rhythm or the pitches? It's probably not the words!

Do it yourself

Try taking the rhythm of a tune you already know and write a new set of pitches to go along with it. For example, take the rhythmic notation for "Skip to My Lou" and write a new melody to that rhythm. Next, use just the pitches to "Skip to My Lou" and create a new rhythm.

▽ **Create a new rhythm**
Use the natural meter of the lyrics and vary it to create a new rhythmic pattern. Try for just the right amount of repetition and contrast.

△ **New melody**
Try out your new melody to see if it's "singable." Are the phrases pleasing, and does the contour of the notes fit within your voice?

Phrasing and phrase marks

Phrases divide melodies into musical sentences. Similar to punctuation marks, they show where a musical thought stops and another one begins. Phrase marks indicate where performers may breathe, or musically regroup for a new idea.

Musical sentences

Musical phrase marks are long, gentle arches that put an entire musical thought under one umbrella. Generally, a phrase sounds relatively complete even when played out of context, especially if it ends on *do* or a tonic chord.

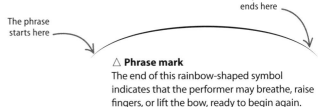

The phrase starts here

The phrase ends here

△ **Phrase mark**
The end of this rainbow-shaped symbol indicates that the performer may breathe, raise fingers, or lift the bow, ready to begin again.

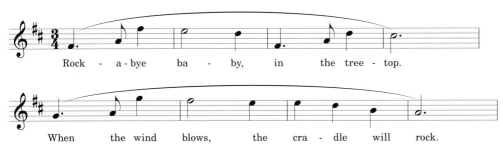

Rock - a - bye ba - by, in the tree - top.

When the wind blows, the cra - dle will rock.

◁ **Phrase marks in a tune**
Sing this lyrical tune, "Rock-a-bye Baby," and observe how the first phrase finishes at the end of the first complete thought.

Places to breathe

Musical phrase marks indicate where singers would naturally take a breath—at the end of an idea. The phrase endings here coincide with commas or periods in the text. Keyboard, wind, and string players observe the same breaks; this helps listeners organize the sounds.

Imagine if there were **no commas** and **no periods** in anything you ever read; it would be so **confusing,** and you would probably have a **hard time understanding** what the **author intended to say.**

A - las! My love, you do me wrong to cast me off—dis - court - eous - ly; And

I have lov - ed you so long,—de - light - ing in——your com pa - ny.

◁ **Phrase marks in a tune**
Longer phrases sound more pleasing and musical than shorter ones, which sound choppy. In this extract from the English folk song "Greensleeves," the phrase extends over the exclamation point and the comma contained in the text.

Phrase lengths

Phrase lengths of four and eight measures are most common in music, and melodies are often composed of several consecutive phrases put together. Regardless of the length, a phrase has meaningful structure, with a beginning, a period of forward motion, and a definite cadence, or stopping point.

Circular breathing

While breathing is typically considered an integral part of musical phrasing, some wind players train themselves to do circular breathing—taking air in through the nose while simultaneously pushing air out through the mouth, removing the necessity of stopping the sound to take a breath. Smooth jazz saxophonist Kenny G once held a note for almost 46 minutes!

◁ **Four-bar phrases**
Shown here are the last eight bars of "Ode to Joy," which has four four-measure phrases. The penultimate phrase ends on an expectant-sounding *so* (scale degree 5), and the quarter rest here makes a clean break before the last phrase.

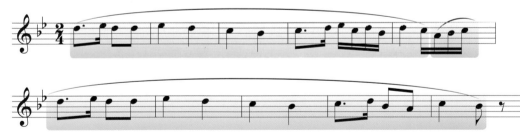

◁ **Other phrase lengths**
Four- and eight-measure phrases are most common, but other phrase lengths can be found, like the five-measure phrases in Haydn's *Variations on a Theme*. The second phrase begins with three quick pick-up notes in measure five.

Phrase endings

Phrase endings are logical places for musicians to break or pause in their playing, signaling to listeners that what follows begins a new musical thought. Musical notation may include symbols directing musicians when to pause.

△ **Comma**
The conventional place to breathe is at the end of a phrase, sometimes also indicated with a comma.

△ **Up-bow**
An up-bow may reinforce a composer's phrasing choices; this symbol may indicate lifting the bow at the end of a phrase.

△ **Down-bow**
The down-bow instructs players to reset the bow on the strings; it may be used for a strong downbeat at the beginning of a phrase.

Types of phrases

Phrases often work together in pairs. The relationship between two phrases may be characterized as question-and-answer, call-and-response, or antecedent and consequent.

Question-and-answer phrases

A question phrase doesn't sound complete on its own. Question phrases end on a more unstable whole note of the scale—usually scale degree 2, 4, 5, or 7—and are followed by an answer phrase, which resolves to scale degree 1 or *do*.

Note that the first phrase of "Mary Had a Little Lamb" ends on scale degree 5, with an upward motion.

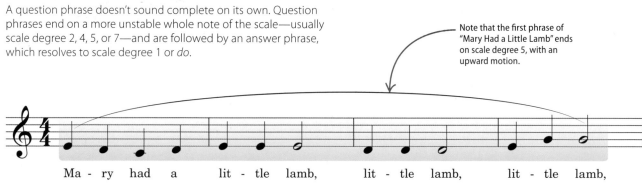

Ma - ry had a lit - tle lamb, lit - tle lamb, lit - tle lamb,

△ **Unfinished melody**
Sing the above question phrase to yourself and observe the feeling of anticipation you get on the last note.

The phrase ends here with downward finality through scale degrees 3, 2, and 1.

Ma - ry had a lit - tle lamb whose fleece was white as snow.

△ **Answering phrases**
Note that the answer phrase is the same length as the question phrase, but it ends on scale degree 1. This gives the phrase ending a sense of finality.

Call-and-response

Call-and-response phrases have been used as communication in various cultures, including many in Africa and India. In these, one player might play or sing a message (the "call") and another performer would reply musically (the "response").

▷ **Yombe children's game song**
In this example, the leader sings, "the slender plantain," and the chorus sing, "pick it up". There is no break between the two parts so it sounds like one phrase.

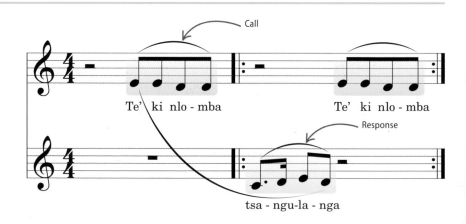

Call

Te' ki nlo - mba   Te' ki nlo - mba

Response

tsa - ngu-la - nga

Antecedent and consequent

When an antecedent and consequent phrase are connected, the entire thing is called a period. Ante is Latin for "before," and consequent is Latin for "following." Antecedent phrases almost always end on a whole note that is part of the V chord, which is built on scale degree 5.

▽ **Parallel period**

This example of Brahm's theme, as well as "Mary Had a Little Lamb," are both parallel periods. This means that the antecedent and the consequent phrases are very similar.

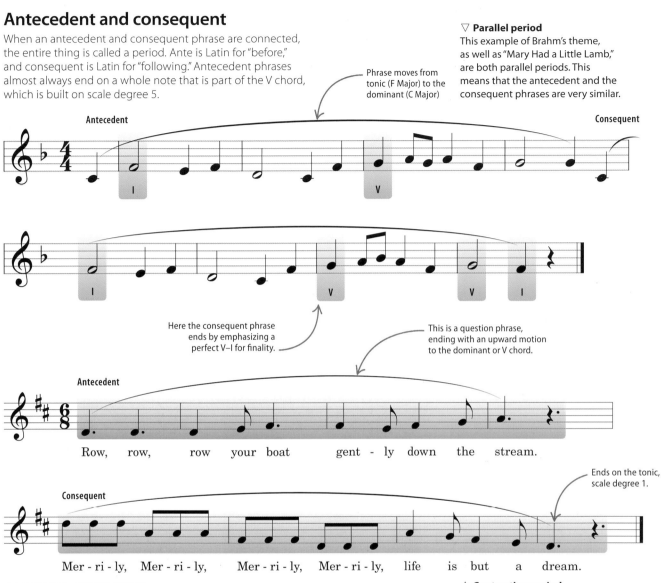

Phrase moves from tonic (F Major) to the dominant (C Major)

Antecedent

I

V

Consequent

I

V

V

I

Here the consequent phrase ends by emphasizing a perfect V–I for finality.

This is a question phrase, ending with an upward motion to the dominant or V chord.

Antecedent

Row, row, row your boat gent - ly down the stream.

Ends on the tonic, scale degree 1.

Consequent

Mer - ri - ly, Mer - ri - ly, Mer - ri - ly, Mer - ri - ly, life is but a dream.

△ **Contrasting period**

Contrasting periods are rhythmically and melodically different from one another. Here phrase one uses longer note values in an ascending contour, while phrase two has shorter notes and travels downward.

Call-and-response

The call-and-response technique has been adopted by many composers. Often the call phrase changes, but the response phrase stays the same. One of the most popular call-and-response tunes is Harry Belafonte's 1956 recording of the "Banana Boat Song." In this traditional Jamaican tune, the call changes frequently, but the response phrase is always "Daylight come and I wan' go home."

Sequences

Sometimes composers repeat melodies note for note, but at a higher or lower pitch than the original. This repetition is called a sequence.

Simple sequencing

In many familiar folk tunes, sequencing at a higher or lower pitch interval is used to vary repetitions of the same material. The reuse of melodic ideas—starting on different pitches, but using similar jumps in pitch between notes—brings cohesion to the music.

▽ **"A-hunting we will go"**
Written in 1777 by Thomas Arne for *The Beggar's Opera*, this tune has become a favorite melody in folk songs and nursery rhymes.

The same melody is sequenced by transposing up a major third to start on scale degree 3, or *mi*.

New material with similar rhythmic character.

Combines the pitches of the first two phrases in a climb back down to 1 or *do*.

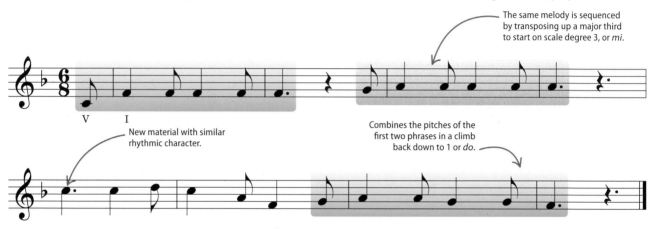

Sequencing at an interval

Composers use sequencing at a variety of intervals. Here a simple ascending scale is sequenced once at an interval of a perfect 4th. The entire motif—melodic fragment or phrase—is repeated, but starts four scale degrees higher.

▽ **Sequence 1**
This fragment starts on scale degree 1 or *do*, moving up the scale. The next fragment maintains upward run of notes motion, beginning on 4 or *fa*.

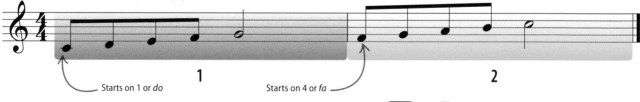

Starts on 1 or *do*   1   Starts on 4 or *fa*   2

🔊 30

▽ **Sequence 2**
The same simple motif is shown below. An upward run of notes is sequenced four times, moving up a whole step each time.

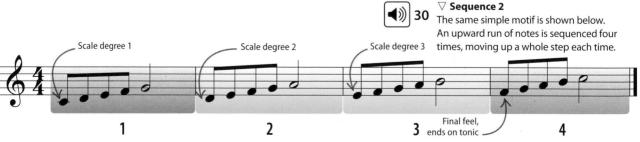

Scale degree 1   Scale degree 2   Scale degree 3   Final feel, ends on tonic

1   2   3   4

Characteristics of sequences

Sequences are identified by a pattern that is restated, two or more times in a row, with each repetition being a consistent distance higher, or lower, in pitch than its predecessor. Sequences are repeated at the same size interval, but the quality of the interval may change. Diatonic sequences generally use the notes in the given key signature, which may change the quality, but not the size of the interval. In pure sequences, the composer may employ altered whole steps to maintain exact interval content.

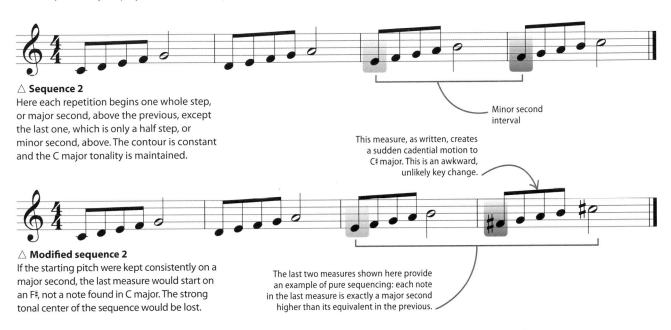

△ **Sequence 2**
Here each repetition begins one whole step, or major second, above the previous, except the last one, which is only a half step, or minor second, above. The contour is constant and the C major tonality is maintained.

Minor second interval

This measure, as written, creates a sudden cadential motion to C♯ major. This is an awkward, unlikely key change.

△ **Modified sequence 2**
If the starting pitch were kept consistently on a major second, the last measure would start on an F♯, not a note found in C major. The strong tonal center of the sequence would be lost.

The last two measures shown here provide an example of pure sequencing: each note in the last measure is exactly a major second higher than its equivalent in the previous.

LOOKING CLOSER

Using sequences

Composers of the Baroque and Classical eras used sequences to a high degree to create repetition and unity within their music. See if you can find the sequences that occur in this example. The sequence in the treble clef, or right hand, is a motif of downward running notes, sequenced at the interval up a minor, or major second. The sequence in the bass clef, or left hand, is an upward sixth motif that is sequenced up one scale degree.

▽ **Mozart's *Piano Concerto in A Major***
This is an excerpt from the first movement, Allegro, of the *Piano Concerto No. 23*, K. 488 (1786).

Ornaments

In aesthetic terms, anything "ornamental" is usually thought of as purely decorative and not necessarily functional. Similarly, ornaments in music are used to decorate, embellish, or emphasize a melody.

Grace notes

A grace note is a simple ornament, which merely decorates the melody. It is notated in smaller type and is placed immediately before the note it ornaments. Attached to the main melodic tone with a small slur, it usually has a diagonal line across its stem and can be performed in several different ways.

 31

▽ **Acciaccatura**
This grace note is played as fast as possible, on, or just before, the beat, producing a "crushed" effect. The aural emphasis is on the main melody note.

△ **Appoggiatura**
Appoggiatura grace notes are half the value of the main melody note. This gives them a higher importance in the melody.

Turns

A turn is a quick, smooth ornament. First the note itself is played, then the note above, back to the main note, followed by the note below, and lastly the main note again. It may be performed as five equal tones, or fitted in quickly and rhythmically at the end of the melody note's value.

 32

▷ **Turns on the staff**
Occasionally composers write out the turn in the desired rhythm—slower equal tones, or quickly executed in a triplet rhythm—to ensure performance consistency.

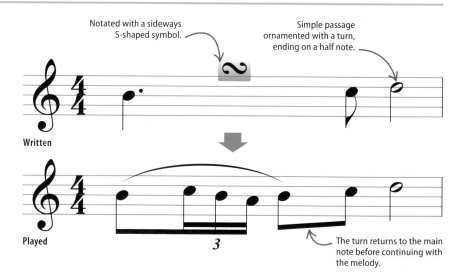

Notated with a sideways S-shaped symbol.

Simple passage ornamented with a turn, ending on a half note.

The turn returns to the main note before continuing with the melody.

Trills

A trill calls for a rapid alternation between the main melody note and the note immediately above it in the scale of the piece. It can be notated with either the *tr* marking, the wavy line, or both. Often the trill concludes with a turn, or a quick use of the note below the main melody note.

△ **Writing trills**
Composers or arrangers may notate a wavy line to indicate that the trill continues for the entire note value.

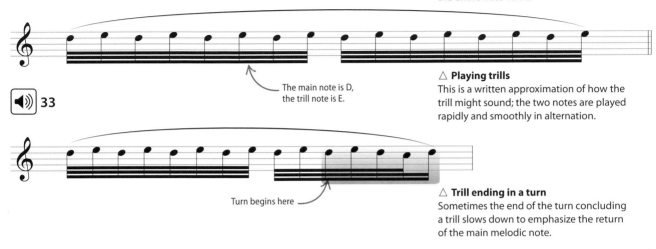

The main note is D, the trill note is E.

 33

△ **Playing trills**
This is a written approximation of how the trill might sound; the two notes are played rapidly and smoothly in alternation.

Turn begins here

△ **Trill ending in a turn**
Sometimes the end of the turn concluding a trill slows down to emphasize the return of the main melodic note.

Mordents

Mordents are like trills with just one shake, or repetition, of the ornamental note. The first mordent symbol means to play the main note with a single rapid alternation with the note above, or below. The second mordent symbol means to play the note below and then return to the main note.

 34

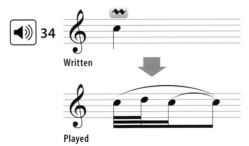

Written

Played

△ **Melody note and the note above it**
A smooth, fast alternation—performed on the beat—between the main note and its upper neighbor.

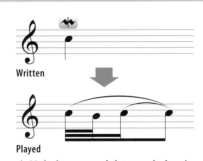

Written

Played

△ **Melody note and the note below it**
The vertical line through the mordent indicates that the lower neighbor of the main note should be played.

Glissando

A trill and a glissando are both denoted with a wavy line, but a glissando is a sweep across all the whole steps between two pitches. Sometimes the performer plays only the notes in the scale that are appropriate for the tonality of the piece.

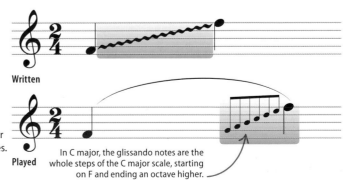

Written

Played

 35 ▷ **Glissando**
The speed of the glissando determines whether the listener can distinguish its individual pitches. Blurring together all the pitches between two whole steps is called a portamento.

In C major, the glissando notes are the whole steps of the C major scale, starting on F and ending an octave higher.

Dynamics

The terms and symbols in music that indicate the quietness or loudness of a sound are called dynamics. While notated, they are relative and somewhat subject to a performer's interpretation.

SEE ALSO	
Musical expression	104–105 ❯
Woodwind	176–177 ❯
What is the score?	194–195 ❯
The Classical period	212–213 ❯

Dynamic terms and symbols

Like many musical expressions, dynamic markings are traditionally provided in Italian. Shown here is a list of the most commonly used dynamic terms, from quietest to loudest. There is often not enough room to note the entire dynamic term in a musical score, so the accompanying symbols are frequently used to denote each dynamic level.

▽ **Dynamic markings**
This shows the relationship between typical sounds you might make to illustrate dynamic levels, ranging from very quiet (*pppp*), to medium (*mf*), all the way to very loud (*ffff*).

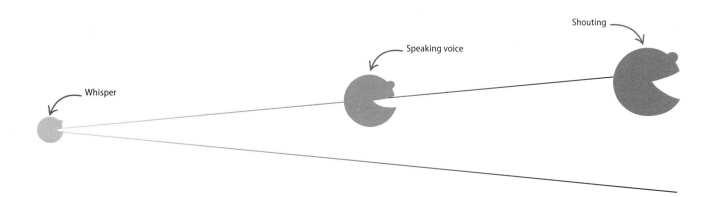

Whisper

Speaking voice

Shouting

pppp	*ppp*	*pp*	*p*	*mp*	*mf*	*f*	*ff*	*fff*	*ffff*
Pianississississimo	Pianissississimo	Pianissimo	Piano	Mezzo piano	Mezzo forte	Forte	Fortissimo	Fortississimo	Fortissississimo

GLOSSARY

Sforzando

This marking instructs the performer to play loud, and then suddenly quiet. Different instruments achieve this in various ways: wind musicians initiate the tone harshly, with lots of air and a hard attack, and then dramatically drop breath support.

◁ **Sforzando**
Abbreviated *sfz*, sforzando, is Italian for "forced."

Musicians and genre determine what **dynamic markings sound like** in a particular piece: a **brass quintet** playing its **quietest** will still be **louder than** a **solo flute**.

Changing dynamic levels

No matter how quiet or muted, or how dramatically loud and bombastic, composers want a performer to play, there is a dynamic term that they can use to indicate their wishes. Dynamics are fluid, and a crucial part of a performer's musical expressivity, so composers use a number of symbols to denote gradual or sudden changes in dynamic levels. This makes the music more interesting, and provides rewarding musical choices for the performer.

▽ **Symbols**
If a composer wants the performer to switch dynamic levels quickly and without warning, the word subito, or "suddenly" (abbreviated sub.) may be written next to the new dynamic marking.

Crescendo

Decrescendo

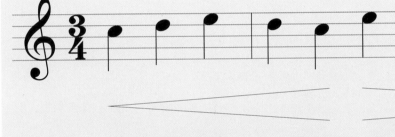

△ **Crescendo on the staff**
Often, composers want the musicians to gradually increase volume. This is called a crescendo, and is marked by a large sideways V under the notes.

 36

△ **Decrescendo on the staff**
A decrescendo is marked by a sideways V pointing the other way, indicating the composer's instruction for the volume to get gradually quieter during that portion.

37

Dramatic dynamics

Composers play with dynamics and dynamic changes to creatively express different moods in music. In his 1893 Symphony No. 6, Pathetique, Pyotr Tchaikovsky called for the bassoon to play *pianississississississimo* (marked *pppppp*). The last movement of Ottorino Resphigi's 1924 tone poem *Pines of Rome* is one of the longest, most gradual, and most dramatic crescendi in all of the orchestral repertoire.

The crescendo in *Pines of Rome* depicts a legion of **Roman soldiers** marching along the Via Appia, triumphantly **ascending** one of Rome's seven hills.

Musical expression

The beauty of a musical performance lies in the infinite variety of ways in which performers can produce sounds. In a similar way, composers can indicate subtle variations in the sounds they want by using certain symbols.

SEE ALSO
❮ **34–35** Rests and ties
❮ **42–43** Tempo

The note connection

Musicians can make their sounds separate, or elongated and attached. Staccato—marked by a dot beneath or above the note head—means the tones should be short and distinct. Legato—a curved line over or under the notes—indicates that the notes should be played smoothly, without breaks in the sound.

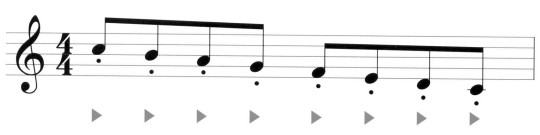

 38

◁ **Staccato**
These notes, marked staccato (Italian for "detached"), should sound clipped and distinct, with a space between each tone.

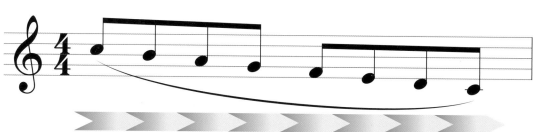

 39

◁ **Legato**
Legato (Italian for "tied together") are notes that are played smoothly, and connected with one air stream, bow stroke, or hand motion.

GLOSSARY

Playing with time

Altering the pace, or tempo, of music, can drastically change the mood and character of a piece. Composers have specific ways of doing this. Think of the effect produced when a musician slows down the last few seconds of a musical piece to signal winding it down, and finally ending it. Alternatively, think of how exciting and rowdy a gradual increase in the speed would sound. Composers have specific terms that indicate to performers the desired musical effect.

ritardando   **rallentando**   **accelerando**   **a tempo**

△ **Ritardando or rallentando**
Slowing down the speed of music is known as ritardando or rallentando (abbreviated rit. and rall. respectively).

△ **Accelerando**
Speeding up the tempo of music, or getting faster, is called an accelerando (abbreviated accel.).

△ **A tempo**
After changing the speed, a tempo indicates that performers should revert to the original pace.

Accent

Musical tones may be played with a varying degree of emphasis, or force. Accents are executed by vocalists and wind players with stronger air; string and keyboard performers use heavier arm or hand motions to produce a weightier tone. Here are the various symbols for different types of accented notes.

△ **Martellato**
This is a hammered, short, and fierce note. It is produced on a string instrument by holding and striking the bow against the string with force.

△ **Marcato**
Marcato, or "accent mark," means that performers should emphasize the note more than the surrounding tones through extra volume or weight.

△ **Sforzando**
This indicates that the performer should strike the note hard with a sudden force, and back away quickly.

△ **Tenuto**
A straight line over or under the notehead implies that performers should take care to hold the note for its full value.

Expression in action

Composers use expressive markings to distinguish notes and phrases. Slurs, staccatos, rests, and different types of accents are indicated to help the performer create interest and drama, such as in this thrilling march excerpt.

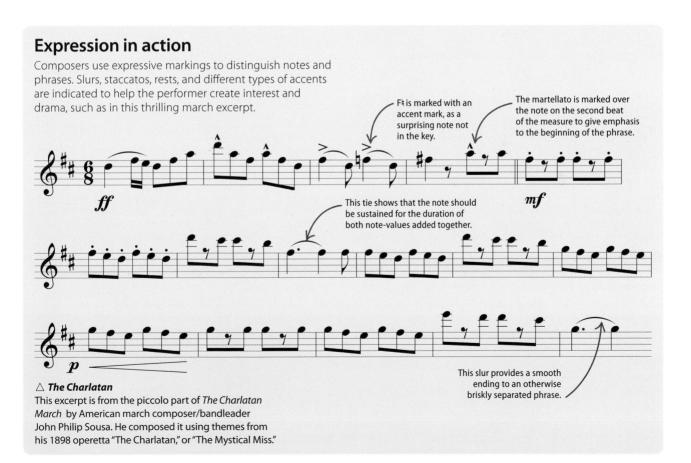

F♯ is marked with an accent mark, as a surprising note not in the key.

The martellato is marked over the note on the second beat of the measure to give emphasis to the beginning of the phrase.

This tie shows that the note should be sustained for the duration of both note-values added together.

This slur provides a smooth ending to an otherwise briskly separated phrase.

△ *The Charlatan*
This excerpt is from the piccolo part of *The Charlatan March* by American march composer/bandleader John Philip Sousa. He composed it using themes from his 1898 operetta "The Charlatan," or "The Mystical Miss."

Musical markings

Composers need to give instructions to musicians on how to perform their musical pieces. Terms and symbols printed on the score relay this information to the performers, who then translate the written notation into sound.

Range and octave information

Sometimes composers may want a performer to play something particularly high, or at the top of an instrument's range. They might also want something to be played at the very bottom of an instrument's range. Notating these extreme ranges on the staves requires many ledger lines, which can be difficult to read.

△ **Ottava**

The marking 8va stands for the Italian word "octave," and when printed above the staff it means to play a note one octave (8 notes) higher than it is written.

△ **Ottava bassa**

The marking 8vb means *ottava bassa*, and indicates to perform notes one octave lower. It is sometimes notated with an 8va marking below the notes.

▷ **Playing 8va**
Here, the sounding pitches look awkward in ledger lines; notating them on the staff with the 8va marking is a clearer direction.

▷ **Playing 8vb**
The pitches to be played on the bass clef are not easy to read below the staff. It is better to place them on the staff and indicate 8vb.

Hold and pause

In music, it is important to have places where forward motion ceases, and where time is held in suspension for a moment. These dramatic breaks and stops are usually indicated with a fermata or pause sign—known colloquially as a "bird's eye"—or a caesura.

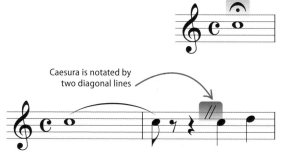

Caesura is notated by two diagonal lines

◁ **Fermata or pause**
A fermata calls for the performer to hold a note longer than its specified value. It is often used to create a sound of finality at the end of a section.

◁ **Caesura**
A caesura is a brief pause of an undefined amount and is open to interpretation. Because it represents a complete stop in musical motion, musicians informally call it "railroad tracks."

Sustaining sounds

Sometimes composers want a more sustained or continuous sound, especially in underlying harmonic parts of a melody. Two typical ways to accomplish this are by using broken chords and, on the piano, the sustaining, or damper, pedal. For an arpeggio sound—notes of a chord played in succession—a wavy line symbol is written beside a chord. This means that rather than playing the entire chord at once, the performer plays each tone one at a time, spreading out the harmony across a longer time in a strumming effect.

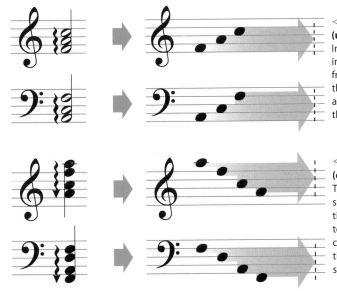

◁ **Arpeggiated chord (upward)**
In this example, each note in the chord will be played from the bottom up, timing the three notes to sound across the two beats of the notated half note.

◁ **Arpeggiated chord (downward)**
These chords are played similarly—one pitch at a time—but starting at the top note and playing them consecutively a bit faster: timing the four notes to sound across one beat.

Piano pedals

On the piano, sustaining tones with the damper pedal is a crucial way to maintain pitches for longer than they would normally last before fading. Pedal marks are notated with a scripted, stylized *Ped.*, or a bracket indicating depress and release times.

The **sustaining/damper pedal** lifts all the dampers on the strings so they keep **vibrating** long after the key is struck on the keyboard.

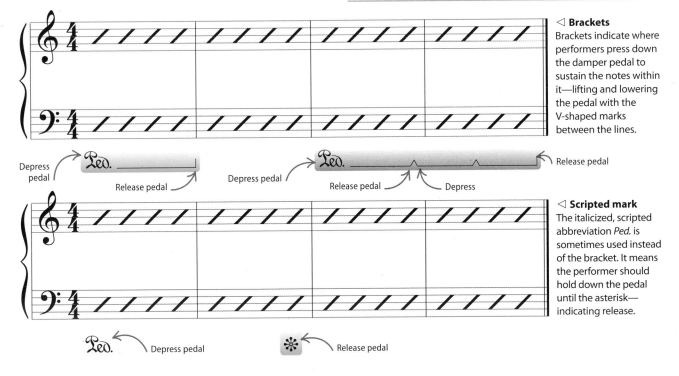

◁ **Brackets**
Brackets indicate where performers press down the damper pedal to sustain the notes within it—lifting and lowering the pedal with the V-shaped marks between the lines.

Depress pedal

Release pedal

Depress pedal

Release pedal

Depress

Release pedal

◁ **Scripted mark**
The italicized, scripted abbreviation *Ped.* is sometimes used instead of the bracket. It means the performer should hold down the pedal until the asterisk—indicating release.

Ped. Depress pedal

✳ Release pedal

Analyzing melodies

Looking closely at how melodies are constructed can help you understand their role and function. In a melodic analysis, always examine elements such as contour, repetition, rhythm, and scale degrees.

Contour

Take an overall look at the melody. What shape does it have—in terms of notes moving upward or downward, or ascending or descending? What is the overall range, from the lowest note to the highest note? Does the melody change the pitch direction frequently, or very little? Look for places where the melody is static with repeated notes, and for unexpected leaps or changes.

▽ **"Down in the Valley"**
Here the pitch range is only an octave. The only octave jump—from low D to high D—occurs near the end of the tune, the most dramatic placement.

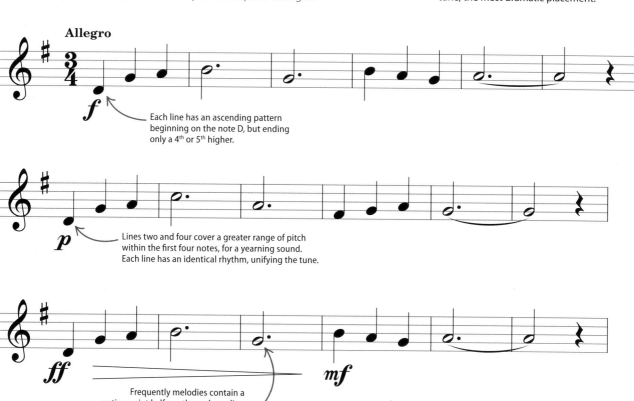

Each line has an ascending pattern beginning on the note D, but ending only a 4th or 5th higher.

Lines two and four cover a greater range of pitch within the first four notes, for a yearning sound. Each line has an identical rhythm, unifying the tune.

Frequently melodies contain a resting point halfway through, ending on *do* or keynote 1, the tonic.

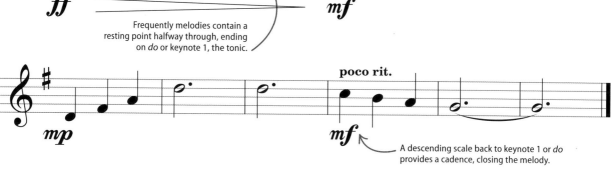

A descending scale back to keynote 1 or *do* provides a cadence, closing the melody.

Repetition

Melodies with some repetition, or a slightly varied reuse of material, sound cohesive and satisfying. Often, as in the first phrase of "When the Saints Go Marching In," a motif (short pattern) will repeat three times. The first two repetitions are identical. The third begins the same, but ends with a more elaborate addition, ornamentation, or closing statement.

▽ **"When the Saints Go Marching In"**
The origins of this American gospel hymn are unknown, but it is now a popular jazz tune, a rallying tune for many sports teams, and a religious anthem.

The first motif is repeated note for note, twice.

The third time, the motive is extended by an outline of the tonic triad, before resting on *re,* or keynote 2.

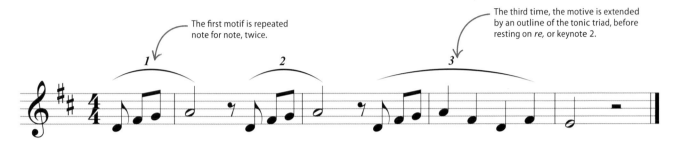

Rhythm

Each subsection of this folk-song melody uses an identical rhythm, unifying the entire tune. Note the "Rule of Three" at work here—the triplet motif is used three times in a row, but the melody steps down, pitch by pitch, to the keynote, to emphasize the return to *do,* or scale degree 1.

▽ **"Sally Go Round the Sun"**
This is an African-American folk tune from the Seal Islands, off the coast of South Carolina.

Tips for analyzing melodies

Ask yourself the following questions about melodic elements to determine if and how they are relevant to understanding the function of the melody.

What is the first note of each phrase? What is the last note?

What is the last note of the melody? How does the last measure function to create a feeling of finality?

Identify notes in terms of scale degrees. Look particularly for tones that are stable (scale degrees 1, 3, 5), and those that need to move to resolve (2, 7).

How many phrases are there? Are any phrases the same? How do they differ?

What rhythmic and melodic patterns repeat themselves? What sections of the melody are notably different? How is the contrast made between same and different?

Does the melody generally flow between notes close to each other, or are the tones drastically different?

If text is present, what elements of the melody seem to interact purposely with the lyrics? Does the melodic structure highlight portions of the tune?

Two or more notes together

Most examples in the Melody chapter of this book have been single lines—just one tone at a time. However, melodies sound richer with even a simple harmony.

Two notes, joined

From one line of notes moving parallel with the melody, to a series of chords accompanying a tune, the harmonic aspect of music enhances melodies in a special way. Music sounds fuller and more rewarding when the underlying chordal structure is brought out through harmonizing the melody; unexpected, surprising harmonies bring interest to even simple tunes. Shown here are some common ways to notate harmonies.

REAL WORLD

Simon and Garfunkel

Paul Simon and Art Garfunkel, a.k.a. the American folk-rock duo "Simon and Garfunkel," learned to write and sing songs together as teenagers. Throughout the 1950s and 60s, their vocal blend and close harmonizations of Simon's song melodies brought beauty and intrigue to relatively simple compositions.

△ **Two notes, close together**
When two tones relatively close in pitch are played together, the simplest way of notating them is to place both note heads on the same stem.

🔊 **42**

When the **notes** to be played simultaneously are **distant**, it is easier to place each voice in its **own clef**, usually treble and bass clefs, and connect them in a **grand staff**.

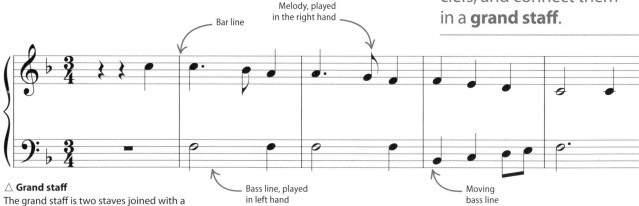

△ **Grand staff**
The grand staff is two staves joined with a brace. It is most commonly used for piano music. Note that the bar lines in both clefs are exactly aligned, making it easy to see which notes are to be played simultaneously.

Chord accompaniment

Another way of creating a more complete sound for a melody is to accompany it with chords, either on a piano, guitar, or ukulele. The chord names are printed above the melody. This style of melodic accompaniment notation is frequently used in jazz or pop music.

▽ **Chord symbols**
These symbols give the name of the root, the chord quality, and any note above the root added to the chord (identified by the size of the interval, such as 7 or 9).

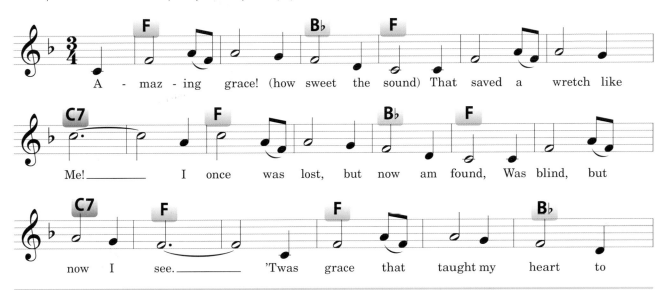

Multiple instruments

Two lines or voices are easily depicted on the grand staff. For more than two, composers use a full score. The example here shows what a piano trio score looks like. Each instrument has its own staff, perfectly aligned with the others.

▽ **Schubert's *Trio* in E♭ Major**
This is the opening of the first movement, an Allegro in sonata form, of Franz Schubert's *Second Piano Trio, Op. 100* (1827).

Writing your own melody

SEE ALSO

❬ **92–93** What is a tune?

❬ **94–95** Phrasing and phrase marks

❬ **96–97** Types of phrases

❬ **108–109** Analyzing melodies

There are always new melodies to be written. Many things can provide inspiration—a mood, the words of a poem, or the sound of an instrument.

Steps and leaps

Most melodies have a mixture of steps and leaps. Moving from one note to another that is a whole note or half note away is known as a step. A leap is when you jump from one note to another that is further away. Scales have steps, and arpeggios have leaps. The mixture of steps and leaps helps to give a melody its shape, or contour.

▽ **"The Mulberry Bush"**
This nursery song has a clear, memorable melody with a distinctive rhythm and a satisfying shape, mixing steps and leaps.

■ Leaps   ■ Steps

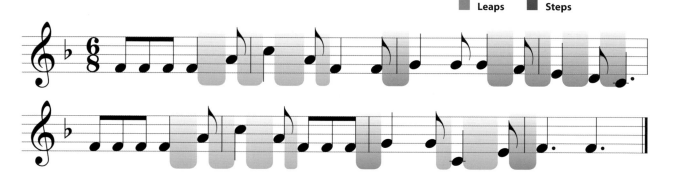

Rhythm

Rhythm, like melodic contour, gives shape to a tune. The rhythm will be determined by various things. Is your melody fast or slow? What is the meter? Does the melody have a distinctive rhythm? Does the rhythm help to bring out the phrase structure? Perhaps the words suggest a strong rhythm. Or is the music intended for dancing or actions of some sort?

The 2/4 time signature sets up a punchy rhythm.

△ **"Heads, Shoulders, Knees, and Toes"**
The rhythm, with its long and short notes, gives a distinctive character to this well-known children's action song.

The second phrase repeats the first one.

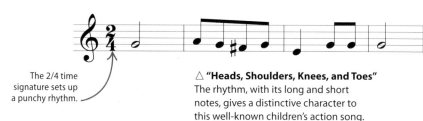

△ **Waltz from** *Swan Lake*
This dance from the ballet *Swan Lake* by Tchaikovsky has a distinctive rhythm, influencing how the dancers move.

The third phrase has the same shape and rhythm, but different pitches.

Phrasing

If you are setting lyrics to music, they will determine the mood, rhythm, and phrasing. But even a melody without lyrics needs a satisfying shape, with balancing phrases and resting points. Phrasing can be regular, like the example shown below, or irregular, but either way it should help the melody to feel well shaped.

▽ **"My Bonnie Lies Over the Ocean"**
The four lines of the verse translate into a four-phrase melody. The melodic shapes are similar, but their slight variations turn the implied harmonies around, leading back to the keynote.

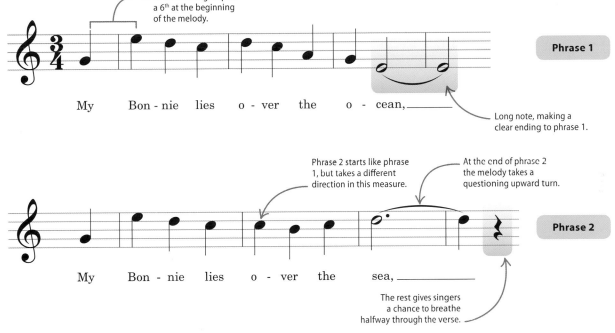

Distinctive big leap of a 6th at the beginning of the melody.

Long note, making a clear ending to phrase 1.

My Bon - nie lies o - ver the o - cean,_____

Phrase 1

Phrase 2 starts like phrase 1, but takes a different direction in this measure.

At the end of phrase 2 the melody takes a questioning upward turn.

My Bon - nie lies o - ver the sea,_____

The rest gives singers a chance to breathe halfway through the verse.

Phrase 2

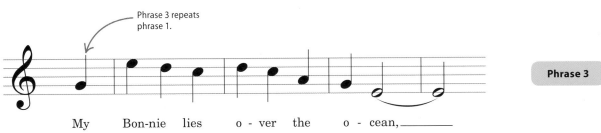

Phrase 3 repeats phrase 1.

My Bon-nie lies o - ver the o - cean,_____

Phrase 3

Phrase 4 starts differently, the first phrase to do so.

Phrase 4 and the whole verse ends on the keynote.

O bring back my Bon - nie to me. _____

Phrase 4

Learning by example

It's good to know lots of good songs and tunes, in different styles and from different periods. Some of the best tunes have a simplicity about them, as if they were there all along, waiting to be discovered.

▽ **"Fuji-san"**
Widely sung in Japanese schools, this is the first half of a song published in 1911. It celebrates the beauty of Mount Fuji.

▽ **"Vltava"**
This melody by the Czech composer Smetana (1824–84) portrays the gathering momentum of the river that flows through the Czech capital, Prague.

▽ **Mozart, *Clarinet Quintet***
This piece ends with a joyous dancing tune. Mozart wrote this, and the equally well-loved *Clarinet Concerto*, for the clarinettist Anton Stadler, whose playing inspired him.

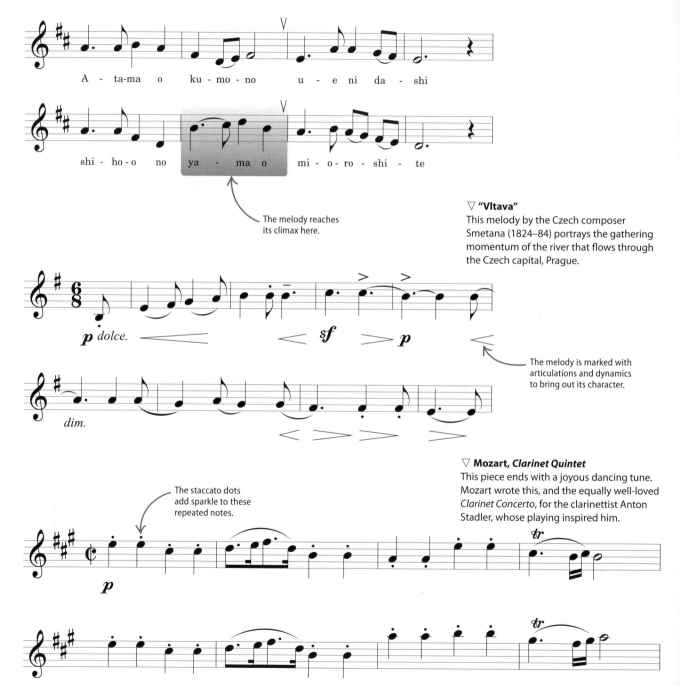

A - ta-ma o ku-mo-no u - e ni da - shi

shi - ho - o no ya - ma o mi - o - ro - shi - te

The melody reaches its climax here.

p dolce.   *sf*   *p*
dim.

The melody is marked with articulations and dynamics to bring out its character.

The staccato dots add sparkle to these repeated notes.

p

What voice or instrument is it for?

What you write must be playable on the instrument for which you are writing. Make sure that the range is right, and try not to create difficulties—consult a player if possible. It helps if you are writing for your own instrument! For voices or wind instruments, allow space to breathe.

A quiet place

To write a good original melody you need peace and quiet, so you can hear it in your head and then work out how to write it down. Gustav Mahler, Edvard Grieg, and Jean Sibelius are examples of composers who had a favored place to which they could retreat when composing. This picture shows Mahler's cabin on the lakeside at Steinbach, Austria, where he wrote his Second Symphony.

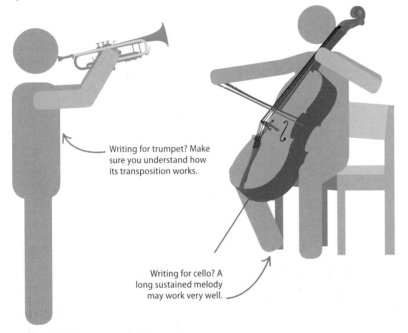

Writing for trumpet? Make sure you understand how its transposition works.

Writing for cello? A long sustained melody may work very well.

△ **The right instrument for the music**
Writing for instruments requires an appreciation of their character—what they do well and what is best avoided. It is always helpful to talk to players and pick up hints as to what works best.

Melody-writing in exam conditions

If you a sitting an exam and the question gives you an opening, first look at the meter (the time signature) and then the tempo, and work out how the rhythm goes. Then look at the key signature, and from the opening notes work out what key it is in, and if it is major or minor. Silently sing the given opening to yourself in your head; then you can imagine how it might continue.

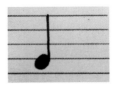

◁ **On the line, or in the space?**
When handwriting your music, be as clear as possible. Never write a note like this. Is it on the line or in the space? Always be 100 percent clear which pitch you want.

◁ **Be clear, be detailed**
Write your music in a clear, well-spaced, accurate way. Add plenty of detail: articulations, dynamics, expression marks, a tempo indication, slurs, or phrase marks.

Chords and harmony

Harmony

Harmony describes the relationship between different notes, whether they are played as part of a melody, or at the same time. If a melody is a line, harmony is the sequence of hooks on which it hangs.

Chords

Notes played at the same time make a chord. Harmony describes the relationship between the notes of a chord, and each chord of a passage of music, such as a phrase. Chords are named after the root—the bottom note—and they are mostly based on triads, the various arrangements of the root and the stack of thirds above it.

 43 ▽ **Harmony**

These arrangements of notes would all have been identified as chords until around 1600. After that time, a chord was identified as having three or more notes. Played separately they are broken chords, but they form a block chord when played together.

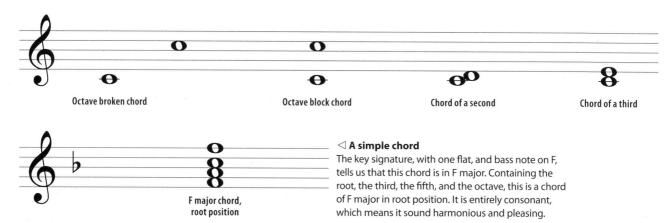

Octave broken chord   Octave block chord   Chord of a second   Chord of a third

◁ **A simple chord**

The key signature, with one flat, and bass note on F, tells us that this chord is in F major. Containing the root, the third, the fifth, and the octave, this is a chord of F major in root position. It is entirely consonant, which means it sound harmonious and pleasing.

F major chord,
root position

Harmonic series

Even single notes have a kind of harmony inside them, known as the harmonic series, or overtones. When you pluck a note on the string of a violin, guitar, harp, or any instrument from the string family, you hear not only the note that is played, but many overtones above that note.

▽ **Harmonic series**

If you played this as a giant chord, it would sound strange and complicated, but all the notes belong to the C at the root.

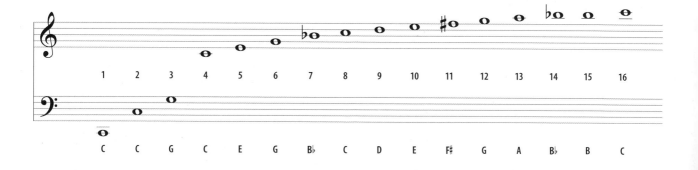

1	2	3	4	5	6	7	8	9	10	11	12	13	14	15	16
C	C	G	C	E	G	B♭	C	D	E	F♯	G	A	B♭	B	C

What is a monody?

A monody—also known as monophony—is a melody with no other notes sounding at the same time. The relationship between these notes is called melodic harmony. In European societies, monodies have been used for many centuries in church music, where they are called plainsong or plainchant. There are simple intervals between each note, so that they may be sung by people together without musical training.

▽ **"Veni Creator Spiritus"**
"Come, Creator Spirit" is one of the oldest plainchants, from the 8th century. All but one of the intervals is stepwise—next to its neighbor—to sound at the same time simple and beautiful.

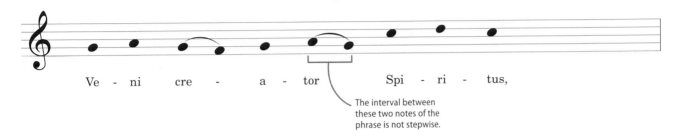

Ve - ni cre - a - tor Spi - ri - tus,

The interval between these two notes of the phrase is not stepwise.

LOOKING CLOSER

The harmony of a melody

Writing music for solo instruments, such as the clarinet or trumpet, that cannot play chords, or string instruments for which a long passage of chords is impractical, presents its own challenges, but harmony can be implied and imagined even when only one note is heard at a time. The music may return often to the tonic to reassert the key signature, as shown in the example below.

▽ **Bach's *Cello Suite 1***
Bach wrote suites and sonatas for the violin and cello, which use the rapid passage of notes across the string to sound like chords. In the opening of his First *Cello Suite,* he creates both a melody and a harmony that is rooted in G major.

REAL WORLD

Harmony of the spheres

In around 500 BCE, the Greek scientist Pythagoras proposed that the movement of the stars and planets was governed by the same mathematical proportions as the intervals between musical notes. This meant that each planet had its own sound, and together they made a "harmony of the spheres." The idea of harmony as a natural phenomenon still influences musicians and composers. Pythagoras discovered that the distance between notes could be expressed in terms of mathematical ratios. He saw these ratios as a reflection of the structure of the universe.

Consonance and dissonance

Consonance is a combination of notes that sound harmonious and pleasing, while dissonance evokes a feeling of tension. The more dissonant the intervals, the greater the tension in the harmony.

SEE ALSO

❰ 56–59 Intervals
❰ 60–61 Major scales
❰ 70–71 The circle of fifths
Modern period   214–215 ❱

Why is an interval consonant or dissonant?

Different musical cultures have their own ideas of what a stable interval is, and what makes a dissonant clash. Western ideas about harmony, outlined here, derive from the works of the ancient Greek scientist Pythagoras, who calculated the relationship between sounds of different pitches.

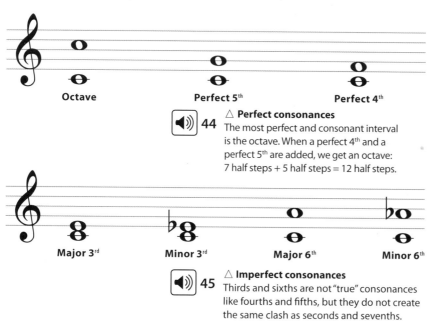

Octave   Perfect 5th   Perfect 4th

🔊 44 △ **Perfect consonances**
The most perfect and consonant interval is the octave. When a perfect 4th and a perfect 5th are added, we get an octave: 7 half steps + 5 half steps = 12 half steps.

Major 3rd   Minor 3rd   Major 6th   Minor 6th

🔊 45 △ **Imperfect consonances**
Thirds and sixths are not "true" consonances like fourths and fifths, but they do not create the same clash as seconds and sevenths.

REAL WORLD

Arnold Schönberg

Arnold Schönberg (1874–1951) was one of the several composers who, around the turn of the 19th and 20th centuries, sought to "emancipate" dissonance. His design of a 12 whole step row was not new, but he created a systematic practice that would influence musicians through the 20th century and beyond. He used it to make music of great beauty and passion, such as his string quartets, which evolved from his earlier "Expressionist" style of composition.

Dissonant intervals

The most dissonant intervals lie a major or minor second apart from each other, though this is still a subjective perception. Some folk music from Hungary and Bulgaria, for example, uses seconds and sevenths, where we would expect to find thirds and fifths.

🔊 46

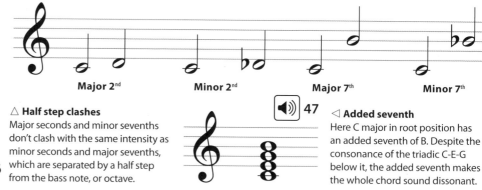

Major 2nd   Minor 2nd   Major 7th   Minor 7th

△ **Half step clashes**
Major seconds and minor sevenths don't clash with the same intensity as minor seconds and major sevenths, which are separated by a half step from the bass note, or octave.

🔊 47 ◁ **Added seventh**
Here C major in root position has an added seventh of B. Despite the consonance of the triadic C-E-G below it, the added seventh makes the whole chord sound dissonant.

Using dissonance

Consonance isn't "good" and dissonance "bad" despite them being referred to as "perfect" and "imperfect" intervals. In 1921, the American composer Charles Ives caught the mood-music of the times with his song "Majority," which uses great dissonance to symbolize revolutionary political ideas. The song begins with the lyrics, "The Masses have toiled. Behold the works of the world".

▽ **Opening of "Majority" by Ives**
The chords in the boxes contain nine different notes of the chromatic scale. You cannot hear each note separately, just as you cannot see each person in a large crowd.

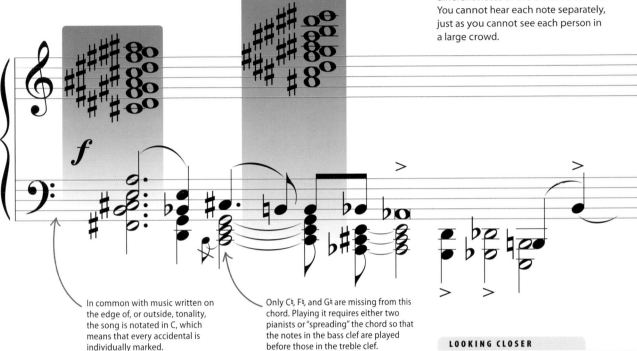

In common with music written on the edge of, or outside, tonality, the song is notated in C, which means that every accidental is individually marked.

Only C♮, F♮, and G♮ are missing from this chord. Playing it requires either two pianists or "spreading" the chord so that the notes in the bass clef are played before those in the treble clef.

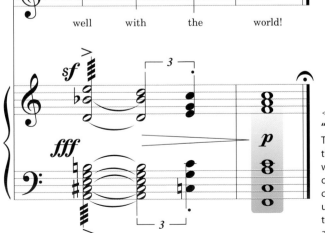

well   with   the   world!

◁ **Conclusion of "Majority" by Ives**
The song ends with the lyrics, "All will be well with the world," on a soft F major chord. Here, Ives is using consonance to symbolize rest and resolution.

LOOKING CLOSER

Tritone

Not all fourths and fifths are perfect. A perfect fourth lies five half steps apart, while a perfect fifth is separated by seven half steps no matter what the scale or starting note is. The note that lies in between is the tritone, an augmented fourth, which is six half steps apart. In most Western music, the tritone creates a fierce dissonance that demands resolution. In jazz, however, the tritone is commonly used as a stable interval.

Augmented 4ᵗʰ

Diatonic and chromatic harmony

SEE ALSO

❮ **16–17** The piano keyboard
❮ **64–67** Keys
❮ **120–121** Consonance and dissonance
The Classical period **210–211** ❯

Diatonic harmony is built from the pitches within a key signature, while chromatic harmony introduces dissonance that either diverges from the given key signature or has no key at all.

Dissonance within a key

It is still possible to write dissonantly within diatonic music. Indeed, the creation and resolution of tension—on which many musical and harmonic narratives depend—demands a degree of dissonance.

▽ **Mozart's *Symphony No. 1***
The opening melody of Mozart's first symphony (which he composed at the age of eight) could hardly be simpler—an E♭ major arpeggio in three octaves. The highlighted notes in the treble clef show minor and major seconds that clash with the E♭ major harmony.

The B in the bass clashes with the A♭ in the treble.

Chromatic harmony

Since chromatic harmony departs from the home key signature, it pulls the music in another direction—toward a different key signature. The term "chromatic" derives from the Greek word for color. Notes outside a given key signature give the melody, or chord, a particular "color" to the ears.

The rests further disrupt continuity and make the phrase feel jagged.

◁ **Mozart's *Symphony No. 40***
In the finale of his penultimate symphony, Mozart writes a unison melody in G minor, which goes through all the 12 half steps of the chromatic scale.

Chords in context

The same interval, or chord, can be diatonic or chromatic depending on its context—the prevailing key signature. In the example below, the C chord in D major would happen in passing unless handled very carefully—too much chromaticism causes music to sound directionless, or random.

C major   D major

△ **When a C chord is chromatic**
A chord based on a root triad of C major becomes chromatic in D major because the C♮ is chromatic in the context of the C♯ of the key signature.

Harmony in color

The term "chromatic" derives from the Greek word *chromos* meaning color, as chromatic harmonies seem more colorful to the ear than purer consonant chords. Color and sound can merge in unexpected ways. Synesthesia is a rare condition that causes people to "see" things like sounds, emotions, and concepts.

△ **Colors in a chord**
For French organist and composer Olivier Messiaen, a chord of transposed inversions on C♯ contained the colors of rock crystal and citrine at the top, copper with gold highlights at the bottom, and sapphire blue rimmed with violet in the middle.

Naming pitches

We decide how to name a given pitch within the rules of diatonic harmony. These names are known as enharmonic equivalents. For example, F♯ and G♭ are the same pitch, but only if we were writing in G♭ major or its subdominant, C♭ major, would the pitch be notated as G♭.

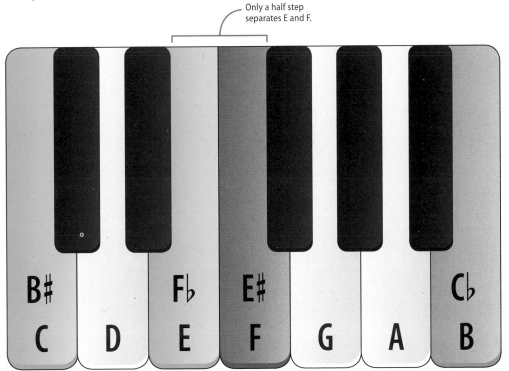

Only a half step separates E and F.

B♯ C D F♭ E E♯ F G A C♭ B

◁ **Enharmonic equivalents**
Note that C♭ is not B♯ because there is only a semitone between B and C. Looking at, or visualizing, a keyboard is a simple way to remember the enharmonic equivalents.

Degrees of the scale

The notes of the major and minor scales are given names and roman numerals to help identify their positions in relation to the keynote, or tonic. These are called degrees of the scale.

SEE ALSO

❮ **60–61** Major scales
❮ **62–63** Minor scales
❮ **64–67** Keys
❮ **74–75** Modulation
Chord types   **130–131** ❯

The keynote

The note the scale starts and ends on is known as the keynote of the scale. In degrees of the scale, this note is called the tonic and is given the Roman numeral I. It does not matter whether it is the starting note or the top note of the scale, both notes are identified in the same way.

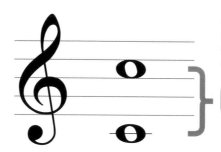

◁ **The tonic**
In a C major scale, the keynote is both Middle C and the C one octave above it. These notes are labeled I and are called the tonic.

Keynote = I = Tonic

Naming degrees of the scale

In an ascending major or harmonic minor scale spanning one octave, the degrees of the scale are tonic, supertonic, mediant, subdominant, dominant, submediant, leading note, and tonic again. Degrees of the scale are also used to identify keys. For example, when C major is the tonic key, the dominant key is G major because its keynote, G, is the fifth note, or dominant degree, of the C major scale.

▽ **Up the scale**
The chart below shows the eight notes of an ascending major or harmonic minor scale, and the Roman numeral and degree of the scale that identifies each note.

The eighth note, one octave above the first note, is also called the tonic.

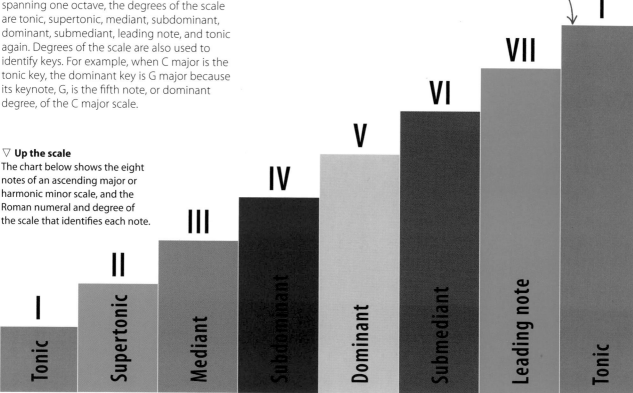

I	II	III	IV	V	VI	VII	I
Tonic	Supertonic	Mediant	Subdominant	Dominant	Submediant	Leading note	Tonic
1st note	2nd note	3rd note	4th note	5th note	6th note	7th note	8th note

Degrees in C

On the staff, each note in a major or harmonic minor scale has both a name and a Roman numeral. Here are the C major and C harmonic minor scales. Each note up the scale is identified with its Roman numeral and degree of the scale.

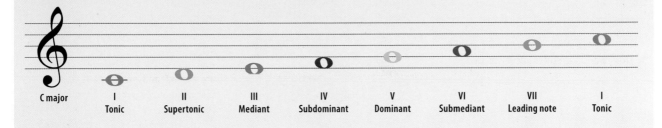

C major	I	II	III	IV	V	VI	VII	I
	Tonic	Supertonic	Mediant	Subdominant	Dominant	Submediant	Leading note	Tonic

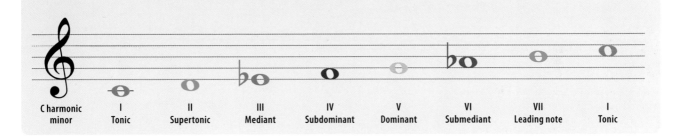

C harmonic minor	I	II	III	IV	V	VI	VII	I
	Tonic	Supertonic	Mediant	Subdominant	Dominant	Submediant	Leading note	Tonic

LOOKING CLOSER

The seventh note

In most scales, the seventh note of the scale is only a half step below the tonic at the top of the scale, and is called the leading note. However, when the seventh note is a whole step below the tonic, it is called the subtonic.

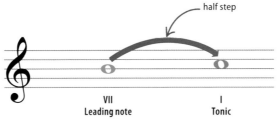

VII
Leading note

I
Tonic

◁ **Leading note**
In major and harmonic minor scales, the seventh note is just a half note below the tonic. Because it leads the melody toward the tonic, it is called the leading note.

▽ **Subtonic**
In natural minor scales, the seventh note is a whole step below the tonic. In this case, the note is called a subtonic. Here the subtonic is shown as part of the C natural minor scale.

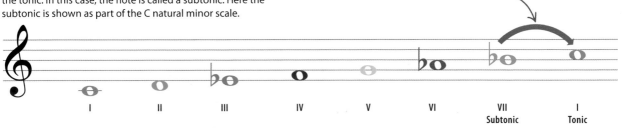

I	II	III	IV	V	VI	VII	I
						Subtonic	Tonic

Triads

A triad is a chord of a given note, a third, and a fifth. It consists of three notes, with two intervals of a third between the notes. The triad is the fundamental basis for making harmony in Western music.

SEE ALSO	
❬ 56–59 Intervals	
❬ 74–75 Modulation	
Chord types	130–131 ❭
Chords	232–233 ❭

Tonic triads

A tonic triad is formed of the root, the third, and the fifth note of the scale in which it appears. The tonic is the name for the first note of a scale. B♭ is the tonic in B♭ major (and minor), and F is the tonic in F major and minor scales, triads, and chords.

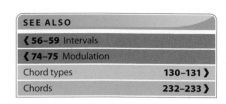

🔊 49

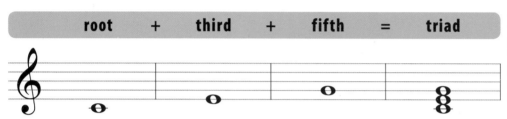

◁ **Triad**
The staff shows the triad as both an arpeggio and a chord. The triad is the chord built by placing the third and the fifth notes above the tonic so that they sound together.

Triads in C major

A tonic triad is built on the first note of a given scale (I), a subdominant triad is built on the fourth (IV, or subdominant) note of the scale, and the fundamental note of a dominant triad is the fifth (V, or dominant) note of the scale. These are the primary triads of any scale.

◁ **Triads of C major**
The three principal triads of C major are shown here. The interval between each note is a major third, or four half steps.

◁ **Triads with multiple meanings**
The same triads can have multiple meanings depending on the chord they are in. So a C major triad may serve as I in C major, IV in G major, V in F major, etc.

LOOKING CLOSER

Arpeggios

Playing the notes of a triad separately produces an arpeggio. It is possible to make great music out of little more than chains of arpeggios, as Bach showed in the C major prelude that opens his sequence of preludes and fugues in each key of the chromatic scale, known as *The Well-Tempered Clavier* ("clavier" is an old-fashioned word for a keyboard instrument).

◁ **Bach's "Prelude in C major"**
Trace the C major arpeggio from the Middle C in the bass clef. The entire prelude is built from these chains of thirds and fourths.

Naming triads

Each triad has a number according to its place in the scale. The number is written in Roman numerals—I is built on the tonic, II is on the second note of the scale, and so on. Major triads are written in capital roman letters (I-II-III), and minor triads are written in lower case (i-ii-iii). Diminished triads are indicated with a superscript circle (vii°).

Tonic	Subdominant	Dominant
i	iv	v
A minor	E minor	D minor

△ **What is the key?**
One triad of the same three notes can have different meanings according to the key. So I of A minor (A-C-E) is composed of the same notes as the subdominant of E minor, and the dominant of D minor.

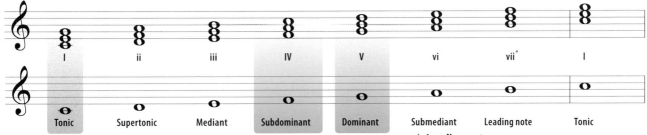

I	ii	iii	IV	V	vi	vii°	I
Tonic	Supertonic	Mediant	Subdominant	Dominant	Submediant	Leading note	Tonic

△ **Leading note**
The seventh note of the scale is known as the leading note because it leads directly into the tonic of the scale, up an octave.

Diminished triads

Diminished triads are separated by intervals of a minor third, or three half steps. They are less stable than perfect triads because the two intervals add up to a dissonant interval, the diminished fifth (known as a tritone) of six half steps.

◁ **Diminished triads**
Formed by the root, the third note of the scale, and the flattened fifth, a diminished triad is indicated with a + sign. The triad shown here is C dim or C°.

diminished triad	=	minor third	+	♭ fifth

Triad	Root	Minor third	Diminished fifth
C dim (Cm (♭5))	C	E♭	G♭
C♯ dim (C♯m (♭5))	C♯	E	G
D dim (Dm (♭5))	D	F	A♭
D♯ dim (D♯m (♭5))	D♯	F♯	A
E dim (Em (♭5))	E	G	B♭
F dim (Fm (♭5))	F	A♭	C♭ (B)
F♯ dim (F♯m (♭5))	F♯	A	C
G dim (Gm (♭5))	G	B♭	D♭
G♯ dim (G♯m (♭5))	G♯	B	D
A dim (Am (♭5))	A	C	E♭
A♯ dim (A♯m (♭5))	A♯	C♯	E
B dim (Bm (♭5))	B	D	F

◁ **Triad or chord?**
These are simply triads, but sometimes the "dim" sign indicates the addition of a diminished seventh. They are especially common in jazz and popular music.

Inversions

Inverting triads, chords, and intervals rearranges them so that the notes appear in a different order, or pitch. Inversions are essential for successful part-writing, and also for being inventive with the musical materials in a given key.

What is an inversion?

A melodic inversion turns a melody upside down by raising or lowering notes up or down the octave, so that a given interval becomes its mirror image in relation to an octave. The intervals can be played separately as part of a melody, or together to make an inverted chord.

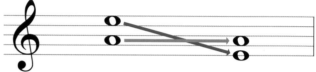

Perfect fifth
The interval between F and C is a perfect fifth.

Perfect fourth
But, when the F is raised an octave, the interval is now a perfect fourth.

Perfect fifth
Reversing the process, if we take the perfect fifth of A–E and lower the E by an octave.

Perfect fourth
...the E–A interval is a perfect fourth. These are common examples of inversions.

More examples of interval inversions

An octave has 12 half steps. Each original interval when added to its inversion must be equal to 12 half steps.

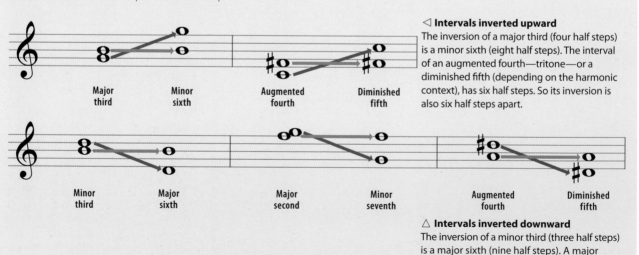

◁ **Intervals inverted upward**
The inversion of a major third (four half steps) is a minor sixth (eight half steps). The interval of an augmented fourth—tritone—or a diminished fifth (depending on the harmonic context), has six half steps. So its inversion is also six half steps apart.

Major third   Minor sixth   Augmented fourth   Diminished fifth

Minor third   Major sixth   Major second   Minor seventh   Augmented fourth   Diminished fifth

△ **Intervals inverted downward**
The inversion of a minor third (three half steps) is a major sixth (nine half steps). A major second (F–G here, two half steps apart) becomes a minor seventh (ten half steps).

Rules for interval inversion

General rules help you to remember the inversions of intervals. The number of half steps always adds up to 12—the number of half steps in an octave.

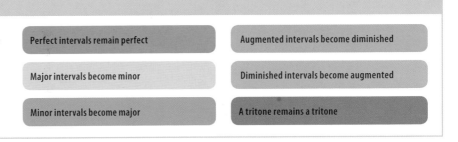

Perfect intervals remain perfect	Augmented intervals become diminished
Major intervals become minor	Diminished intervals become augmented
Minor intervals become major	A tritone remains a tritone

Chord inversions

Inverting a diatonic chord means starting it on another note of the triad of the key signature on which it is based. The first inversion starts the chord on the third, and the second inversion starts the chord on the fifth. A third inversion would bring the tonic back to root position, so the term is redundant.

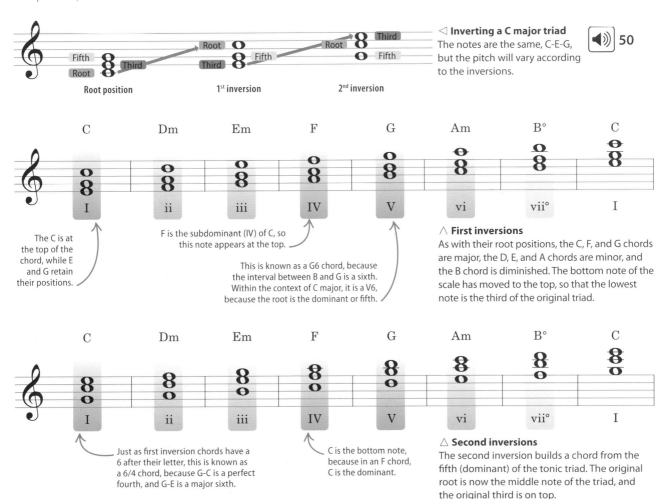

◁ **Inverting a C major triad** 50
The notes are the same, C-E-G, but the pitch will vary according to the inversions.

Fifth
Root
Third
Root position

Root
Third
Fifth
1st inversion

Third
Root
Fifth
2nd inversion

C Dm Em F G Am B° C
I ii iii IV V vi vii° I

The C is at the top of the chord, while E and G retain their positions.

F is the subdominant (IV) of C, so this note appears at the top.

This is known as a G6 chord, because the interval between B and G is a sixth. Within the context of C major, it is a V6, because the root is the dominant or fifth.

△ **First inversions**
As with their root positions, the C, F, and G chords are major, the D, E, and A chords are minor, and the B chord is diminished. The bottom note of the scale has moved to the top, so that the lowest note is the third of the original triad.

C Dm Em F G Am B° C
I ii iii IV V vi vii° I

Just as first inversion chords have a 6 after their letter, this is known as a 6/4 chord, because G-C is a perfect fourth, and G-E is a major sixth.

C is the bottom note, because in an F chord, C is the dominant.

△ **Second inversions**
The second inversion builds a chord from the fifth (dominant) of the tonic triad. The original root is now the middle note of the triad, and the original third is on top.

Chord types

Chords can be categorized into different types, which are determined by the intervals between the notes of the chord. These intervals give each chord type a distinctive sound quality.

SEE ALSO	
⟨ **56–59** Intervals	
⟨ **126–127** Triads	
Suspension	**140–141** ⟩
Chord symbols	**148–149** ⟩

Triads

Triads consist of three distinct notes—the root, third, and fifth. There are four basic types of triadic chord—major, minor, augmented, and diminished. Triads can be broken down into two intervals of a third, or one interval of a fifth. The quality of the intervals between the root, third, and fifth of a triad determines to which of these chord types it belongs.

Triad type	Interval between root and third	Interval between third and fifth	Interval between root and fifth
Major	Major third	Minor third	Perfect fifth
Minor	Minor third	Major third	Perfect fifth
Augmented	Major third	Major third	Augmented fifth
Diminished	Minor third	Minor third	Diminished fifth

△ **Triad types and their intervals**
You can determine the chord type of a triad by observing the quality of the thirds between its individual notes, and the quality of the fifth between its root and fifth.

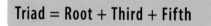

Triad = Root + Third + Fifth

Color code

 Major third

 Minor third

 Perfect fifth

Diminished fifth

Augmented fifth

 51

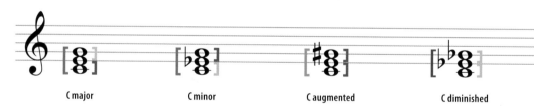

C major   C minor   C augmented   C diminished

◁ **C triads**
Shown here are major, minor, augmented, and diminished triads, with a root of C. Note the intervals between their notes.

B diminished   F♯ augmented   F diminished   A♭ major   G♯ minor

△ **Triads on other notes**
Shown here are triads with a root other than C. Like the C triads, these triads are also broken down into two thirds and one fifth, and the quality of these thirds and fifths determines the triad type.

Doubling up

Chords with four notes are sometimes made by taking a simple triad and doubling one of its existing notes an octave higher or lower. Composers might choose to double the root, third, or fifth of a triad depending on the effect they want to create. Doubling the root, for example, emphasizes a chord's tonal center.

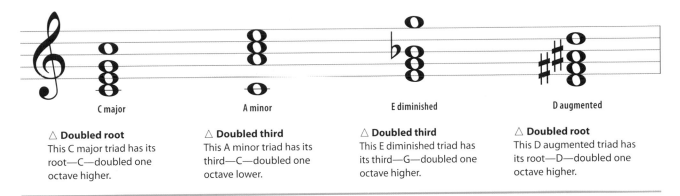

C major　　　　　A minor　　　　　E diminished　　　　　D augmented

△ **Doubled root**
This C major triad has its root—C—doubled one octave higher.

△ **Doubled third**
This A minor triad has its third—C—doubled one octave lower.

△ **Doubled third**
This E diminished triad has its third—G—doubled one octave higher.

△ **Doubled root**
This D augmented triad has its root—D—doubled one octave higher.

Suspended chords

Suspended chords are exceptions to the general rule that chords are triadic. The interval between the first two notes in a suspended chord is not a third, but a fourth (sus4) or, less often, a second (sus2). Suspended chords are so called because the second and fourth create dissonances, or suspensions, which then appear to require resolution back to the third.

▽ **On the staff**
If the third of a C major triad (E) moves down to a second (D), the chord becomes Csus2. If the third moves up to a fourth (F), the chord becomes Csus4.

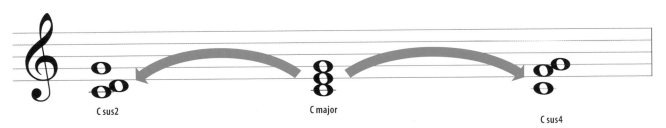

C sus2　　　　　C major　　　　　C sus4

REAL WORLD

Michael Jackson

Suspended chords are commonly heard in pop music. A famous example is Michael Jackson's hit single "Black or White." The opening riff of the song features the chord sequence Esus4, E major, Esus2, E major. The fourths and seconds of the suspended chords can clearly be heard resolving onto the third of the major chord.

The **augmented triad** is often used as a **substitute for** the **dominant** in **pop songs** that are in a **major key**.

Other chords

There are many variations of chords other than triads based on the standard degrees of the scale. Triads can have extra notes added to them or—in the case of the Neapolitan sixth—can be based on a flattened degree of the scale.

How do you make a seventh chord?

Seventh chords are one of the most common types of added note chord. They are formed by taking a triad and adding a note that is a major, minor, or diminished seventh above the root. Several types of seventh chords are possible from these combinations of triads and seventh intervals.

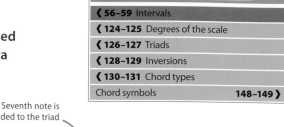

Seventh note is added to the triad

D major triad

◁ **Seventh chord on D**
This seventh chord, starting on D, consists of a D major triad and an added note a seventh above the root of the triad.

Type of seventh chord	Type of triad on which chord is based	Quality of interval between root of triad and added seventh note
major	major	major
minor	minor	minor
dominant	major	minor
(fully) diminished	diminished	diminished
half-diminished	diminished	minor
minor major seventh	minor	major

◁ **Common types of seventh chord**
These chords are named according to the type of triad on which they are based, and the quality of the interval between the root of the triad and the added seventh note.

Color code

■ Major third	■ Perfect fifth	■ Major seventh	■ Diminished seventh
■ Minor third	■ Diminished fifth	■ Minor seventh	

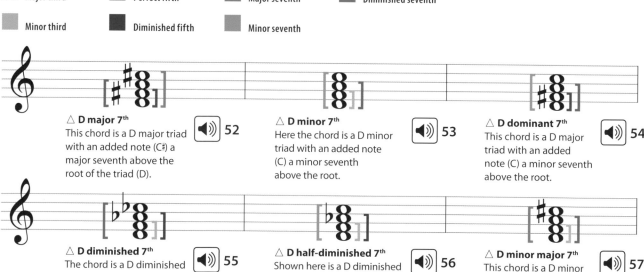

△ **D major 7th**
This chord is a D major triad with an added note (C♯) a major seventh above the root of the triad (D). 🔊 52

△ **D minor 7th**
Here the chord is a D minor triad with an added note (C) a minor seventh above the root. 🔊 53

△ **D dominant 7th**
This chord is a D major triad with an added note (C) a minor seventh above the root. 🔊 54

△ **D diminished 7th**
The chord is a D diminished triad with an added note (C♭) a diminished seventh above the root. 🔊 55

△ **D half-diminished 7th**
Shown here is a D diminished triad chord with an added note (C) a minor seventh above the root. 🔊 56

△ **D minor major 7th**
This chord is a D minor triad with an added note (C♯) a major seventh above the root. 🔊 57

Inversions of a seventh chord

Seventh chords have four different notes—the root, third, fifth, and seventh—and can thus have three different inversions. As with triads, the seventh chord is in first inversion if its third is the bass note, and in second inversion if its fifth is the bass note. However, it can also be in third inversion, with its seventh as the bass note.

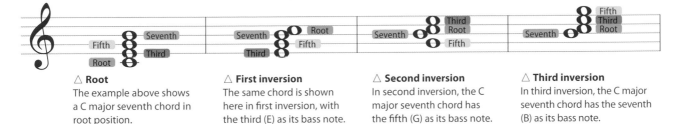

△ **Root**
The example above shows a C major seventh chord in root position.

△ **First inversion**
The same chord is shown here in first inversion, with the third (E) as its bass note.

△ **Second inversion**
In second inversion, the C major seventh chord has the fifth (G) as its bass note.

△ **Third inversion**
In third inversion, the C major seventh chord has the seventh (B) as its bass note.

Neapolitan sixth

The Neapolitan chord is a major triad built on the note a minor second above the tonic. For example, if the music is in C major, D♭ is a minor second above the tonic, so the Neapolitan chord is a D♭ major triad. Neapolitan chords are usually found in first inversion, so they are called Neapolitan sixths because their top note is a minor sixth above their bass note.

D♭ major triad in first inversion

Neapolitan 6th in C major
In C major, the Neapolitan chord is a D♭ major triad, and the Neapolitan sixth is D♭ major in first inversion.

C major

Minor 2nd above tonic = D♭

D♭ major triad = Neapolitan chord

Interval = minor 6th

In first inversion = Neapolitan sixth

Bay of Naples

The Neapolitan sixth is called "Neapolitan" because it is particularly associated with the 18th-century composers of Italian opera who were active in and around the city of Naples, such as Giovanni Battista Pergolesi, Giovanni Paisiello, Domenico Cimarosa, and Alessandro Scarlatti. These composers used the Neapolitan sixth to create emotional and dramatic tension in their music.

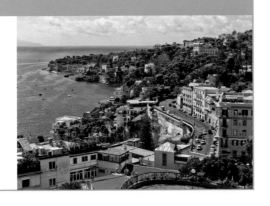

The **dominant seventh** is the most **common seventh chord** because it naturally **resolves onto** the **tonic**.

»

Extended chords

Extended chords are formed by taking a seventh chord and continuing to add notes beyond the seventh in patterns of thirds. The ninth, eleventh, and thirteenth chords, shown below, are examples of extended chords. In practice, the fifth, and the note between the seventh and the top note (such as the ninth in an eleventh chord), might be omitted from an extended chord to make the chord easier to play. However, extended chords must always contain a root, third, and seventh, as well as the top note beyond the seventh (ninth, eleventh, or thirteenth).

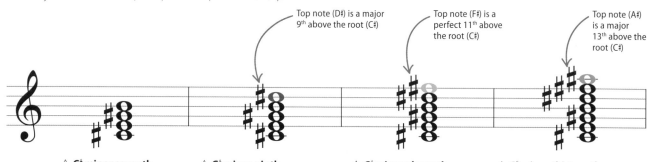

Top note (D♯) is a major 9th above the root (C♯)

Top note (F♯) is a perfect 11th above the root (C♯)

Top note (A♯) is a major 13th above the root (C♯)

△ **C♯ minor seventh**
The C♯ minor seventh is the bass seventh for C♯ minor extended chords.

△ **C♯ minor ninth**
This chord is formed by taking a C♯ minor seventh chord and adding a major ninth.

△ **C♯ minor eleventh**
By adding a perfect eleventh to a C♯ minor ninth chord we get a C♯ minor eleventh.

△ **C♯ minor thirteenth**
Adding a major thirteenth to a C♯ minor eleventh chord gives us a C♯ minor thirteenth.

Type of extended chord	How it is formed
Major	1 3 5 7 + extension
Dominant	1 3 5 ♭7 + extension
Minor	1 ♭3 5 ♭7 + extension

◁ **Types of extended chords**
The most common extended chords are major, dominant, or minor. The type of extended chord depends on the type of seventh chord on which it is based.

REAL WORLD

The "Hendrix Chord"

The dominant seventh chord with an added augmented ninth was a particular favorite of the guitarist, singer, and songwriter Jimi Hendrix. He usually featured it in his music as an E7♯9 chord—an E dominant seventh chord with a top note of F✗ (or enharmonically, G♮), an augmented ninth above the root note of E. Hendrix's influence brought this chord, which had previously been associated mainly with jazz, into much wider use in rock music, and it became known as the "Hendrix Chord."

The **thirteenth chord** is the **largest** possible **extended chord** in **diatonic harmony**.

Added note chords

Added note chords consist of a triad and what is known as a non-tertian extra note. In other words, the extra note means that the chord is not built up in patterns of thirds. This distinguishes added note chords from extended chords. Added note chords either include an extra note that is not a seventh, ninth, eleventh, or thirteenth (such as a fourth or a sixth), or they omit the third or the seventh, which means the chord is no longer built up in thirds.

> The **most common added note chords** are those with an **added fourth** or **added sixth**.

Added note (C) is a 4th above the chord's root (G)

Added note (D) is a 6th above the chord's root (F)

9th chord with a 7th note omitted—this is an added note chord.

7th (B♭) makes this an extended chord—all the notes are a 3rd apart.

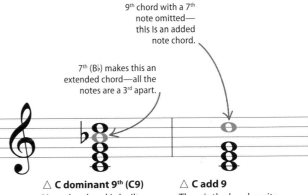

△ **G add 4**
This G major triad has an added note of a fourth (C). This makes it an added note chord.

△ **Fm add 6**
The F minor chord is an added note chord because it has an added note of a sixth (D).

△ **C dominant 9th (C9)**
Here the chord is built up in thirds, which makes it an extended chord, not an added note chord.

△ **C add 9**
The ninth chord omits the seventh, disrupting the pattern of thirds and making it non-tertian.

Chord substitution

Chord substitution involves using one related chord in place of another. It is commonly found in jazz music. Looking at extended chords helps us understand how chords are related and might be substituted for one another, because one extended chord can contain the notes of several triads. For example, a C major ninth chord contains the notes of a C major, E minor, and G major triad.

▽ **Chords within chords**
Breaking these triads and extended chords down into their individual notes shows that many different chords can share common tones.

Chord	Individual notes
C major	C E G
C major 7th	C E G B
C major 9th	C E G B D
E minor	E G B
E minor 7th	E G B D
G	G B D

The Rolling Stones

Added note chords are a common feature of popular guitar music. Many of the songs by bands such as The Beatles and The Rolling Stones include added note chords. One of the most famous examples is The Rolling Stones' 1969 hit "You Can't Always Get What You Want"—the song's harmonies are centered around the C add 9 chord.

Cadences

The term "cadence" describes how a phrase or a piece of music comes to a conclusion. Derived from the Latin verb *cadere,* which means "to fall," a cadence is a type of settling, or rounding off.

SEE ALSO

❬ **124–125** Degrees of the scale

❬ **130–131** Chord types

The Baroque period **208–209** ❭

Perfect cadence

The simplest and most conclusive cadence is a perfect cadence, where the feeling of completion comes from moving down from a chord on the dominant (the fifth) to the tonic (root), reasserting and strengthening the key signature.

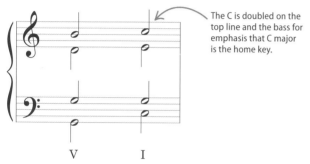

The C is doubled on the top line and the bass for emphasis that C major is the home key.

V   I

△ **The 5–1 cadence**
The dominant chord of C is G, which is arranged here to allow for a stepwise movement into a C chord (D to E and B to C).

 58

Imperfect cadence

In an imperfect cadence the last chord is chord V (the dominant) creating an unfinished effect. In the key of C, the second chord of an imperfect cadence would be the chord of G.

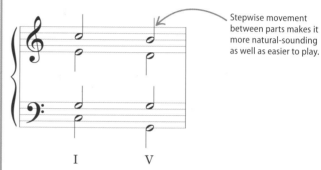

Stepwise movement between parts makes it more natural-sounding as well as easier to play.

I   V

△ **What next?**
This reverses the movement of the perfect cadence, moving from C to G in C major. It would be strange or unusual to conclude an entire piece this way.

 59

Plagal cadence

A plagal cadence is often found in chorale harmonies and hymns. The subdominant (IV) has a greater feeling of openness than the dominant (V).

The top line does not have to change because the C is also part of a subdominant chord (F-A-C).

IV   I

△ **"Amen"**
In the Christian tradition, this type of cadence in sacred music is often used for the final "Amen."

60

Interrupted cadence

A cadence that completes the phrase but suspends resolution by moving to a vi chord rather than I or V is called an interrupted cadence.

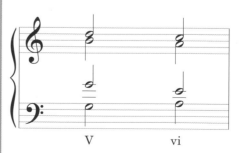

V   vi

△ **Cliffhanger**
Although the VI chord in C major shares both C and E with the tonic, the A resolves to a different and slightly unexpected place, turning away from the expected tonic.

 61

Tierce de Picardie

This is a cadence in a minor key that ends in a major chord, creating an expected change of mood. The origins of the French name are debated, but it indicates that the point of tension lies within the third of the chord moving from minor to major. Baroque music with a figured bass often leaves the decision open to the performer, whether to close with a major or minor resolution.

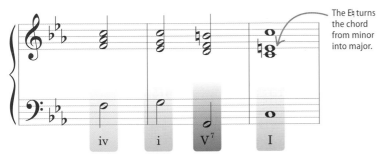

The E♮ turns the chord from minor into major.

iv   i   V⁷   I

△ **Surprise!**
The Tierce de Picardie is often found after an extended sequence of intense minor-key phrases, but even Chopin concludes many of his Nocturnes with a gentle Tierce de Picardie.

Going gently

A Tierce de Picardie need not sound false or abrupt. If the tempo of a piece is slow and the expression is sad or tender, the cadence into the minor can intensify a feeling of gentle rest. Bob Dylan's album *Modern Times* ends with "Ain't Talkin'" in E minor, which subsides and then quietly twists into E major for the last chord.

Cadences in action

The final measures of the concluding chorale to the *St John Passion* by Bach illustrate several different kinds of cadence. Bach uses each one to give a different kind of stress, or emphasis, with the last one being the strongest of all, to reinforce the sense of homecoming in E♭. The shaded areas in the extract show each cadence, with the pause mark above the end of each phrase.

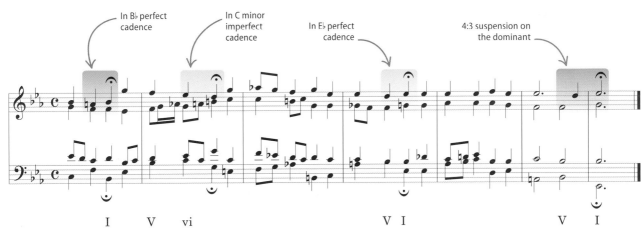

In B♭ perfect cadence

In C minor imperfect cadence

In E♭ perfect cadence

4:3 suspension on the dominant

I   V   vi   V   I   V   I

△ *St John Passion*
After two hours of music, telling the story of the trial and crucifixion of Jesus, the lyrics sung to this line are: "Lord Jesus Christ, hear me, I will praise your name for ever!"

Passing notes

Passing notes are so called because they pass the harmony of a sequence from one chord to another. They break the rhythmic and harmonic regularity of a series of chords, and add decoration and tension to a phrase.

Non-harmony notes

Passing notes and suspensions are known as non-harmony notes because they do not belong to the harmony of a particular chord. They fill in the gaps between the chords, even though other notes may be sounding at the same time. A simple passing-note sequence outline fills in the interval of a third between two notes, moving stepwise between them.

ii   v   i

△ **Passing notes in the melody and bass**
The highlighted passing note creates a dissonance. Passing notes can occur in any part of a chordal texture, not just the melody line.

 62   63

v   i

△ **Passing notes in the harmony**
Here the passing note is in the alto line. Note that the C♯ in the tenor line creates a dissonance, before falling down to D.

More than one passing note

Two or more passing notes can be used to link the harmony notes, to go chromatically, half step by half step, through the interval of a third, or to link the interval of a fourth.

▽ **Chopin's "Étude Op.10, No.2"**
Chopin wrote an entire study in which pianists can perfect the smoothness of their passing notes through the chromatic scale in the right hand.

Weak and strong passing notes

Most passing notes are rhythmically weak, and would sound odd if played with an accent. However, an accented passing note can give tension to a chord, which is quickly resolved. In this way, the function of a passing note can be similar to a suspension.

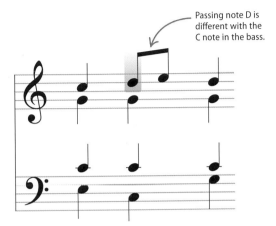

Passing note D is different with the C note in the bass.

△ **A strong passing note**
The shaded passing note D is dissonant with the note C in the bass, but it is placed at the beginning of the chord, giving it extra emphasis.

Neighbor notes

A neighbor note lies only a major or minor second away from the harmony note—and after visiting its neighbor, the harmony always returns home. The neighbor may lie either above or below the chord tone, and at any place within the harmony (melody, bass, or inner parts). Unlike neighbor notes, passing notes are non-harmonic in nature and pass the harmony from one chord to the other, without returning to the initial note.

△ **What does it do?**
A neighbor note tends to strengthen rather than destabilize the sense of the prevailing tonality. Here from D or B, back to the tonic C.

"The **sonatas** of **Mozart** are **unique**: too **easy for children**, too **difficult for adults**." Artur Schnabel

A party of passing notes

In these eight measures of Piano Sonata K 457, finale in C minor, Mozart writes several kinds of passing notes. The tempo marking for this music is allegro assai or "very quickly." Thus, the passing notes and suspensions touch in little dabs of dissonance, giving momentum and tension to the melody without disturbing its C minor key center.

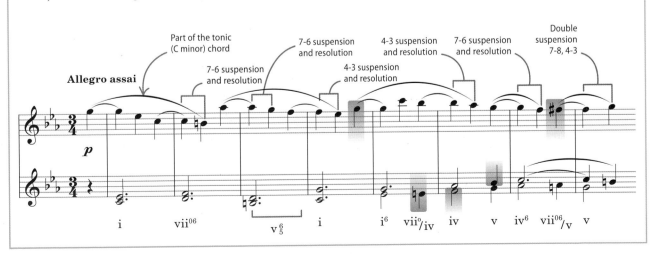

Suspension

A suspension is a musical device for creating and resolving tension. A note is suspended from one chord over the next to create a temporary dissonance, which is then resolved when the suspended note falls to make the chord consonant.

SEE ALSO

❮ 72–73 Accidentals
❮ 120–121 Consonance and dissonance
❮ 136–137 Cadences
❮ 138–139 Passing notes
The Romantic period 212–213 ❯

How do you make a suspension?

The music examples below show two imperfect cadences in F major. They both move from an F chord (I, or root) to a C chord (V, the dominant of F major). But in the second example, the fourth of the C chord, F, is suspended over the C and G, creating a 4:3 suspension, until it moves down to the E, which is the third of the chord.

▽ **Character of a suspension**
Suspensions occur on strong beats and resolutions on weak beats. Here the strong beat is the first beat of the measure. The suspended note tends to fall, not rise, to its consonant resolution.

The cadence is identical, but the F is suspended over C and G.

E

G

C

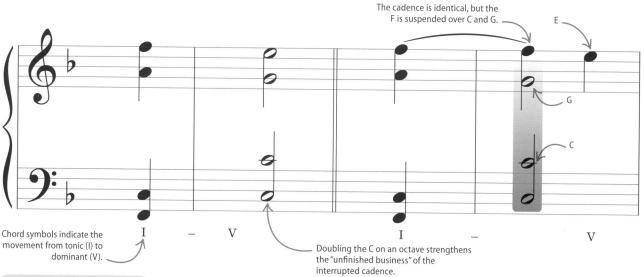

Chord symbols indicate the movement from tonic (I) to dominant (V).

I — V

I — V

Doubling the C on an octave strengthens the "unfinished business" of the interrupted cadence.

Crucifixus

Many composers of choral music, old or new, use suspension to portray in music the "Crucifixus" text, which describes Jesus hanging on the cross. Italian Baroque composer Antonio Lotti wrote a particularly painful example, which uses suspended dissonance across eight separate vocal lines.

"A **cluster of notes** which opened the **door** to **modern music**."
Stephen Fry on the Tristan chord

When is a suspension not a suspension?

The harmonic effect is the same for both the musical examples shown here, but in the first example, the shaded dissonance is an appoggiatura, a grace note that is played on the beat, or even slightly before it, lightly crushing into the consonance of the I–V progression.

▷ **Suspended timing**
Suspensions tend to behave like ornaments—their effect is passing. If the dissonance is prolonged, the sense of the key is threatened.

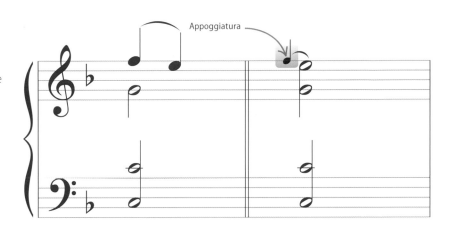

Appoggiatura

6–5 suspensions

Another common type of suspension is 6–5, where the dominant (V) is delayed. In the example shown here, the key signature has three flats, and the root is C in the final chord. This means that this is a C minor progression, not E♭ major. Thus, the chord in the middle, with the B in the bass, is a chord on the seventh degree of the scale, comprising B in the bass, D and F in the treble, with an added diminished seventh on the bass staff in the tenor part.

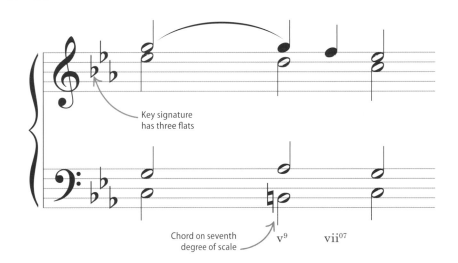

Key signature has three flats

Chord on seventh degree of scale

v^9 vii^{o7}

Tristan chord

Richard Wagner's opera *Tristan und Isolde* derives much of its particular soundworld and feeling from the effect of the opening chord sequence. It has been analyzed in different ways, but it is essentially a chain of suspensions. Wagner does not resolve these suspensions until the end of the opera, so that all the music in between is heard in a state of expectation.

▷ **Tristan und Isolde, opening**
Since the first note is A, the second note, F, is a suspended sixth that creates the need to resolve on to the dominant of A, the E at the end of the first complete measure.

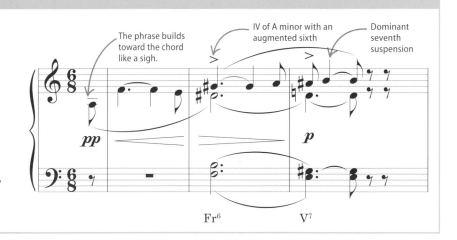

The phrase builds toward the chord like a sigh.

IV of A minor with an augmented sixth

Dominant seventh suspension

Fr^6 V^7

Modal harmony

A mode is another way of ordering pitches to create a particular harmonic structure. They give structure to melodies, especially unaccompanied melodies, but they can also be used within diatonic music.

SEE ALSO

❮ **62–63** Minor scales

❮ **86–87** Modes

❮ **118–119** Harmony

Blues and jazz   **220–221** ❯

Mode in practice

Each mode begins on a different note of the diatonic scale, which lends it an individual character. Because of their origins, they are sometimes known as church modes or Gregorian modes, but they have been used outside religious contexts for centuries in different musical genres. For example, Scottish and Irish folk music often use modes, not only for the melodies but the harmonic accompaniments, too, and this is what lends them their "folky" character.

Mode name	Starting note
Dorian	D
Phrygian	E
Lydian	F
Mixolydian	G
Aeolian	A
Locrian	B
Ionian	C

The structure of a mode

All the modes have their own structure of whole steps and half steps, which gives them their specific character, so that they do not sound like a minor or a major scale. In the diatonic system, a major scale is divided into successive intervals of whole step-whole step-half step-whole step-whole step-whole step-half step—represented in numbers of half steps as 2212221. A natural minor scale is divided as whole step-half step-whole step-whole step-half step-whole step-whole step, or 2122122. The arrangement of the modes in this scheme is shown below.

REAL WORLD

Modes in jazz

Miles Davis used modes rather than chord progressions. "So What?"—the first number on *Kind of Blue*—is a superb example of modal jazz, where the bassist works up and down a modal scale and the other musicians improvise in complementary harmony.

Ionian	Whole step	Whole step	Half step	Whole step	Whole step	Whole step	Half step
Dorian	Whole step	Half step	Whole step	Whole step	Whole step	Half step	Whole step
Phrygian	Half step	Whole step	Whole step	Whole step	Half step	Whole step	Whole step
Lydian	Whole step	Whole step	Whole step	Half step	Whole step	Whole step	Half step
Mixolydian	Whole step	Whole step	Half step	Whole step	Whole step	Half step	Whole step
Aeolian	Whole step	Half step	Whole step	Whole step	Half step	Whole step	Whole step
Locrian	Half step	Whole step	Whole step	Half step	Whole step	Whole step	Whole step

◁ **Ionian mode**
The Ionian mode does sound like a major scale, because it has the same arrangement of whole steps and half steps.

△ **Dorian mode**
The example on the staff shows the Dorian mode, starting not on its "natural" note of D, but on C.

Using modes

Due to its dramatic potential in sound and image, the Dies Irae plainchant has fascinated composers for centuries. Shown below is the original chant, and a parody of it made by the French composer Hector Berlioz in the finale of his *Symphonie Fantastique*. Berlioz uses the chant both as a narrative device within his story (an artist who is in love and has a nightmare that he has gone to hell), but also for its clash with the musical language of his own time.

▽ **Dies Irae**
This famous medieval plainchant describes in graphic terms the Day of Wrath that will announce the Last Judgement. It is in the Dorian mode.

Di-es i - rae di - es il - la,   Sol- vet _saye - lum in fa- vil- la: Tes-te _ Da- vid cum Si- byl-la

▽ **Symphonie Fantastique, finale**
Here the Dies Irae is quoted in the treble clef. It reappears in the bass later on, but moves much more slowly.

Standard practice is not to write in parallel thirds. Berlioz deliberately breaks the rules.

Berlioz uses a syncopated-style rhythm with the modal melody, completely out of keeping with its original character.

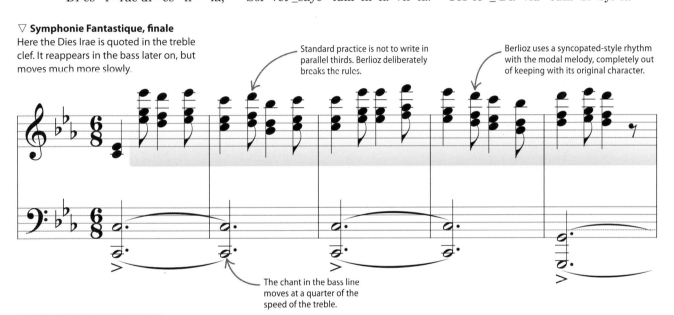

The chant in the bass line moves at a quarter of the speed of the treble.

The Day of Judgement

The "Dies Irae" is a medieval Latin hymn that formed part of the Catholic mass for the dead. Translating as "Day of Wrath," it describes the Last Judgement, which in the Catholic religion marks the end of the world. This Renaissance mural shows Christ, surrounded by the saints, sending believers to heaven and casting unbelievers down to hell.

"**Passionate subjects** must be dealt with in **cold blood**."
Hector Berlioz

Music for choirs

Choirs typically sing in four parts—soprano, alto, tenor, and bass—known as SATB. Learning to write in four parts is excellent training in composition because each part has to have its own direction and interest.

SEE ALSO	
❮ 14–15 High and low	
❮ 18–19 Notes on the staff	
❮ 126–127 Triads	
Voices	192–193 ❯

Ranges

Each person's voice has its own range, but for the sake of practicality in both composition and performance, music for choirs tends to work within set boundaries for each voice. Note that the 8 below the treble staff indicates that the tenor part sounds an octave below the notated pitch.

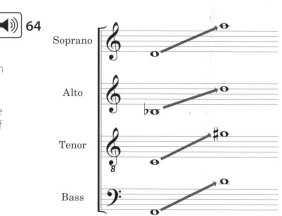

◁ **Soprano**
The soprano range typically spans from the D above Middle C to a top A.

◁ **Alto**
Alto ranges from B♭ below Middle C to D in the treble staff.

◁ **Tenor**
The range from C to the G above Middle C is tenor.

◁ **Bass**
The bass part ranges from a bottom F to the D above Middle C.

Closed score

A closed score indicates that the music is laid out on two staves with a treble and bass clef. The layout of the tenor part helps differentiate between open and closed scores. A tenor part in an open score with four staves has to be transcribed from treble to bass clef.

▽ **"Jesu, Joy of Man's Desiring"**
On the treble staff, the soprano part is written at the top with the stems upward; the alto part is beneath it with stems pointing downward. On the bass staff, the tenor is at the top and the bass part is beneath it.

Voice leading

Voice leading describes how a part moves from one note to the next.

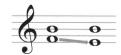

△ **Contrary motion**
In contrary motion, the parts move in opposite directions.

△ **Oblique motion**
Here, one part remains on the same note, while the other moves up or down.

△ **Similar motion**
In similar motion, both the parts move in the same direction.

△ **Parallel motion**
Here, both the parts move up or down by the same interval.

Writing four-part harmony

Writing your own chorale harmony will help you judge your understanding of the subject. You can make your own melody or choose a famous one, but the melody should be in a regular 4/4 or 3/4, and in a fairly simple key signature.

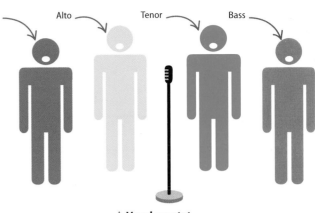

△ **Vocal quartet**
Much Baroque music often performed by choirs was originally written for one voice per part—a vocal quartet. In the 20th century, jazz, barbershop, and Gospel music revived the tradition of writing for vocal quartets.

Recommendations for writing a four-part harmony

Avoid sequences of parallel octaves and fifths, which sound clumsy.

Stay within the range of each voice part.

Do not overload the harmony with complexity and interest if you want the melody line to be followed throughout.

Avoid crossing voices on the same chord.

Use stepwise motion as much as possible. Do not include an interval leap wider than an octave.

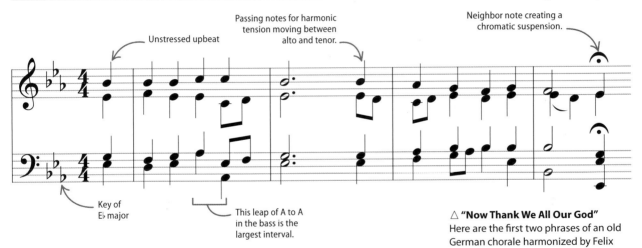

△ **"Now Thank We All Our God"**
Here are the first two phrases of an old German chorale harmonized by Felix Mendelssohn. Note how he observes all the "rules" of harmonization in this example.

LOOKING CLOSER

Doubling voices

If you are using triadic harmony, it is likely that one note in every four-part chord will be a double of the other. Often the top and bottom notes will be doubles of each other, especially the first and last notes of a phrase, but it is important to make each part independent. Some guidelines are listed here.

In root position triads, double the root, except in diminished triads, double the third, otherwise the tritone interval is too prominent.

In V-vi of minor keys, double the third of the vi chord.

In first-inversion triads, double the root of the chord rather than the bass.

In second-inversion triads, double the bass.

Resolve a dominant seventh chord downward by a step.

Bass

The bottom line of the harmony is called the bass. The ear is drawn to the top and bottom lines more easily than the parts in between. So the melody is commonly placed on the top line, and the harmony has its foundation in the bass part.

Bass instruments

It is most common to hear the bass part on a double bass (in classical music and jazz) or a bass guitar (in popular music). However, the left hand of the keyboard, such as a piano, electric keyboard, organ, or harpsichord, also plays the bass part in any music with more than one voice. Other instruments that play the bass part include cello (string), bassoon (wind), and tuba (brass).

> "As the **earth** is the **foundation** of the **other elements,** so the **bass** is the **foundation** of the **harmony...**"
> Gioseffo Zarlino, 1558

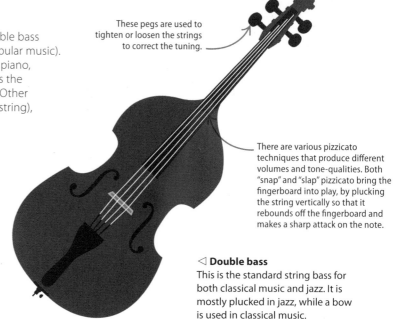

These pegs are used to tighten or loosen the strings to correct the tuning.

There are various pizzicato techniques that produce different volumes and tone-qualities. Both "snap" and "slap" pizzicato bring the fingerboard into play, by plucking the string vertically so that it rebounds off the fingerboard and makes a sharp attack on the note.

◁ **Double bass**
This is the standard string bass for both classical music and jazz. It is mostly plucked in jazz, while a bow is used in classical music.

Drone bass

The simplest type of bass is a drone bass, which sustains a single note over a long period. This restricts the harmony that can be placed above it, if the harmony isn't to sound random or too dissonant. Except for passing notes and suspensions, only those notes that sound consonant with the drone can be used for any length of time. The drone is either the tonic or the dominant of the key.

▽ **Haydn, Symphony No.104**
This drone bass opens the finale of Haydn's last symphony. The opening is deliberately plain, with no harmony between melody and bass. This conveys a rustic effect.

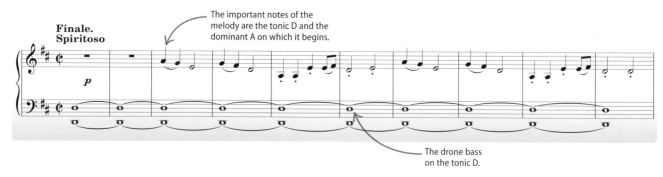

The important notes of the melody are the tonic D and the dominant A on which it begins.

The drone bass on the tonic D.

Pedal bass

A pedal bass is a single note repeated or held throughout a passage. In the context of organ music, a pedal is played by the feet on the pedals of the instrument, but all bass instruments will play a pedal to anchor the harmony from time to time.

▽ **Bach,** *Fantasia in G major* **BWV572**
The climax to this organ fantasia features a powerful, repeated pedal note in the bass, extending for many measures beneath quick chromatic progressions until the final cadence.

Ground bass

A ground bass is a pattern of notes repeated throughout a movement or work. Rather than the standard practice of "hanging" the harmony from a melody—like clothes on a line, in a ground bass, the rest of the harmony must fit with the ground bass. Sometimes the bass itself is the melody.

▽ **Pachelbel,** *Canon in D major*
This piece by Pachelbel has a two-measure ground bass and a canon in three voices above it. The ground bass is repeated throughout the piece and never deviates from a 1-4-5 cadence.

Figured bass

A figured bass uses chord symbols to indicate the notes to be played. This is used in Baroque music and in popular music, especially for guitar, both as a shorthand notation and as a way of indicating the harmonic direction of a melody, but leaving the bass player free to add notes around the chords.

▽ **Corelli, "La Folia"**
This arrangement of an Italian folksong is scored for violin and keyboard (harpsichord). The numbers represent the chords in the treble staff above the bass.

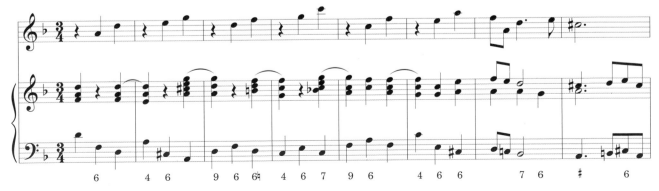

Chord symbols

Chord symbols are used in most genres of popular music. A chord name and its corresponding symbol indicates the root and type of the chord. If chords include added notes, they can also be indicated by chord symbols.

SEE ALSO

⟨ **110–111** Two or more notes together

⟨ **124–125** Degrees of the scale

⟨ **130–131** Chord types

Blues and jazz   **220–221** ⟩

Basic chord symbols

The five main chord types in popular music are major, minor, augmented, diminished, and half-diminished. The table shows the symbols that are used to indicate these chord types. A minimum of two alternative symbols are possible for each chord type.

Major chord	Letter name (e.g., C), M, maj, or Δ
Minor chord	m or min
Augmented chord	+ or aug
Diminished chord	° or dim
Half diminished chord	∅ or Ø

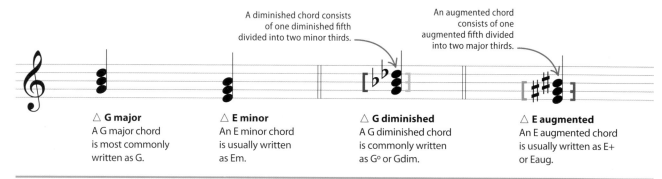

A diminished chord consists of one diminished fifth divided into two minor thirds.

An augmented chord consists of one augmented fifth divided into two major thirds.

△ **G major**
A G major chord is most commonly written as G.

△ **E minor**
An E minor chord is usually written as Em.

△ **G diminished**
A G diminished chord is commonly written as G° or Gdim.

△ **E augmented**
An E augmented chord is usually written as E+ or Eaug.

Seventh chords

A seventh chord is a triad plus an added note that is a seventh above the root of the triad. Chord symbols for seventh chords indicate the type of triadic chord and the quality of the seventh between the root of the triad and the added seventh note, as shown in the table.

Major seventh	Major chord symbol + 7 i.e. M7
Minor seventh	Minor chord symbol + 7 i.e. m7
Dominant seventh	7 (composed of a major 5th and a minor 7th)
Diminished seventh	Diminished chord symbol + 7 = °7
Half-diminished seventh	Half-diminished chord symbol + 7 = ∅7
Minor major seventh	Minor triad + major seventh = mM7
Augmented major seventh	Augmented triad + major seventh = +M7

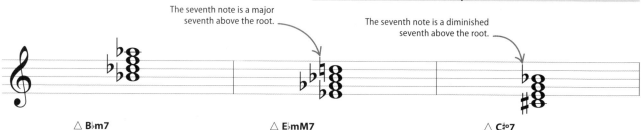

The seventh note is a major seventh above the root.

The seventh note is a diminished seventh above the root.

△ **B♭m7**
Since a minor seventh is added to the B♭ minor triad, the chord symbol is B♭m7.

△ **E♭mM7**
With a major seventh added to the E♭ minor triad, the chord symbol becomes E♭mM7.

△ **C♯°7**
The diminished seventh chord, starting on C♯, has the chord symbol C♯°7.

Extended chords

Chords can have added notes beyond a seventh note—for example, notes that are a ninth, an eleventh, or a thirteenth above the root of a chord can be added to it. These notes would be indicated by the numbers 9, 11, and 13 respectively in chord symbols, as shown below.

Ninth chord	Chord name + 9
Eleventh chord	Chord name + 11
Thirteenth chord	Chord name + 13

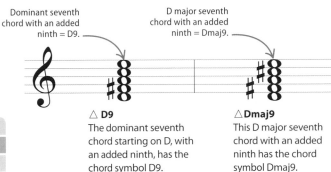

Dominant seventh chord with an added ninth = D9.

D major seventh chord with an added ninth = Dmaj9.

△ **D9**
The dominant seventh chord starting on D, with an added ninth, has the chord symbol D9.

△ **Dmaj9**
This D major seventh chord with an added ninth has the chord symbol Dmaj9.

Tone chords

Those chords where a particular note has been raised or lowered by a half step are known as tone chords. The chord symbol includes an indication as to which note has been altered, and whether it has been raised or lowered. For example, the symbol (♭5) shows that the fifth of a chord has been lowered.

Raised note	Chord name + sharp symbol (♯, +, Δ) before the altered tone of the chord
Lowered note	Chord name + flat symbol (♭, or -) before the altered tone of the chord

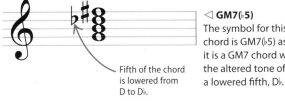

◁ **GM7(♭5)**
The symbol for this chord is GM7(♭5) as it is a GM7 chord with the altered tone of a lowered fifth, D♭.

Fifth of the chord is lowered from D to D♭.

Slash chord

A slash chord has a bass note that is not the root of the chord. Its chord symbol is indicated by the root note, a slash, and then the bass note. The bass note can belong to the chord (in which case the slash chord is an inversion), but this is not always the case.

Symbol	Chord	Bass note
C/G	C major	G (a C major second inversion)
D/F♯	D major	F♯ (a D major first inversion)
Am/G	A minor	G

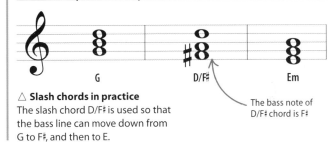

G

D/F♯

Em

△ **Slash chords in practice**
The slash chord D/F♯ is used so that the bass line can move down from G to F♯, and then to E.

The bass note of D/F♯ chord is F♯

Blues harmonies

What makes the blues blue? The 12-bar blues is built on a I-IV-V progression that flattens the fifth, giving a kink to what would otherwise be a straightforward major chord pattern. This means that blues music uses lots of diminished chord symbols. Leonard Bernstein's *West Side Story* is heavily influenced by jazz, and it features many blues harmonies.

No one knows who **invented chord symbols,** but some **musicologists believe** they were **first used** by the **American** composer, arranger, and pianist **Ferde Grofé** (1892–1972).

Harmonizing a song melody

Harmonizing can be as simple as adding chords to the notes of a melody. There are rules to make harmony pleasant and interesting, but, unlike math, there is no "right" answer.

SEE ALSO	
❰ 16–17 The piano keyboard	
❰ 130–131 Chord types	
❰ 136–137 Cadences	
Bass	146–147 ❱

Accompanying a melody

This old folksong from Croatia is a melody in two parts. It is so simple that the two parts are identical, except for the last measures (measures 4 and 8). The harmony could also be simple accordingly. The first half of each part can be identical, and then the second half can differ.

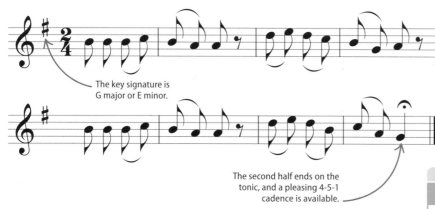

The key signature is G major or E minor.

The second half ends on the tonic, and a pleasing 4-5-1 cadence is available.

"The **trouble** with **music appreciation** in general is that people are **taught** to have **too much respect** for music; they should be taught to **love it instead**."
Igor Stravinsky

◁ **Choose another melody?**
Try harmonizing for yourself, but pick a singable melody with lots of stepwise intervals and a regular structure in groups of four measures: "Twinkle, Twinkle, Little Star" is a well-known example.

▽ **Rules and when to break them**
George Orwell's advice to anyone writing English: "Break any of these rules rather than write something outright barbarous."

Do's	Don'ts
Do keep the harmony as simple as you can when starting out.	Don't change the harmony on every note.
Do begin and end with a tonic chord in the root.	Don't overuse III, VI, and VII chords because they will destabilize the sense of the key.
Do keep in mind the instrument(s) you are writing for and their tessitura range.	Don't write huge leaps between chords.
Do think about what cadence (and half-cadence) you will use according to the style of your melody and harmony.	Don't worry about using simple chord combinations. 1-4-5 chords have served just fine for hundreds of years.

REAL WORLD

Joseph Haydn (1732–1809)

The greatest musicians and composers have made some of their best music from basic materials. Haydn wrote 104 symphonies that were highly sophisticated and cheerful compositions. He knew how to shape a folk melody to allow it to bear more sophisticated harmony, and when to keep things simple.

Create your own harmony

Here is a two-part harmonization of the melody shown on p.150. For a piano, two chords per measure will keep the harmony interesting; fewer than that and the song may fall flat or sound too plain. Harmonizing every note, however, will rob the song of its simple character. The song has a strong accent on the first beat of the measure, so that is where the harmony should be the strongest. Watch out for overcomplicating the harmony on a weak beat because that will introduce an unwanted stress on the beat.

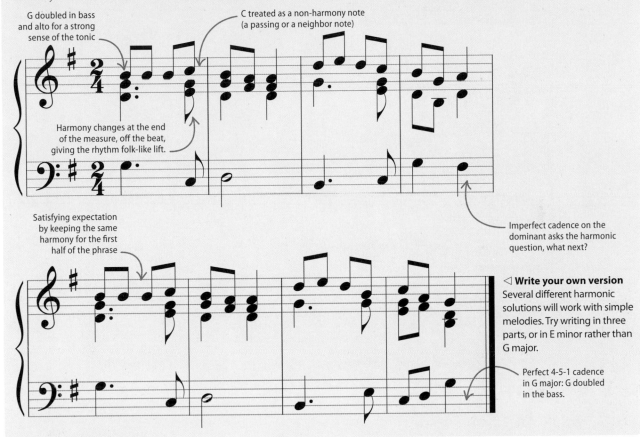

G doubled in bass and alto for a strong sense of the tonic

C treated as a non-harmony note (a passing or a neighbor note)

Harmony changes at the end of the measure, off the beat, giving the rhythm folk-like lift.

Satisfying expectation by keeping the same harmony for the first half of the phrase

Imperfect cadence on the dominant asks the harmonic question, what next?

◁ **Write your own version**
Several different harmonic solutions will work with simple melodies. Try writing in three parts, or in E minor rather than G major.

Perfect 4-5-1 cadence in G major: G doubled in the bass.

LOOKING CLOSER

How and where?

Most composers, in the past and present, have used a piano to experiment with music. For some pianists, especially the ones who are good in their own right, the piano shapes the harmony of the music even if it is written for other instruments. Beethoven and Stravinsky used the piano to explore a range of ideas.

▽ **"Augurs of Spring"**
Written for strings, but clearly conceived on the piano, the sound of Stravinsky's savage ballet "Augurs of Spring" is summed up in these chords. Try them for yourself.

Tempo giusto ♩ = 50

Form

Repeats

Repetition is one of the important unifying aspects of music. Most musical forms employ some degree of repetition, whether on a small scale—a few measures—or repeating entire sections.

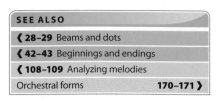
Simple repeat symbol

The repeat symbol, a double bar preceded by two dots, means to return to wherever you see the inverted, or reversed, repeat symbol and repeat the material in between. If there is no reversed repeat sign, go back to the beginning and repeat.

◁ **Repeat symbol**
The repeat symbol is notated by a double bar, like the one that ends a piece, but with two preceding dots.

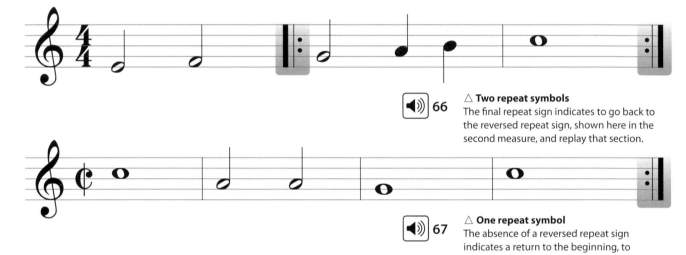

🔊 66

△ **Two repeat symbols**
The final repeat sign indicates to go back to the reversed repeat sign, shown here in the second measure, and replay that section.

🔊 67

△ **One repeat symbol**
The absence of a reversed repeat sign indicates a return to the beginning, to replay the entire section.

Repeat one or two measures

A one-measure repeat is notated by a single slash with two dots, within the measure immediately after the measure to be repeated. There is no limit to the number of one-measure repeats that composers may use, although for ease in performance the number of measures to be repeated is usually placed over the measure, if greater than one.

🔊 68

◁ **Repeating a measure**
If only one measure of music is to be repeated, you will see this symbol indicating to repeat the previous measure one time.

🔊 69

◁ **Repeating two measures**
If two measures are to be repeated, the symbol used has two slashes and the number 2 above it. This means to repeat the previous two measures one time.

Same tune, different ending

First and second endings are used when a composer or arranger wants a section of music repeated, but with a different end portion. The first ending is performed the first time through the piece, and the second ending is used for the final repetition. Third and fourth endings are rarely used.

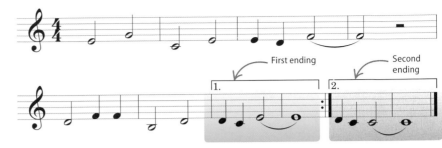

First ending   Second ending

1.   2.

△ **"Mary Ann"**
Different endings are used for this eight-measure Calypso tune of the Caribbean islands. The first six measures are identical and repeated twice.

D.C.: back to the beginning

Da Capo ("back to the head" in Italian) is abbreviated D.C. When this is notated in the course of a piece, it means to go back to the beginning and repeat a large section. D.C. usually appears in one of the following two usages—D.C. al Fine, or D.C. al Coda, explained below.

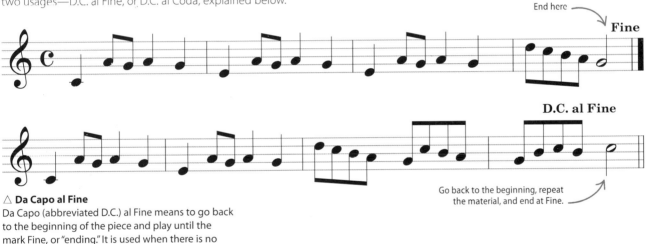

End here

Fine

D.C. al Fine

△ **Da Capo al Fine**
Da Capo (abbreviated D.C.) al Fine means to go back to the beginning of the piece and play until the mark Fine, or "ending." It is used when there is no new ending material.

Go back to the beginning, repeat the material, and end at Fine.

D.C. al Coda

Da Capo al Coda is used when there is unique musical material that ends the piece. D.C. al Coda tells the performer to go back to the beginning of the piece and play until the word Coda, or the coda symbol, and then jump to the end portion (coda) of the piece.

◁ **Coda symbol**
Coda means "tail" in Italian. When the performer sees the coda symbol it is a signal to jump over the next section of the music and play a special ending.

D.C. al Coda

CODA

◁ **"Hot Cross Buns"**
In this tune written in the D.C. al Coda format, the two repetitions are the same except for the last two measures.

D.S.: back to the sign

Not all repeats in music involve going all the way back to the beginning of the piece. Sometimes composers want to send you to a certain point in the piece, which is when dal segno (Italian for "back to the sign") is used. Dal segno is abbreviated as D.S.

◁ **Dal segno al fine (D.S. al fine)**
The instruction dal segno al fine means to go back to the segno (sign, shown here) and play until the fine mark, or ending.

◁ **Dal segno al coda**
Here, play to the end of line two, then return to the sign at measure six. At measure 13 (the double measure), skip to the coda and play the last seven measures as written.

Types of repeats

This musical illustration contains several types of repeats that performers encounter in various pieces of music. Repeat signs save space, and therefore reduce printing and typesetting costs because identical musical segments do not have to be written out.

▽ **Repeats 1**
To avoid getting lost in a piece with many complicated repeats, always remember the performer should go back to the previous repeat sign or the beginning, whichever is closest.

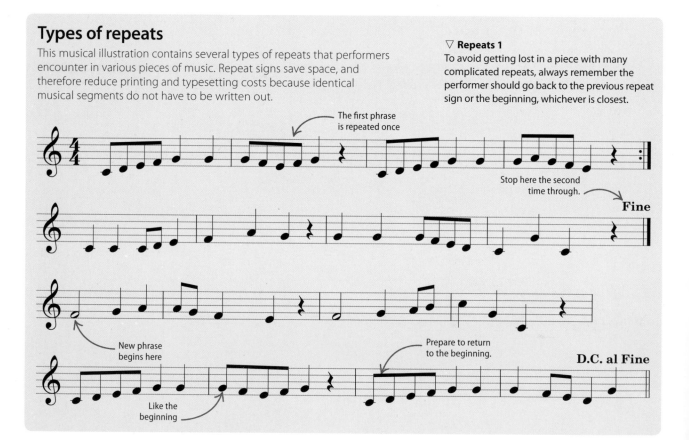

The first phrase is repeated once

Stop here the second time through.

Fine

New phrase begins here

Prepare to return to the beginning.

D.C. al Fine

Like the beginning

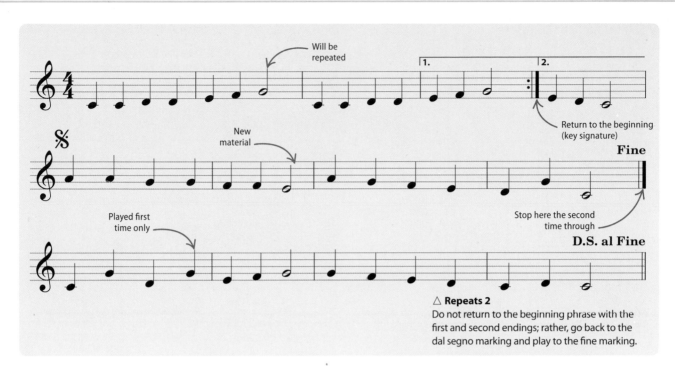

△ **Repeats 2**

Do not return to the beginning phrase with the first and second endings; rather, go back to the dal segno marking and play to the fine marking.

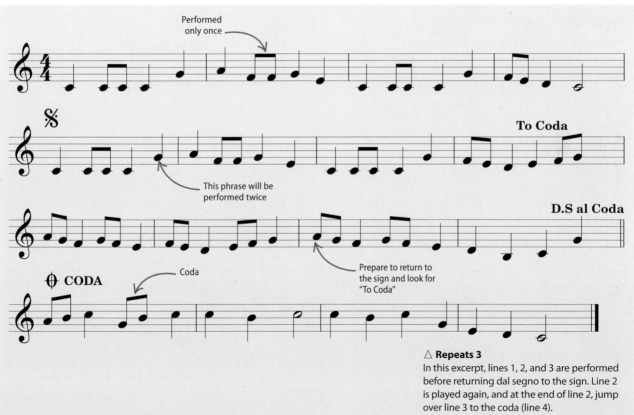

△ **Repeats 3**

In this excerpt, lines 1, 2, and 3 are performed before returning dal segno to the sign. Line 2 is played again, and at the end of line 2, jump over line 3 to the coda (line 4).

Binary form

The word "binary" means having two parts. A musical piece in binary form has two large sections, usually labeled A and B. For this reason, binary form is also known as the AB form.

SEE ALSO
❰ 124–125 Degrees of the scale
❰ 154–155 Repeats
Ternary form   160–161 ❱

How are A and B different?

The A and B parts of a piece in binary form are usually similar in terms of melodic and rhythmic material. The major difference between the two is that the B section modulates, or moves, to a different but related key. If the key of the A section is a major key, usually the B section will modulate to the key of the fifth scale degree, or *sol*—also known as the dominant key.

▽ **AB**
This diagram shows how a binary piece contains two sections, with a corresponding move from tonic to a closely related key, and then back again. Each portion is repeated, and the B section modulates to the tonic key.

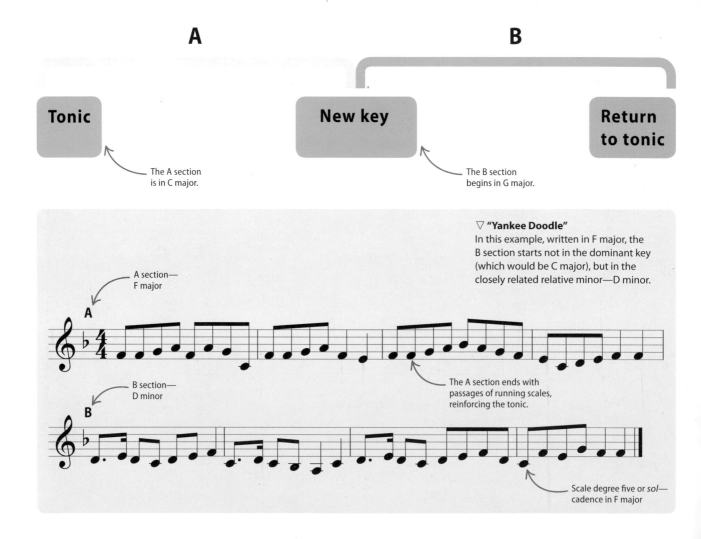

A

B

| Tonic | New key | Return to tonic |

The A section is in C major.

The B section begins in G major.

▽ **"Yankee Doodle"**
In this example, written in F major, the B section starts not in the dominant key (which would be C major), but in the closely related relative minor—D minor.

A section— F major

A

B section— D minor

B

The A section ends with passages of running scales, reinforcing the tonic.

Scale degree five or *sol*— cadence in F major

AABB

In the *Orchestral Suite No. 2* by J. S. Bach, the Badinerie—or the quick, light movement in a suite—is an example of binary form. The A section is in B minor, and the B section is in D major. The B section transitions back to B minor, to end the piece in the key in which it began. For a fuller, more complete piece, composers often call for each section of the binary piece to be repeated.

▽ **Badinerie**
In 18th-century music, a Badinerie is commonly found as a light instrumental piece in duple meter—usually the final movement of a dance suite. This 1739 Badinerie was written for solo flute, strings, and continuo.

Outlines the tonic B minor triad

Cadence in B minor

Trill

Highlighting F♯, the dominant of B minor

Cadence in B minor

A

Elaborating D major

Firmly in D major

Appoggiatura

F♯, the dominant of B minor

The B section modulates back to the tonic, B minor.

Transitions back to B minor

B

Ternary form

Ternary form is any musical structure with three separate, identifiable sections. The most common are ABA—or ABA'—and the minuet and trio. Just like binary form, the B section of a ternary form contrasts A in style or tonality.

SEE ALSO
❮ 40–41 Syncopation and swing
❮ 124–125 Degrees of the scale
❮ 154–157 Repeats
❮ 158–159 Binary form

ABA

In ABA form, a contrasting middle section, B, is "sandwiched" between two identical strains. ABA' (or "A Prime") denotes a concluding A section—similar to the first A section, but differing slightly. Often the ending of the A' section is written to sound definitively final.

▽ **Three sections**
The diagram below shows how a ternary piece contains three sections, with nearly identical outer portions. The B section may be in a new key.

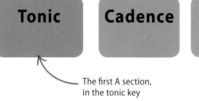

A (may be repeated)　　　　　**B**　　　　　**A**

| Tonic | Cadence | New key | Cadence | Tonic | Final cadence |

The first A section, in the tonic key

▽ **"Shoo Fly"**
This popular American tune is an example of ABA'. It was first published in 1869 and has been widely recorded and performed as a children's song.

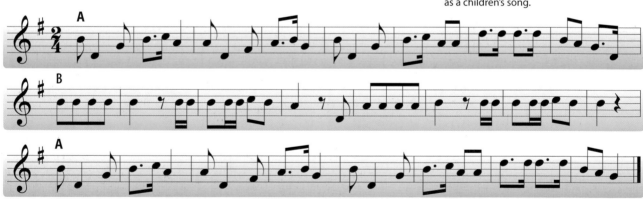

▽ **Last phrase of "Shoo Fly"**
In this version, the final A section ends with an extended final cadence, with half notes leading from scale degree 3 to 1 (*mi* to *do*).

Minuet and trio

A well-known use of the ABA form can be found in the "minuet and trio" structure. The minuet is a short dance-like form in 3/4 time, with a strong downbeat and a waltzlike sound. The trio is usually more lyrical, with legato phrases to contrast with the minuet. Often the second appearance of the minuet is not written out, but the entire form is printed as Minuet, Trio, Da Capo al Fine.

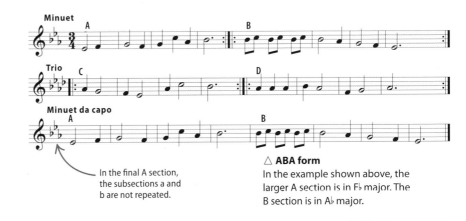

In the final A section, the subsections a and b are not repeated.

△ **ABA form**
In the example shown above, the larger A section is in F♭ major. The B section is in A♭ major.

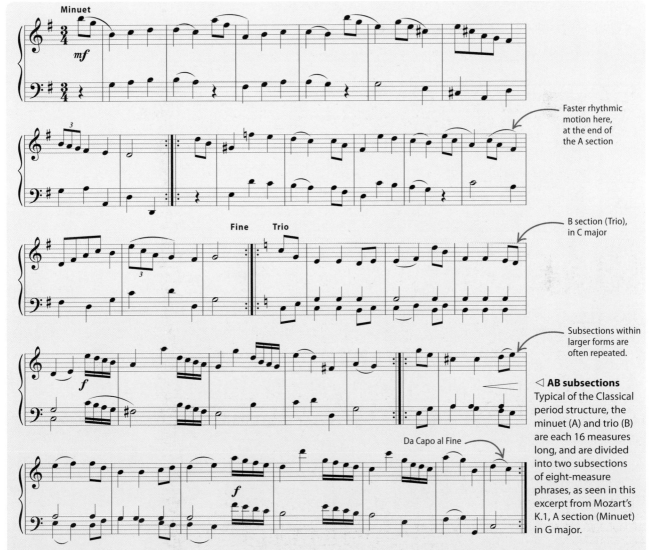

Faster rhythmic motion here, at the end of the A section

B section (Trio), in C major

Subsections within larger forms are often repeated.

◁ **AB subsections**
Typical of the Classical period structure, the minuet (A) and trio (B) are each 16 measures long, and are divided into two subsections of eight-measure phrases, as seen in this excerpt from Mozart's K.1, A section (Minuet) in G major.

Counterpoint

The term "counterpoint" comes from the Latin *contra punctus contra*, or point-against-point. Musical counterpoint emphasizes individual musical lines—these independently structured parts interact to create a fuller harmonic texture.

SEE ALSO

❰ 96–97 Types of phrases
❰ 98–99 Sequences
Musical texture 200–201 ❱
The Baroque period 208–209 ❱

Partner songs

Simple counterpoint results when two unique songs with similar harmonic structure and complementary melodies are sung or played together. These tunes stand on their own as unique pieces, but are also performed as "partner songs"—the two independent lines create a polyphonic, contrapuntal effect.

▽ **"Hey ho"/"Ah poor bird"**
In counterpoint, the combination of two or more familiar folk tunes, like these two old English rounds, is also called a *quodlibet*.

Rounds

A tune composed to allow two or more voices to sing or play the exact same melody beginning at different intervals of time is called a round, or canon. Rounds are composed to be repeated multiple times, unlike canons, which have definite endings.

▷ **"Frère Jacques"**
This French nursery rhyme (called "Brother John" or "Are You Sleeping?" in English) is one of the world's best-known rounds.

Canon

Canons are similar to rounds, but the voices that enter the canon following, or imitating, the lead voice may differ in rhythm or pitch. While these variations allow for more creativity, the various presentations of the canon theme are still closely tied to the original statement.

▽ **Pachelbel's Canon**
Composed c.1694, but unpublished until 1919, Johann Pachelbel's *Canon in D* is the most famous canon ever written. It is scored for three violins and a bass instrument, which repeats the same eight-note motif, or ground bass, 28 times.

Voice 1

Voice 2

Voice 2 repeats voice 1 from two measures earlier.

Voice 3

Voice 3 repeats the material from voice 2.

Voice 4

Fugue

Just like a canon, a fugue theme (subject) is introduced and then imitated by two or more voices. Each entrance of the subject starts on a different pitch. After each voice performs the theme once, the exposition of the piece is over. Then, "episodes" or "development" sections appear, which employ strict contrapuntal compositional techniques.

▽ **Fuga I, Bach's *The Well-Tempered Clavier***
This keyboard fugue written in 1722 (BWV 846) is a textbook example of fugal counterpoint. The 14-note subject appears 24 times, evenly spread among the four voices.

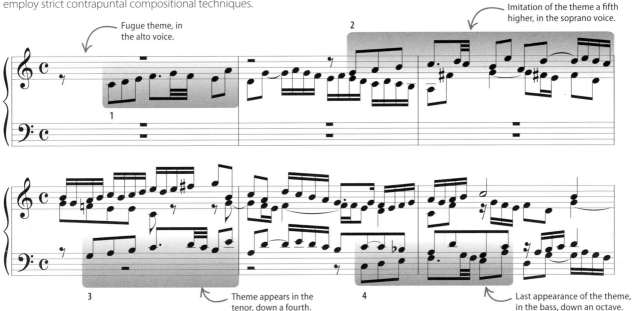

Fugue theme, in the alto voice.

Imitation of the theme a fifth higher, in the soprano voice.

Theme appears in the tenor, down a fourth.

Last appearance of the theme, in the bass, down an octave.

Theme and variations

Theme and variations is a musical form in which one melody provides continuity for the whole piece. The composer presents the theme repeatedly, but varies it each time in tempo, tonality, texture, dynamics, instrumentation, or overall style.

SEE ALSO
❮ **44–45** Tempo
❮ **104–105** Musical expression
❮ **154–157** Repeats
Orchestral forms **170–171** ❯

The same, but different

Theme and variations has been popular since the 17th century. One melody (typically 8 to 32 measures long) is creatively altered by the composer for a series of subsequent variations. Coherence is achieved because the theme is almost always recognizable in its new form.

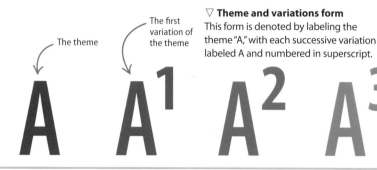

The theme

The first variation of the theme

▽ **Theme and variations form**
This form is denoted by labeling the theme "A," with each successive variation labeled A and numbered in superscript.

Goldberg Variations

While Renaissance composers often wrote themes followed successively by more rhythmically difficult variations, Baroque composers solidified the form. J. S. Bach's most famous theme and variations, the 1741 *Goldberg Variations* for solo harpsichord (BWV 988), contains 30 versions of one simple aria. The piece is probably named after its first performer, Johann Goldberg.

△ **Goldberg theme**
This is a peaceful tune in G major. It is 32 measures long, and corresponds to the 32 sections of the entire piece (theme + 30 variations + theme).

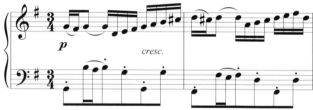

Allegro moderato (♩= 108)

△ **Variation 1**
The first variation contains lively running passages, but retains the same harmonic progression of the theme as well as the triple meter.

△ **Variation 11**
A virtuosic variation with close, even overlapping hand position, it is in the unusual time signature of 12/16 (doubling the more common 6/8).

Moderato

△ **Variation 30**
This variation, the last in the piece, cleverly intersperses German folk song material with the theme in a jokey *quodlibet* (see p.162).

Piano variation by Mozart

Mozart wrote 12 solo piano variations of a French folk song, "Ah! vous dirai-je, Maman" (K. 265, ca. 1781). Only variations 11 and 12 have tempo indications—Adagio and Allegro. Variation 8 is in a minor key, and variation 12 is in triple meter.

▽ **"Twinkle, Twinkle, Little Star"**
You may know this theme as "Twinkle, Twinkle, Little Star," "Baa Baa Black Sheep," or even "The Alphabet Song."

THEME

mf

Modern variations

Many modern composers have created theme and variations, sometimes using another composer's tune for inspiration. The mid-20th century tour de force for orchestra by Benjamin Britten, *Young Person's Guide to the Orchestra*, features 13 variations (and a grand closing fugue) on a theme by Henry Purcell (1659–95). Each variation features a different instrument section in the orchestra. Britten even wrote narration to precede each variation, introducing the instrument families and explaining how they make sound.

"**Composing** is like driving down a foggy road toward a **house**. Slowly you see details of the house, the color of the slates and bricks, the shape of the windows. The **notes are** the **bricks** and the **mortar** of the house." Benjamin Britten

Ostinati, loops, and riffs

A piece of musical material repeated over and over may be called a riff, an ostinato, or a loop. While they are essentially the same thing, the different terms are used within different genres of music.

SEE ALSO	
❮ 38–39 Triplets and tuplets	
❮ 162–163 Counterpoint	
Rock bands	**190–191 ❯**
Blues and jazz	**198–199 ❯**

Ostinato

Italian for obstinate, ostinati are brief phrases that are repeated over and over in a piece of classical music. Ostinati may be varied or transposed, but their similarity is their hallmark. "Open" rhythmic ostinati are less restrictive, whereas melodic ("closed") ostinati are more limited as melodies are restricted by their harmonic implications.

 70

▽ **Rhythmic ostinati**
One of the most famous rhythmic ostinati ever written is this snare drum rhythm, which underpins the melody in Maurice Ravel's *Bolero* (1928).

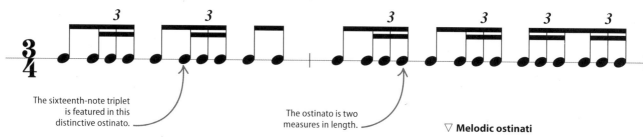

The sixteenth-note triplet is featured in this distinctive ostinato.

The ostinato is two measures in length.

▽ **Melodic ostinati**
In Frédéric Chopin's *Berceuse*, D-flat major, Op. 57 (1843), one of the most well-known melodic ostinati appears in the left hand.

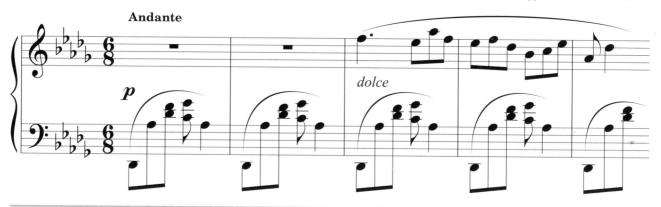

Ground bass

A type of ostinato, ground bass consists of a repeated harmonic motif in the bass part of the music. One of the most famous ground bass lines is the lowest part of *Canon in D*, written by Johann Pachelbel in the 17th century. This eight-note ground bass pattern occurs 28 consecutive times in the piece.

 71

△ *Canon in D*, **Johann Pachelbel**
These eight simple notes imply the following rich harmonic progression: D major, A major, B minor, F♯ minor, G major, D major, G major, A major.

Loop

When an ostinato is used in electronic music it is called a loop. Short sections of music can be created and repeated easily in composing software programs, synthesizers, or sequencers. Often composers will sample (or digitally appropriate a portion of sound from) a small bit of music from an existing piece, to use as a loop in a new piece.

▽ **A software loop**
Here is an example of synthesizer, bongo drum, and DJ beat loops premade and layered on top of each other. The synth and bongo loops are one four-count measure.

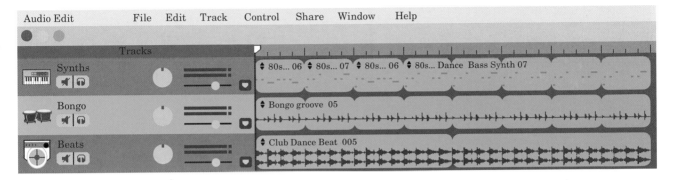

Riff

The term "riff" is used in pop, rock, and jazz music. Riffs are usually repeated material used as a melody, accompanied by instruments that play the changing harmonies underneath. Also known as "the hook" or a "lick," riffs can be extremely catchy and memorable, as in Eric Clapton and Cream's 1967 hit "Sunshine of Your Love." They do not repeat as many times in a row as an ostinato, unless they are accompanimental, as seen below.

 72

▽ **Bluesy riff**
Riffs may be repeated over and over if they serve as the background to a melodic improvisation, as shown in this example from the blues style.

Eric Clapton

British singer-songwriter and guitarist Eric Clapton's most famous riffs are so revered by guitar enthusiasts that entire books and websites are devoted to dissecting and analyzing his blues, pop, rock, and folk performances. In addition to the tune discussed above, Clapton's 1970 song "Layla," recorded with his band Derek and the Dominoes, features some of the most iconic, recognizable guitar riffs of all time.

"I'd love to **knock** an **audience cold** with **one note,** but what do you do for the rest of the **evening?**"
Eric Clapton

Breaks and fills

Breaks and fills are used in dance music and jazz as a way of creating contrast with the established musical flow. They stop the forward momentum of the piece, in order to focus the listener on rhythm, a solo, or even silence.

SEE ALSO

‹ 146–147 Bass

Rock bands 190–191 ›

Breaks

In a tune, brief departures from the melodic flow are called breaks. Sometimes they can be two or three measures of silence, or they may feature one solo instrument. Breaks can place the listener's focus on the dancing, rather than the music, or they can highlight a quick improvised and flashy solo.

▽ **"Tiger Rag"**
In this example of a traditional Dixieland tune, the break occurs in the last line, with suggested clarinet or tenor sax notes.

Melody shown here with note stems in the upward direction.

Slurred material is the suggested solo.

Clar. solo

Tenor solo

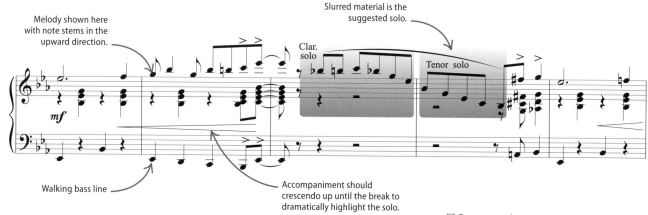

Walking bass line

Accompaniment should crescendo up until the break to dramatically highlight the solo.

▽ **Dance music**
Breaks are the places where the melody and harmony wind down for a minute, usually to give the percussionist a place to shine.

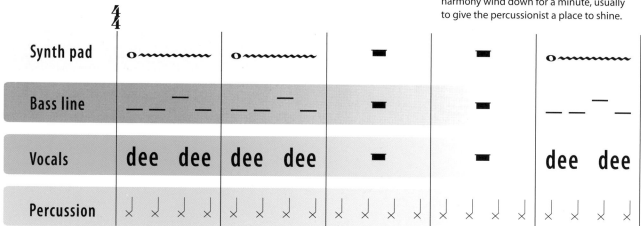

Fills

Fills are short and simple rhythmic passages played by musicians to "fill in" or "fill up" the space between phrases. Most fills are typical of a certain genre. Drummers may use fills as a chance to perform a mini-solo, but for the most part fills are not especially notable. This quality distinguishes them from riffs, which tend to be memorable, even unforgettable, hallmarks of a particular tune.

▽ **Fill**

In this example of a fill, a bass player fills two measures between phrases with a short, flashy transitional move from C major to F major, and then back again.

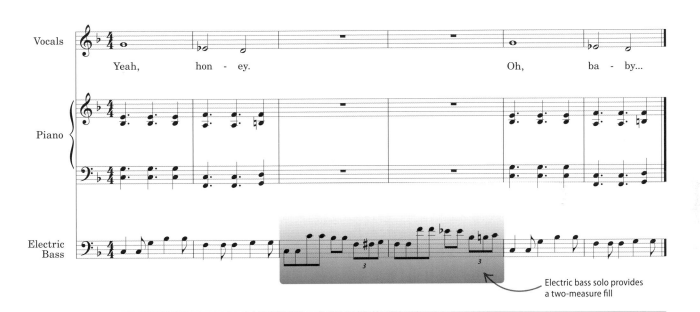

Electric bass solo provides a two-measure fill

Dizzy Gillespie (1917–1993)

Flashy, impressive breaks on solo trumpet were a hallmark of Dizzy Gillespie's trademark bebop style. His style featured fast tempi, amazing virtuosity, and breathtaking improvised instrumental solos by him and his bandmates.

Vamps

A vamp is a simple two-, four-, or eight-measure harmonic pattern (even a single chord) played in the same rhythm over and over until a cue. "Vamp till ready" is a musical command in musical theater scores. Vamps allow for in-the-moment improvisations in live performances of rock or blues music.

△ **Classic vamp**
This repeated C minor chord over a descending bass line, from scale degree 1 to scale degree 5 or *sol*, is typical of a vamp.

🔊 73

Orchestral forms

Many orchestral works of music are written in a specific form that is particular to a genre or time period. The structural organization within musical works helps the listener make sense of the piece.

SEE ALSO

❬ **30–31** Time signatures

❬ **44–45** Tempo

❬ **164–165** Theme and variations

The orchestra **184–185** ❭

Symphonies

Large-scale orchestral pieces are called symphonies. Traditional symphonic forms date from the Classical period, and usually feature a four-movement architecture. Each movement is formally structured and, although separated from the others by a pause, has a strong relationship with the entire symphony.

▽ **Four-movement form**
Later composers still favored the typical four-movement symphony structure, but expanded upon it by adding movements, using different forms, or unifying their work.

I	II	III	IV
Fast tempo (in sonata form)	**Slow tempo** (in ABA form)	**Medium to Fast tempo** (in dance form)	**Fast tempo** (rondo form)

LOOKING CLOSER

Haydn's *Symphony No. 88* in G Major

An energetic, optimistic piece in the Classical four-movement architecture, Haydn's *Symphony No. 88* in G Major (1787) illustrates his creativity while working within strict Classical forms. The first movement is a sonata form, followed by a graceful theme and variations. The third movement is a rustic, dance-like minuet and trio, and the last a rondo, with the surprising insertion of a delightful canon in the middle.

Adagio-Allegro (sonata form)

I

◁ **First movement**
A short, stately introduction in triple meter, followed by a lively duple meter Allegro in sonata form.

Largo (theme and variations)

II

◁ **Second movement**
Solo oboe and cello present a legato theme in D Major, triple meter, followed by six variations.

"As **conductor** of an orchestra I could **make experiments...** and was thus in a position to **improve, alter,** make **additions or omissions,** and **be** as **bold** as I pleased." Franz Joseph Haydn

Rondo

A rondo, or rondeau, consists of the same theme (A) repeatedly inserted between new material. Many, but not all, Classical rondos are fast and vivacious, using folk themes, and featured as the last movement in the symphony form.

▽ **Rondo form**
Rondos can be extended by adding new sections, as long as the A section is interspersed throughout. Rondos are often symmetrical, in an overall ABA form.

a	b	a	c	a	b	a
Theme 1	Theme 2	Theme 1	Theme 3	Theme 1	Theme 2	Theme 1
A			B		A	

Sonata

A sonata is a three-movement work for solo keyboard, or solo instrument with keyboard accompaniment. The first movement has a structure called "sonata form" (also used in the first movement of symphonies). The second movement is a slower, ternary form; the last movement is a rondo, theme and variations, or another sonata form.

△ **Beethoven's *Appassionata* sonata**
Shown here are the opening measures of Beethoven's famous sonata for solo piano, *Sonata No. 23* in F minor, Op. 57, 1805.

Exposition				Development	Recapitulation				Coda
First theme	Bridge	Second theme	Closing theme	Expansion and variation on themes, freely composed,	First theme	Bridge	Second theme	Closing theme	(Optional)
Key : tonic	Modulation	New key		moves through several tonalities: eventual strong pull back to tonic	Tonic				
Larger form: A				**B**	**A' (A prime)**				
a		b			a		b		c

△ **Sonata form**
Essentially a large ternary form, the sonata form employs a relatively tight structure of themes and tonalities, like the one shown here.

Concerto

Written to showcase one or more instrumental soloists accompanied by an orchestra, a concerto is normally three movements long, in a fast-slow-fast pattern. This enables the soloist to dazzle the audience with flashy pyrotechnics in the outer movements while lulling listeners into a lyrical mood in between.

▷ **Haydn's *Cello Concerto* in D Major**
An improvisatory-sounding virtuosic solo, a cadenza usually occurs near the end of a concerto's first or last movement. The orchestra drops out to highlight the soloist's technique, re-entering on cue upon the cadenza's characteristic ending, which is the resolution of an extended, dramatic trill.

Instruments and voices

Strings

The "twang" of a huntsman's bow thousands of years ago inspired the development of a stringed instrument. A simple harp evolved with more strings and a resonating box. By adding a bow to sound the strings, the forerunners of modern orchestral strings were born.

Orchestral strings

Violins, violas, violoncellos (usually called cellos), and double basses are the backbone of classical music. When played together, they blend particularly pleasingly because they all make their sound in the same way. They all have similar body shapes and four strings, which are normally played with a bow, but which may also be plucked.

Range

◀)) 74

△ **Violin**
Violins play the highest notes in the orchestral string family. They are divided into two groups known as firsts and seconds.

Range

◀)) 75

△ **Viola**
The viola has a larger body and longer strings than the violin, giving its deeper notes a distinctively rich, dark quality.

◀)) 76

△ **Violoncello**
The cello body is supported on a spike on the floor. Its beautiful tone quality makes it a favorite for soloists as well as for orchestra members.

Range

◀)) 77

Range

◁ **Double bass**
The player normally stands up or perches on a stool to play this large instrument. Occasionally, a fifth string is fitted for very low notes.

REAL WORLD

Violin

The vibrations of the violin strings are transmitted to its wooden body through the bridge—a narrow piece of wood over which the strings pass. Strings are tuned by adjusting the pegs at the scroll.

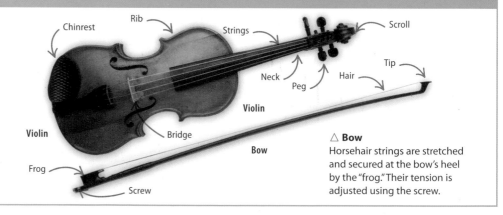

Chinrest · Rib · Strings · Scroll · Neck · Peg · Hair · Tip · Violin · Violin · Bridge · Bow · Frog · Screw

△ **Bow**
Horsehair strings are stretched and secured at the bow's heel by the "frog." Their tension is adjusted using the screw.

Producing the sound

All stringed instruments produce sound through the vibration of their strings. The strings of the guitar and harp are plucked, while the orchestral strings—violin, viola, cello, and double bass—are vibrated with a bow.

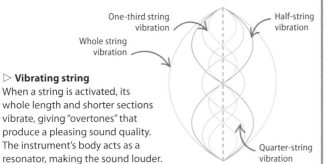

One-third string vibration

Half-string vibration

Whole string vibration

Quarter-string vibration

▷ **Vibrating string**
When a string is activated, its whole length and shorter sections vibrate, giving "overtones" that produce a pleasing sound quality. The instrument's body acts as a resonator, making the sound louder.

LOOKING CLOSER

String techniques

While the guitar and harp are always played with the fingers, orchestral strings are played with a bow, or "con arco." Other techniques can be used to vary the sound and produce special effects, ranging from comic to spooky.

Down-bow Up-bow

◁ **Bowed**
The direction in which the player draws the bow across a string is indicated by these symbols.

trem.

◁ **Tremolo**
To play tremolo, the player moves the bow in rapid short strokes across the string.

◁ **Portamento**
This swooping effect is created between two notes when the finger slides up the fingerboard.

pizz.

△ **Plucked**
When playing "pizzicato," the player leaves the bow aside and plucks the string.

con sord.

△ **Muted**
To deaden the sound, a three-pronged wooden mute (sordino) is clamped across the bridge of the instrument.

Guitar

The guitar is heard in folk, pop, jazz, and classical music across the world. It has a violin-type body, wire or nylon strings, and a fretted neck. It is played with fingertips or a plectrum (pick), and it may often be heard as a strumming accompaniment to a song or a dance.

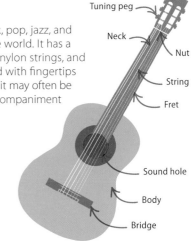

Tuning peg

Neck

Nut

String

Fret

Sound hole

Body

Bridge

▷ **Acoustic guitar**
The acoustic guitar has long associations with Spain, especially with the gypsy-inspired flamenco dance music in which the guitar body can be slapped loudly like a drum.

Changing the pitch

The pitch of a string is changed by altering its length, or by increasing or decreasing its tension. If the string is shortened or tightened, the pitch is raised; if it is lengthened or loosened, the pitch is lowered.

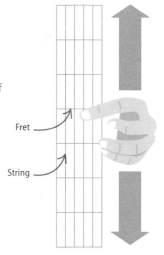

Fret

String

▷ **Stopping a string**
Pressing down the fingertip on the fingerboard shortens the string and changes its pitch. Guitar necks have narrow raised frets indicating where the player should press.

Harp

Harps have sturdy frames and a resonating chamber with a soundboard to project the sound. Strings are played with the thumb and fingers of both hands, though the little finger is not used. Small harps used in folk music may rest in the player's lap.

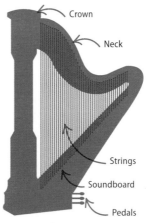

Crown

Neck

Strings

Soundboard

Pedals

◁ **Concert harp**
The large concert harp has 47 strings of different lengths. The pitch of any string can be raised by a half or whole step by pressing down a foot pedal.

Woodwind

Woodwind instruments are wood or metal tubes with holes that, when covered by fingertips or finger-operated keys, create different pitches. The instruments range from simple whistles to those used in modern orchestras and bands.

Orchestral woodwinds

Pairs of flutes, oboes, clarinets, and bassoons form the heart of an orchestra. Smaller or larger versions feature occasionally—especially the piccolo, cor anglais, bass clarinet, and contrabassoon—extending the range of notes available in the woodwind section, and adding special colors, or timbres, to the texture.

Orchestral family
From the contrabassoon to the piccolo, woodwind instruments cover a vast range of pitches.

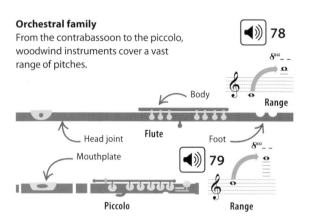

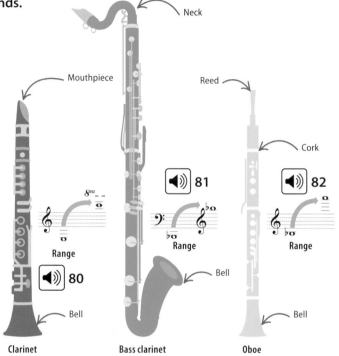

Saxophones

Invented around 1840 by Belgian Adolphe Sax, the saxophone is a "hybrid" instrument with a brass body, a single reed like the clarinet, and a conical tube like the oboe. Widely used in jazz and band music, saxophones are occasionally used in orchestras to play distinctively warm, lyrical solos.

Sounding pitches for saxophones
Saxophones are made in several different sizes, the most popular ones being soprano, alto, tenor, and baritone. Together, they cover a wide range of pitches.

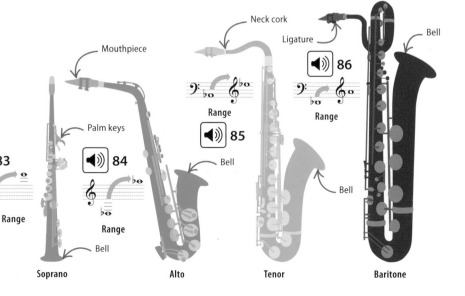

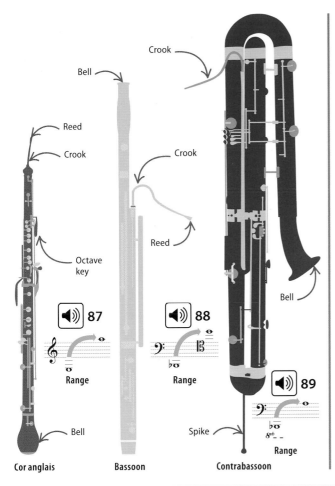

Crook

Bell

Reed

Crook

Crook

Reed

Octave key

Bell

🔊 **87**

Range

Spike

Bell

🔊 **88**

Range

Cor anglais

Bassoon

🔊 **89**

Range

Contrabassoon

Producing the sound

When the column of air in a woodwind instrument's tube is made to vibrate, sound is produced. A short, narrow tube gives a higher pitch than a long, wide one. The holes in the tube allow the air to escape, effectively shortening the tube.

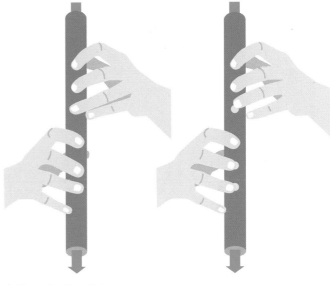

△ **Changing the pitch**
The player's fingers cover the holes in various combinations, creating different pitches. The holes beyond the reach of the player's fingers may be closed or opened by finger-operated keywork.

Reeds and mouthpieces

Woodwind players blow into a cane reed or a mouthpiece to make the column of air in the tube vibrate. This gives each woodwind instrument its distinctive tone color, or timbre. The sweet breathiness of the flute and clarinet contrast well with the penetrating, edgy quality of the double-reeds.

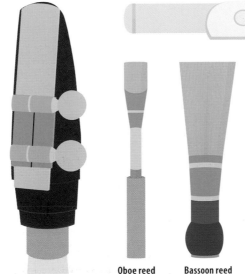

Oboe reed   **Bassoon reed**

▷ **Single reed**
The air blown into the mouthpiece of a clarinet and saxophone causes a single piece of thin cane, the reed, to vibrate against the hard lower surface of the mouthpiece.

△ **Flute mouth plate**
The player directs air against the sharp metal edge of the mouth plate. This causes the column of air to vibrate, producing a sound like blowing across the top of a bottle.

◁ **Double reeds**
Oboes and bassoons are played with double reeds, two lengths of cane bound together at the base. Air is blown at high pressure through a tiny aperture between the two blades of cane.

Brass

Brass instruments are some of music's oldest and most versatile instruments—at home, in orchestras, bands, and jazz ensembles. The instruments consist of a length of brass tubing with a flared bell to project the sound.

SEE ALSO

❮ **76–77** Transposition

The orchestra	**184–185** ❯
Ensembles	**188–189** ❯
What is the score?	**194–195** ❯

The brass family

Trumpets, French horns, trombones, and tubas form the brass section of the orchestra, providing a rich, weighty core to large symphonic works. The trumpet and its similar-shaped relations—the cornet and flugelhorn—are popular and versatile instrumental soloists in all genres, particularly in all genres, particularly jazz. The tenor horn, euphonium, and sousaphone—played upright like the tuba—feature in marching bands.

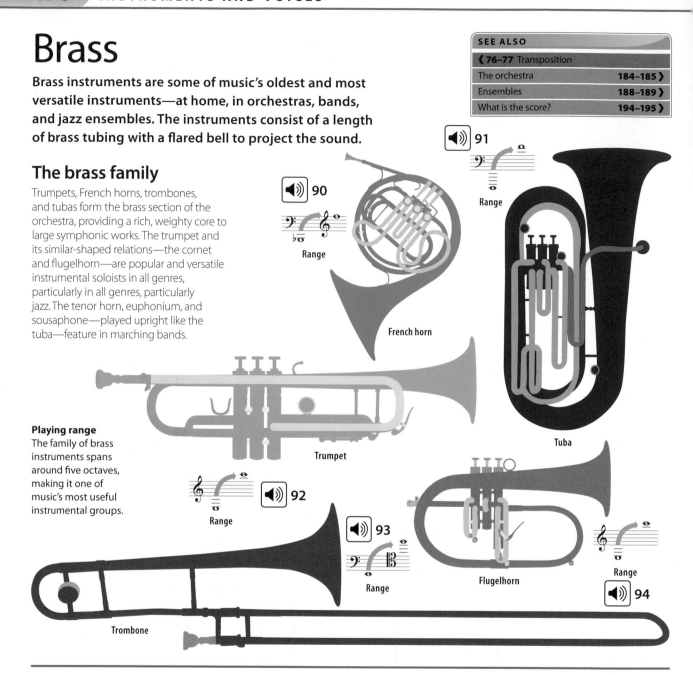

🔊 90

Range

French horn

🔊 91

Range

Tuba

Trumpet

Playing range
The family of brass instruments spans around five octaves, making it one of music's most useful instrumental groups.

Range

🔊 92

🔊 93

Range

Flugelhorn

Range

🔊 94

Trombone

Brass mouthpieces

The sound of any brass instrument begins at the mouthpiece. The player's mouth is placed against the round metal rim of the mouthpiece – a technique called "embouchure". By "buzzing" the lips, air is forced into the tube of the instrument, causing it to vibrate and sound a note.

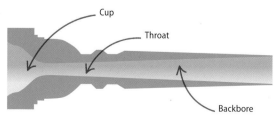

Cup

Throat

Backbore

◁ **Cup-shaped mouthpiece**
All brass instruments have cup-shaped mouthpieces. The backbore is inserted at the top of the instrument. French horns use a small, deep cup, while trombonists prefer larger, flatter mouthpieces.

Changing the pitch

A brass player changes notes by increasing the force of the air stream entering the instrument, except with a trombone, or a brass instrument with keys. This is done by loosening or tightening the embouchure. Without keys or valves, the player is limited to the notes of the "harmonic series"—these are the notes played by a brass tube—which get higher in pitch as the air flow in the tube intensifies.

▽ **Harmonic series**
A harmonic series can be defined as a series of notes that are produced while playing any instrument. The lowest note of this series is called a "fundamental." The other/higher notes are known as "overtones," "harmonics," or "partials."

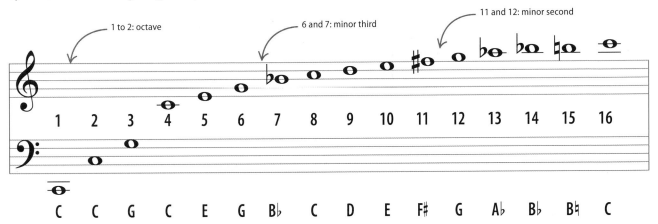

1 to 2: octave

6 and 7: minor third

11 and 12: minor second

1	2	3	4	5	6	7	8	9	10	11	12	13	14	15	16
C	C	G	C	E	G	B♭	C	D	E	F♯	G	A♭	B♭	B♮	C

Lengthening the tube

The fundamental note of a brass instrument can be altered by lengthening the tube. This makes the "harmonics," or higher notes, available. Trombones do this by means of a slide, which can be extended. Trumpets, horns, and tubas use special mechanisms to divert air into extra tubing, temporarily lowering the fundamental note.

▷ **Piston mechanism**
Systems of pistons or valves are used to divert the air into the extra tubing. The player presses down a key to operate a piston, and the air is diverted into a special loop, elongating the vibrating length.

Key to operate piston

Extra tubing lengthens the tube

Air is diverted once key is pressed

Airflow

Up position

Down position

Transposing instruments

Instruments that use music written in a different key (called "concert" pitch) from that of the actual sound are called transposing instruments. This distinction between written and sounding notes makes it easier for the player to read the music, and is most often used for brass instruments, clarinets, and saxophones.

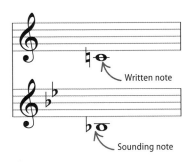

Written note

Sounding note

△ **B♭ trumpet**
A written C, when played on a B♭ trumpet, sounds as B♭.

Special effects

Brass instruments produce special effects by inserting a metal or wood mute into the bell of the instrument. Straight and cup-shaped mutes are used to produce a quiet, nasal sound.

▷ **Mutes**
A conical mute deadens the sound of a trumpet or trombone, making its sound less prominent in the ensemble.

Keyboards

Though keyboards seem to be instruments in their own right, in reality they activate sound produced by other means—by strings (piano, harpsichord), by wind (organ), and by electronics (keyboards and electric pianos).

The piano

The most popular of all instruments, the modern pianoforte ("soft-loud") has its origins in the early 18ᵗʰ-century fortepiano ("loud-soft"). It features as a soloist in recitals and concertos, and is central to most chamber music.

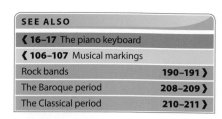

Stick

Raising the lid allows the sound to project across large halls.

Music stand

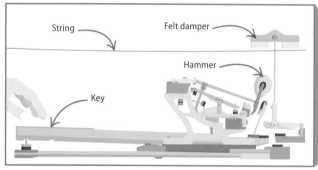

△ **Hammer mechanism**
When a key is pressed, the hammer strikes the strings and a felt "damper" is lifted, allowing the strings to vibrate. When the key is released, the damper returns to its initial position, preventing further vibrations.

String

Felt damper

Hammer

Key

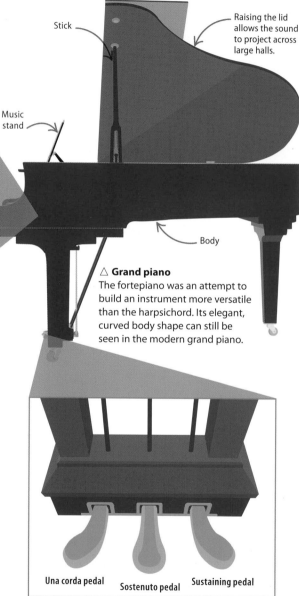

Body

△ **Grand piano**
The fortepiano was an attempt to build an instrument more versatile than the harpsichord. Its elegant, curved body shape can still be seen in the modern grand piano.

REAL WORLD

Inside a piano

While the strings in a grand piano run horizontally, they are vertical in an upright piano. Made of steel, the strings are secured to the frame at high tension by pins. Most notes have two or three strings tuned identically to add power. When the "una corda" (one string) pedal is pressed, the hammers move sideways, striking only one of the strings.

Una corda pedal   Sostenuto pedal   Sustaining pedal

△ **Piano pedals**
Depressing the sustaining pedal joins sounds together smoothly, while the middle pedal sustains only certain pitches. The una corda pedal softens the sound.

Electronic keyboards

The keys of an electronic keyboard activate digital sound modules, producing a huge range of sampled sounds and musical effects at the touch of a button. They usually have a single keyboard, or "manual," and a selection of switches, "stops," to alter the tone color of a melody, play preselected harmonies, or add a rhythmic drumbeat effect.

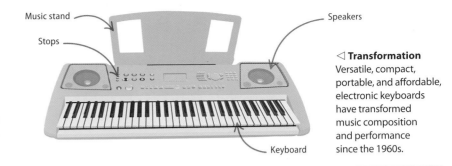

Music stand

Speakers

Stops

Keyboard

◁ **Transformation**
Versatile, compact, portable, and affordable, electronic keyboards have transformed music composition and performance since the 1960s.

Organ

The pipe organ is a box of whistles sounded by the air blown from a windchest. It is played from one or more keyboards, or "manuals," and a pedalboard. Air is allowed into the pipes by pulling out the "stops." The pipes are arranged in "ranks," each producing a different kind of sound and pitch range.

"For my **eyes and ears,** the **organ** is the **king of instruments.**" Mozart, 1777

▷ **Small pipe organ**
While many organs are built into buildings and powered by electricity, the 18th-century organ (still replicated today) is often freestanding, using electricity only to power the windchest.

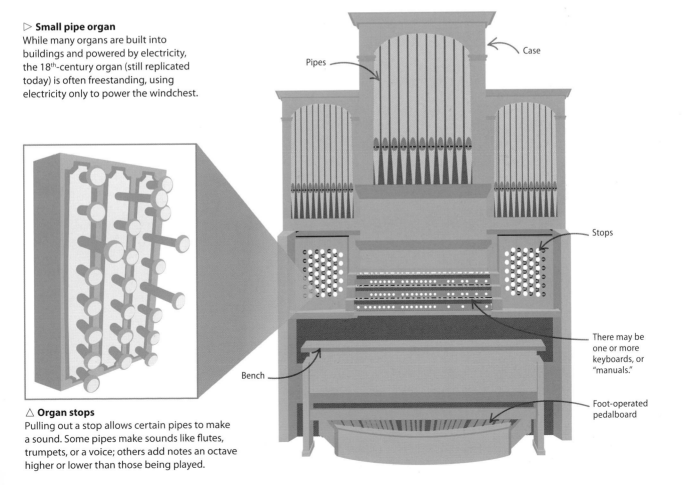

Pipes

Case

Stops

There may be one or more keyboards, or "manuals."

Bench

Foot-operated pedalboard

△ **Organ stops**
Pulling out a stop allows certain pipes to make a sound. Some pipes make sounds like flutes, trumpets, or a voice; others add notes an octave higher or lower than those being played.

Percussion

Percussion instruments are not only important soloists but they also form the heart of bands and orchestral ensembles, playing melodies, providing harmony, color, and texture, and driving forward the rhythm.

SEE ALSO	
❮ 10–11 What is music?	
The orchestra	184–185 ❯
What is the score?	194–195 ❯
Folk, world, and roots	202–203 ❯

Orchestral percussion

Orchestral percussion players have to master dozens of different instruments and often have to play them all in one performance. Tuned instruments, such as tubular bells, xylophone, marimba, and vibraphone, mostly play melodies and add color. They are played with sticks or mallets, unlike the celesta, which is operated by a keyboard. Occasionally, one-offs such as a triangle, cowbells, or a thunder sheet may feature for special effects.

△ **Xylophone**
The wooden bars of a xylophone are arranged like the keys of a piano keyboard. It is played with two mallets and produces a distinctively hollow sound, effective for solos.

▷ **Tubular bells**
Also called orchestral bells or chimes, tubular bells are a series of tuned brass tubes graded in length. They are struck with a wooden hammer to produce a sound that easily penetrates the densest musical texture.

▷ **Snare drum**
Snare drums are double-headed, with string "snares" stretched across one of the drum heads. When the other head is struck, it produces a rattling effect.

△ **Timpani**
Timpani, or kettledrums, are tuned by a mechanism that tightens the skin of the head. They are used in pairs, or larger groups in orchestras, to play a range of pitches.

△ **Cymbals**
Cymbals are plates of brass with a narrow rim and a convex center. They can either be clashed together, or struck with a stick or brush.

△ **Celesta**
The celesta consists of a set of steel bars which are struck with hammers by means of a simplified piano mechanism.

Rhythm percussion

Supporting the overall musical texture, rhythm percussion drives forward the music and provides a consistent beat throughout a piece. Most rhythm percussion instruments are untuned. Their key role is to emphasize particular rhythms, especially those associated with certain styles, or genres, of music—for example, Latin dance rhythms such as tango.

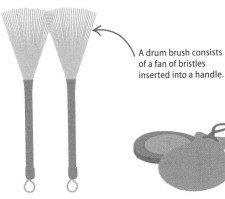

A drum brush consists of a fan of bristles inserted into a handle.

△ **Brushes**
A drum "brush" can be drawn across the drum head to create a soft rustling effect rather than the hard strike of a wooden stick.

△ **Castanets**
Castanets are a pair of shell-shaped wooden clappers joined with a string on one edge, and clashed between the thumb and forefinger.

△ **Conga drums**
These tall, single-headed, South American drums are played with the palms and fingers, and usually feature in groups of two or four.

△ **Hi-hat cymbals**
An essential part of a drum kit, the hi-hat consists of a pair of cymbals that can be clashed together and opened by a foot-operated pedal.

LOOKING CLOSER

Writing for percussion

Percussion parts are arranged in different ways depending on the style of the music. Tuned instruments need to use treble and bass staves, while untuned, rhythm-only instruments, like most drums, use symbols on a staff with no clef. Occasionally, percussionists will find they need to play several instruments, all notated on the same part of the staff.

▽ **Orchestral notation**
In orchestral music, each instrument is notated separately in its own part, so that players can move around the platform from one instrument to the next as required. Shown below is the snare drum part of Ravel's *Boléro*.

Snare drum solo in Ravel's famous *Boléro*

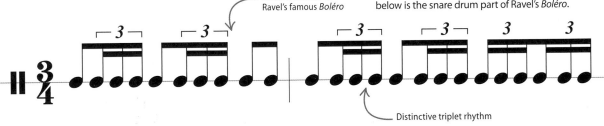

Distinctive triplet rhythm

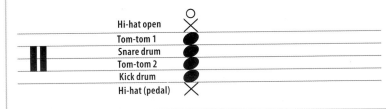

Hi-hat open	○ (×)
Tom-tom 1	●
Snare drum	●
Tom-tom 2	●
Kick drum	●
Hi-hat (pedal)	×

◁ **Drum kit notation**
Drum kit players usually have all their instruments notated in one part, using different symbols to identify which instrument is needed at any point.

The orchestra

A favorite large ensemble for classical music, orchestras provide a flexible, richly varied, and colorful palette of sounds and textures for a composer to work with.

Orchestra

Large orchestras of 50 or more players are called "symphony" orchestras, while smaller ensembles are known as "chamber" orchestras. Symphony orchestras have the full range of woodwind, brass, and percussion, and also a large number of orchestral strings—first and second violins, violas, cellos, and double basses. There may be one or more harps, and sometimes even a piano or an organ. A chamber orchestra mainly consists of strings, with limited wind or brass instruments occasionally added.

Timpani are placed close to the trumpets.

▽ **Seating plan**
Strings sit at the front of the orchestra, nearest to the conductor. Woodwind sit as a group in the center of the orchestra, with brass, percussion, and harps ranged around the back of the orchestra.

French horn bells point away from the body of the orchestra.

Harps sit behind the violins.

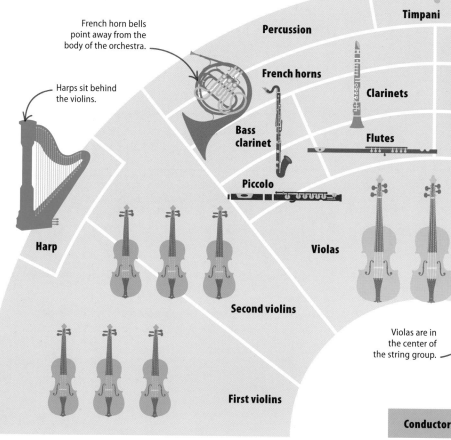

Timpani

Trombones

Percussion

Trumpets

Tuba

French horns

Clarinets

Bassoons

Contrabassoon

Bass clarinet

Flutes

Oboes

Cor anglais

Piccolo

Harp

Violas

Cellos

Second violins

Violas are in the center of the string group.

First violins

Conductor

History of the orchestra

The earliest orchestra, established by French composer Lully in 1626, consisted of five sizes of violin-type instruments. During the Baroque era, flutes, oboes, bassoons, horns, trumpets, and drums were added to the basic string ensemble. In the Classical era, clarinets and trombones appeared regularly, joined by the tuba and various percussion instruments in the Romantic period, until the modern symphony orchestra was finally established by around 1900.

Lully 1626	Baroque	Classical	Romantic	From 1900
24 violins of five different sizes	2 first violins	4 first violins	8 first violins	12 first violins
	2 second violins	4 second violins	8 second violins	12 second violins
	2 violas	4 violas	8 violas	10 violas
	1 cello	2 cellos	6 cellos	8 cellos
		1 double bass	4 double basses	6 double basses
	harpsichord			piano
				synthesizer
	2 recorders	2 flutes	2 flutes	3 flutes
			1 piccolo	1 piccolo
	2 oboes	2 oboes	2 oboes	3 oboes
			1 cor anglais	1 cor anglais
		2 clarinets	2 clarinets	3 clarinets
			1 E flat (small)	1 E flat (small)
			1 bass (large)	1 bass (large)
				1 alto sax
	1 bassoon	2 bassoons	2 bassoons	3 bassoons
			1 contrabassoon	1 contrabassoon
	2 timpani	2 timpani	3 timpani	5 timpani
			side drum	side drum
			bass drum	bass drum
			triangle	triangle
			celeste	celeste
			xylophone	xylophone
			tubular bells	tubular bells
			cymbals	cymbals
				vibraphone
				marimba
				tambourine
		2 French horns	4 French horns	4 French horns
	2 trumpets	2 trumpets	4 trumpets	4 trumpets
			3 trombones (2 tenor, 1 bass)	3 trombones (2 tenor, 1 bass)
				1 tuba

Double basses play the lowest string notes.

Double basses

△ **Growth of the orchestra**
The orchestra has grown in size from a small court ensemble to a massive—and expensive—musical entity, which sounds its best in a large concert hall or first-class recording studio.

The conductor

A conductor guides members of an orchestra or choir through a musical work to achieve an accurate and effective interpretation. Conductors have individual styles, using fine movements or large gestures depending on the type of music.

SEE ALSO

❰ **24–25** Beats and measures

❰ **30–31** Time signatures

❰ **32–33** Compound time

What is the score? **194–195** ❱

Why do we need conductors?

After 1800, as compositions became more complex and their rhythms and speeds more flexible, it became necessary to have a conductor. Orchestras are now larger, making it difficult for players to hear one another. The conductor gives visual cues for the players to follow, making the overall performance unified.

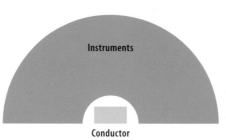

Instruments

Conductor

◁ **Conductor's position**
Most conductors stand in the center on an elevated rostrum, or podium, so that they can easily be seen by the performers.

The conductor's score

As well as choosing the music that the orchestra plays, the conductor also studies the musical score in advance, marking instructions on it to convey to the orchestra during a rehearsal. Some conductors memorize these instructions, using no score in concerts.

▽ **Section of score**
In the score of the opening of "Sinfonia Concertante for Violin and Viola," Mozart places the solo instruments between the orchestral oboes and horns and orchestral strings.

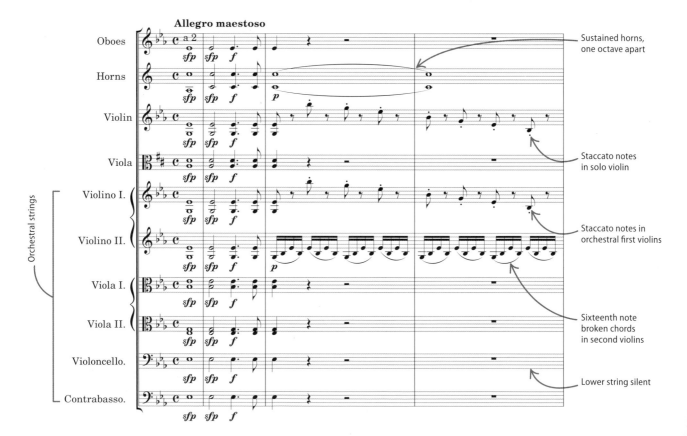

Sustained horns, one octave apart

Staccato notes in solo violin

Staccato notes in orchestral first violins

Sixteenth note broken chords in second violins

Lower string silent

Taking the lead

A conductor's work on the rostrum is done through hand gestures, facial expressions, and movement of the whole body. The right hand generally provides the beat to indicate the basic pulse of the music, while the left hand concentrates on the expression. The first beat of each measure is indicated by a downbeat flick with the right hand. The remaining beats in the measure follow particular patterns.

Baton

The conductor uses a baton to act as an extension of the arm. It is a narrow wooden or fiberglass rod, with a bulb at its wider end. It is usually held in the right hand, between the thumb and forefinger, with the bulb in the palm of the hand. Some conductors, especially when working with choirs, prefer to conduct using their hands alone.

One in a measure

For one beat in a measure, the conductor makes a downbeat with the baton (or hand), flicking an imaginary "click" before bouncing back up immediately, ready for the next measure.

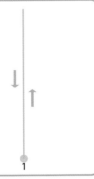

Two in a measure

For two beats in a measure, the conductor makes a downbeat with a click for the first beat and then repeats the click, bouncing the arm up again immediately, ready for the next measure.

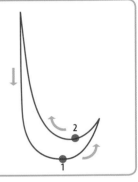

Three in a measure

After the first downbeat click, the conductor moves his arm to the right for the second click, flicking back toward the center for the third beat before returning to the top.

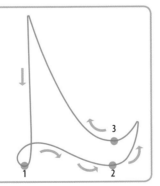

Four in a measure

After the first downbeat click, the conductor moves his arm to the left for the second click, across to the right for the third, flicking back slightly toward the center for the fourth beat before returning to the top, ready for the next measure.

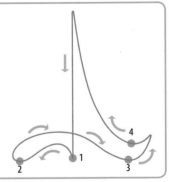

Five in a measure

Five beats in a measure is unusual. The conductor begins by moving his arm down for the first beat, left for the second. For the third and fourth beats, he moves his arm to the right, then flicks upward for the fifth beat, before returning to the top for the next measure.

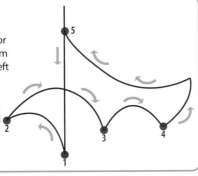

Six in a bar

After the first downbeat click, the second and third beats are clicks to the left, the fourth and fifth clicks are to the right, while the sixth is a final flick before returning to the top, ready for the next measure.

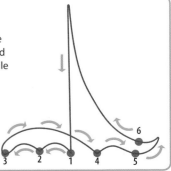

Ensembles

Certain combinations of instruments work particularly well together. This is because their individual sounds blend pleasingly, or because the contrast of different sounds they produce creates varied musical colors and textures.

Favorite combinations

Conductors are rarely needed for small ensembles. As a result, the instruments are laid out so that the players can see and hear one another, and ensure the sound produced by the different instruments is blended and well-balanced by the time it reaches the ears of an audience.

Violin 1

Violin 2

Viola

Cello

△ **String quartet**
The two violins, viola, and cello form a string quartet. Sometimes a fifth instrument, usually a second cello, is added to form a string quintet.

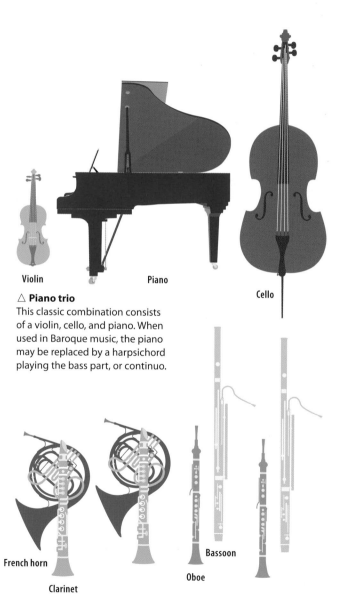

Violin

Piano

Cello

△ **Piano trio**
This classic combination consists of a violin, cello, and piano. When used in Baroque music, the piano may be replaced by a harpsichord playing the bass part, or continuo.

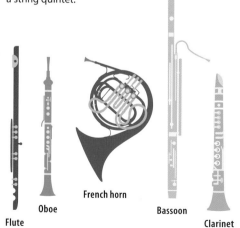

French horn

Oboe

Bassoon

Flute

Clarinet

△ **Wind quintet**
The French horn sits in the center of the semicircle, with the flute and clarinet nearest to the edge of the platform, producing a well-balanced overall sound.

French horn

Bassoon

Oboe

Clarinet

△ **Wind octet**
In a wind octet setup, the players sit in pairs, as they do in an orchestra. They either sit in two rows, or in a semicircle of eight if space permits.

Big band

Originating in the USA in the 1920s, the big band specializes in jazz and swing music. It lacks stringed instruments, but features a four-piece rhythm section (drums, piano, bass guitar, and electric guitar) instead, brass—trumpets, trombones, and occasionally flugelhorn or cornet—and woodwind, particularly saxophones, and sometimes clarinets and flutes. Its music is either newly written or arranged, with jazz-type improvisations to showcase the talent of instrumentalists.

▽ **Seating plan**
The players sit in rows—saxophones in front of the brass. The drum kit, piano, and guitars form a tight rhythm group on the other side of the stage.

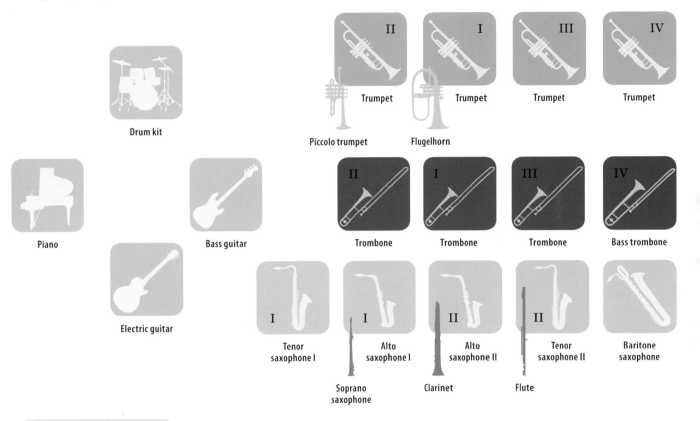

Drum kit

II Trumpet   I Trumpet   III Trumpet   IV Trumpet

Piccolo trumpet   Flugelhorn

Piano

Bass guitar

II Trombone   I Trombone   III Trombone   IV Bass trombone

Electric guitar

I Tenor saxophone I   I Alto saxophone I   II Alto saxophone II   II Tenor saxophone II   Baritone saxophone

Soprano saxophone   Clarinet   Flute

REAL WORLD

Music on the move

Originating from 16th-century military bands, marching bands today assume various forms and feature in both celebratory and ceremonial settings. They comprise a wide range of instruments, though rarely include strings. While the drums maintain the marching speed and musical beat, brass and woodwind instruments play the melodies.

The world's **largest marching band,** consisting of **800 members,** gathered at **Allen School, Texas,** in **2013.**

Rock bands

Rock bands are an iconic symbol of popular music in the 20th century. The combination of guitars, drums, keyboard, and vocals have made countless bands rich and famous, including the Beatles, Rolling Stones, Queen, and Led Zeppelin.

SEE ALSO

❮ **174–175** Strings

❮ **180–181** Keyboards

❮ **188–189** Ensembles

Popular music   **222–223** ❯

Set up

A rock band's setup varies according to the number of performers, the shape of the stage, and the size of the venue. The drummer, driving the rhythm, normally sits in the center at the back of the group. The bass guitarist stands to one side near the keyboard, with guitars and vocals in the front line. Microphones can be positioned in front of each performer, with amplifiers and speakers at the side.

Guitars

There are usually three guitars in a rock band—lead, rhythm, and bass—each with a different function. Powerful electric guitars are normally used instead of the quieter acoustic type.

The cymbal is struck by the drummer with a drumstick or brush.

Drums are the rhythmic heart of a rock band, maintaining a steady beat, adding syncopations (off-beats), and "swinging" the rhythm where necessary.

Drums

Lead guitar plays solos, melodies, or riffs, and improvises embellishments around the rhythm guitar part.

Rhythm guitar reinforces the music's rhythmic pulse and adds harmony with chords.

Lead guitar

Rhythm guitar

LOOKING CLOSER

Electric guitars

The slim, solid body of an electric guitar does not resonate, so the instrument's natural sound is quiet. Connecting it to an amplifier makes the sound powerful. The bass guitar sounds an octave lower than the lead and rhythm instruments.

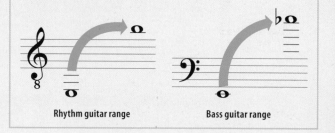

Rhythm guitar range

Bass guitar range

Special sounds

Other instruments, including the harmonica, accordion, extra percussion, saxophones, and even violin, occasionally feature in rock bands. This not only adds variety to the general sound, but can also become a musical "signature"—such as Mick Jagger's harmonica playing with the Rolling Stones.

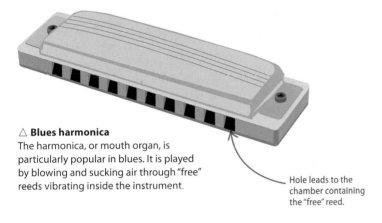

△ **Blues harmonica**
The harmonica, or mouth organ, is particularly popular in blues. It is played by blowing and sucking air through "free" reeds vibrating inside the instrument.

Hole leads to the chamber containing the "free" reed.

The Beatles

The most universally recognized of all rock bands, the Beatles were formed in Liverpool, England, in the 1960s. Paul McCartney, John Lennon, George Harrison, and Ringo Starr were accomplished performers, and Lennon and McCartney were gifted songwriters as well. The Beatles' musical style originated in rock 'n' roll, but they later explored a range of other styles, including ballad, experimental, psychedelic rock, and Indian music.

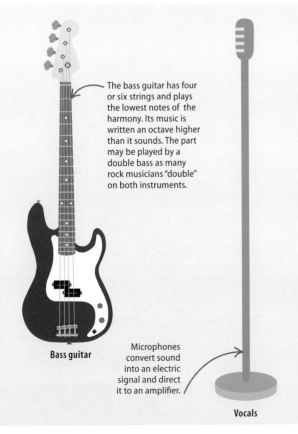

The bass guitar has four or six strings and plays the lowest notes of the harmony. Its music is written an octave higher than it sounds. The part may be played by a double bass as many rock musicians "double" on both instruments.

Bass guitar

Microphones convert sound into an electric signal and direct it to an amplifier.

Vocals

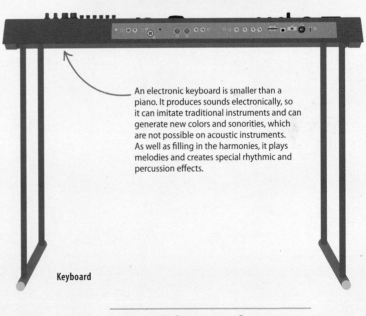

An electronic keyboard is smaller than a piano. It produces sounds electronically, so it can imitate traditional instruments and can generate new colors and sonorities, which are not possible on acoustic instruments. As well as filling in the harmonies, it plays melodies and creates special rhythmic and percussion effects.

Keyboard

"I **won't** be a **rock star**.
I **will** be a **legend**."
Freddy Mercury, Queen

Voices

The voice is a universal instrument. From the earliest times, humans have used their voices to call, warn, express emotion, and entertain. Singing is part of music-making in all cultures, both as a solo and group activity.

How we sing

Correct breathing is the key to good singing. Singers breathe in through the nose and out through the mouth and nose. The lungs, diaphragm, and head provide support, power, tonal quality, and resonance to the sound produced by the vocal folds, or "cords." To change the pitch or volume of a note, a singer uses ligaments in the larynx to control the vibration of the vocal cords.

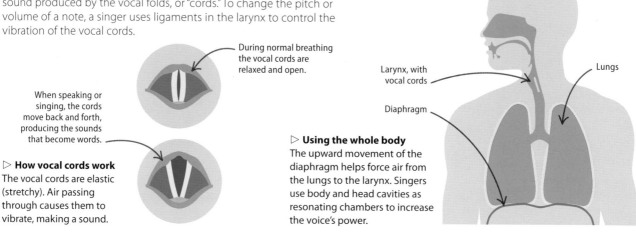

During normal breathing the vocal cords are relaxed and open.

When speaking or singing, the cords move back and forth, producing the sounds that become words.

▷ **How vocal cords work**
The vocal cords are elastic (stretchy). Air passing through causes them to vibrate, making a sound.

▷ **Using the whole body**
The upward movement of the diaphragm helps force air from the lungs to the larynx. Singers use body and head cavities as resonating chambers to increase the voice's power.

Larynx, with vocal cords

Lungs

Diaphragm

Different voices

When placed together, male and female voices can cover a range of around five octaves. Like a fingerprint, every voice has its own sound—with a distinctive color, or "timbre." Soloists need individual power, while group singing usually requires voices to blend.

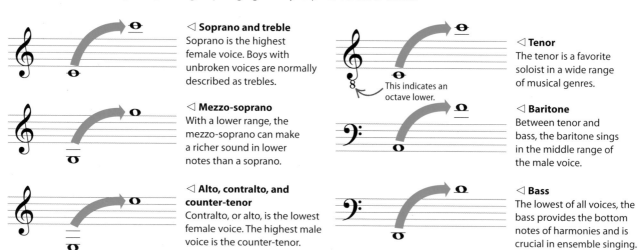

◁ **Soprano and treble**
Soprano is the highest female voice. Boys with unbroken voices are normally described as trebles.

◁ **Mezzo-soprano**
With a lower range, the mezzo-soprano can make a richer sound in lower notes than a soprano.

◁ **Alto, contralto, and counter-tenor**
Contralto, or alto, is the lowest female voice. The highest male voice is the counter-tenor.

This indicates an octave lower.

◁ **Tenor**
The tenor is a favorite soloist in a wide range of musical genres.

◁ **Baritone**
Between tenor and bass, the baritone sings in the middle range of the male voice.

◁ **Bass**
The lowest of all voices, the bass provides the bottom notes of harmonies and is crucial in ensemble singing.

Beyond extreme

Some singers have a particularly wide pitch range. A soprano may be able to sing "coloratura," which involves rapid, brilliantly articulated passages high in the voice, such as that found in the Queen of the Night's aria in Mozart's opera *The Magic Flute*. Tenors with strong top notes are also popular in opera, often playing the heroic roles.

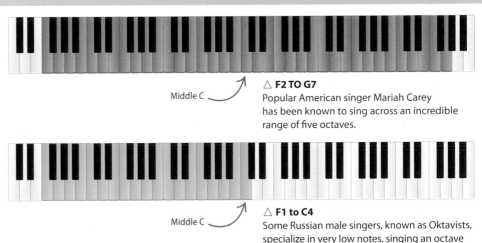

Middle C

△ **F2 TO G7**
Popular American singer Mariah Carey has been known to sing across an incredible range of five octaves.

Middle C

△ **F1 to C4**
Some Russian male singers, known as Oktavists, specialize in very low notes, singing an octave lower than the usual bass line.

Performing

Singing is the most popular form of music-making in the world. Groups, choirs, and choruses are found everywhere—in halls, clubs, places of worship, and on recordings—singing all sorts of music. Most choirs are grouped with the four main voice types, and come in sizes ranging from eight to more than one thousand voices.

▽ **Choir**
Choirs can be grouped in different ways. Normally the higher voices are placed at the front, and the lower voices at the back.

■ **Tenors** ■ **Baritones** ■ **Basses**
■ **Sopranos** ■ **Mezzo-sopranos** ■ **Altos**

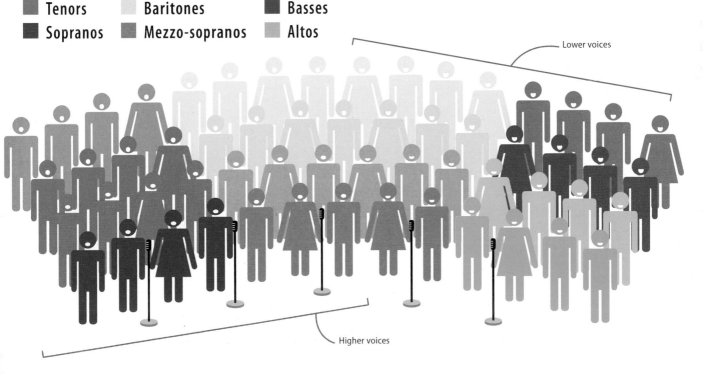

Lower voices

Higher voices

What is the score?

A score is the written version of a piece of music. In a full score, each instrument or voice involved has its own part written on an individual staff. Players perform their individual parts, which contain only their own line of music.

SEE ALSO

❮ **184–185** The orchestra
❮ **186–187** The conductor
Classical music   **204–207** ❯

Orchestral score

Conductors use full scores for study, rehearsal, and performance. On the first page of the score, each part is labeled with the Italian name of the instrument. The instruments are grouped in families from top to bottom, with the highest-pitched instrument of each family first.

▽ **Beethoven's *Symphony No. 2* in D major**
Scores provide a graphic representation of the sound. Beethoven's *Symphony No. 2* opens with all the instruments playing together (tutti), followed by wind and brass, and then the strings.

Piano score

Music for a piano is normally written on two staves, treble and bass. The staves are bracketed together to indicate that the notes are to be played by one player. This is called a piano score, or piano reduction. Orchestral music is occasionally arranged for this instrument.

▷ **Joseph Haydn's** *Sonata No. 34* **in E minor**
In this piano sonata by Haydn, the left hand plays the notes in the bass clef, and the right hand plays those in the treble clef.

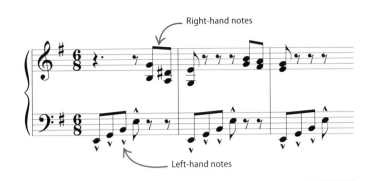

Right-hand notes

Left-hand notes

String quartet score

String quartet music has parts for the first violin, second violin, viola, and cello. Similar to orchestral music, all the parts appear together in the full score, but each player has an individual part for performance. As a viola is a transposing instrument, its part is written in the alto clef.

Violins play a triple-stopped chord

▷ **Four or more**
The *Eine kleine Nachtmusik* serenade by Mozart can be played by a string quartet with one player to each part, or by a small chamber orchestra.

Violins play in unison

Violas and cellos play one octave apart.

Italian	English	French	German
Violino	Violin	Violon	Violine
Viola	Viola	Alto	Bratsche
Violoncello	Violoncello (Cello)	Violoncelle	Violoncello
Contrabasso	Double bass (Contrabass)	Contrebasse	Kontrabass
Arpa	Harp	Arpe	Harfe
Timpani	Timpani	Timbales	Pauken
Piatto	Cymbal	Cymbale	Zimbel
Flauto	Flute	Flûte	Flöte
Oboe	Oboe	Hautbois	Oboe
Clarinetto	Clarinet	Clarinette	Klarinette
Fagotto	Bassoon	Basson	Fagott
Corno	French horn	Cor	Horn
Tromba	Trumpet	Trompette	Trompete
Trombone	Trombone	Trombone	Posaune
Tuba	Tuba	Tuba	Tuba
Pianoforte	Piano	Piano	Klavier
Organe	Organ	Orgue	Orgel

◁ **Music's languages**
Most printed music uses the Italian names for instruments and also for indications of speed and expression. Occasionally composers or publishers use other languages.

Words and music

The voice is music's natural instrument. Fusing words and music is one of humankind's oldest and most important pastimes.

SEE ALSO
‹ 24–25 Beats and measures
‹ 192–193 Voices
The Baroque period   208–209 ›
The Romantic period   212–213 ›

Meter

The natural rhythm of words is called meter. When setting text, composers generally aim to observe its natural meter. By elaborating selected words or phrases with extra notes or shifting the stress on certain words, sections of the text can be highlighted for the listener.

▷ **"As I walked down the road one day…"**
Here the natural stress of the words suggests a two-beats-in-a-bar or duple rhythm.

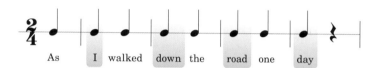

▷ **"Singing and dancing we ran down the road…"**
In this example, the natural stress of the words suggests a three-beats-in-a-bar or triple rhythm.

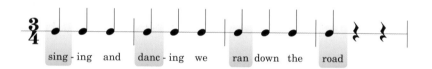

Syllabic setting

When a melody has exactly one note matched to each syllable it is called syllabic. A clear and simple approach, it works well for traditional folk songs and some hymns, when it is important that all the words are clearly heard.

▽ **"Scarborough fair"**
It is important that the listener can easily follow the words of this traditional folk song, so its simple tune and straightforward syllabic setting work well.

Melismatic setting

A melisma is a group of notes sung to one syllable. It produces a very expressive musical effect, and is used to draw special attention to a word or phrase. It has been used as a technique from earliest times in church music right up to contemporary pop music.

▽ **Mozart's *Requiem***
The "Dona nobis pacem" (Give us peace) section from Mozart's *Requiem* features melismatic settings in each voice in turn. Shown here is an extract in the tenor voice.

Word-painting

Illustrating a particular word or phrase literally in music is called word-painting. This technique is common in Renaissance and Baroque vocal music (c.1550–1750), especially in madrigals—secular part-songs for several voices. It brings the music to life, not only in the performance, but also visually on the page.

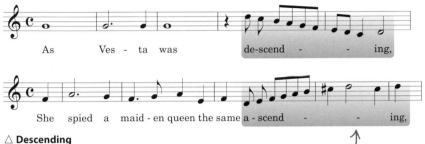

As Ves - ta was de-scend - - - ing,

She spied a maid - en queen the same a - scend - - - ing,

△ **Descending**
In Thomas Weelkes' madrigal "As Vesta Was From Latmos Hill Descending," rising and falling melodic phrases visually represent the meaning of the words.

Rising melodic phrase representing the word ascending

LOOKING CLOSER

Writing for singers

Some vowel sounds are more difficult to sing than others, especially on a long or high note. For example, on high notes singers prefer to sing the vowels "oo" or "ee." The main singing vowel sounds are:

Ah as in farther

Eh as in let

Ee as in greet

Oh as in phone

Oo as in blue

Accompaniment

Piano and guitar are the most popular instruments for accompanying the voice because they provide chords to underpin the harmony and support the vocal line. Composers try to reflect the sense of the text and meaning of specific words in the accompaniment.

▽ **Coloring words**
In Schubert's song "Mein!" about a brook, the rippling piano part vividly depicts the watery sounds of a flowing stream.

Bäch_lein, laß dein Rauschen sein! Rä - der, stellt euer Brausen ein!

Recitative

Operas and oratorios use a special kind of musical word setting called recitative. It is a declamatory rather than melodic style, used to move on the story, or when every word of dialogue must be heard clearly.

Dido

Thy hand, Be - lin - da; dark - - - - ness shades me,

Basso continuo

△ **Purcell's *Dido and Aeneas***
In this recitative from *Dido and Aeneas*, the speechlike melodic line is underpinned by simple harmonies improved by the continuo.

Styles and genres

Musical textures

Texture is a vital part of musical composition. A solo is the simplest texture, but extra parts—similar or contrasting—can be added to include harmony and color to the finished work.

SEE ALSO

❮ 92–93 What is a tune?
❮ 118–119 Harmony
❮ 196–197 Words and music

Plainchant

Plainsong, or plainchant, is an ancient form of solo melody that has been used in church rituals for more than 1,000 years. Heard today in the singing of psalms, it is notated on a staff, but there is no indication of a rhythm or pulse.

▽ **Christmas chant**
This plainchant is a setting of a joyful Christmas text and uses only five different tones, the first five notes of the Dorian mode.

Ver - bum   ca - ro   fac - tum   est,   Al -le - lu - ia,   al - le - lu - ia.

Solo melody

A solo is the oldest and simplest form of melodic music, and can be the most expressive way of conveying the meaning of words. From the simplest lullaby sung to soothe a child, to a rousing football song—the solo has a unique place in music.

◁ **"She Moved Through the Fair"**
Notated here is a typical example of a folk song. It is sung with rhythmic freedom to ensure that the text is projected with near speechlike clarity.

My   young   love said to me   "My mo-ther won't mind,

Homophony

Meaning "same voices," homophony is the word for describing music that moves in block chords. Usually, the upper line has the melody, while the lower parts provide harmonic accompaniment. Homophony is most often heard in hymns and barbershop quartets.

▷ **"Gaudeamus igitur," Brahms**
Set homophonically, this popular song tune—"Gaudeamus igitur" ("Let us therefore rejoice")—is included in Brahms' *Academic Festival Overture.*

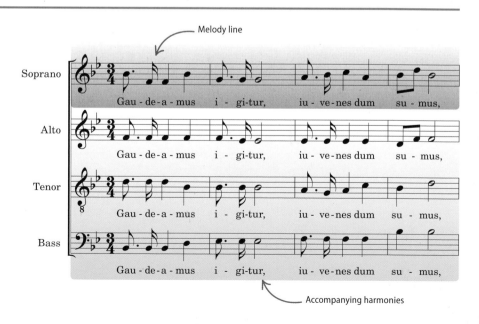

Melody line

Soprano

Gau - de - a - mus   i - gi-tur,   iu - ve - nes dum   su - mus,

Alto

Gau - de - a - mus   i - gi-tur,   iu - ve - nes dum   su - mus,

Tenor

Gau - de - a - mus   i - gi-tur,   iu - ve - nes dum   su - mus,

Bass

Gau - de - a - mus   i - gi-tur,   iu - ve - nes dum   su - mus,

Accompanying harmonies

Polyphony

Literally meaning "many voices," polyphony is a musical device in which several melodic lines are woven together. The parts are independent and equally important, although they tend to imitate one another. Known from the Middle Ages, polyphony reached the height of its popularity in 16th century choral music.

▽ **"Amen"**
In this setting of "Amen," each of the three voices enter in turn with a similar pattern of four notes—a rising fourth followed by two downward steps.

A cappella

A cappella means "in the manner of the chapel" because it originally described church music. It now refers to several voices singing together without accompaniment. Their music may be unison, homophonic, or polyphonic. While most a cappella choirs use all four voices—soprano, alto, tenor, and bass—barbershop quartets are all male.

▽ **"Sing We and Chant It"**
This attractive Baroque a cappella piece by Thomas Morley can be sung by five solo voices, or a choir.

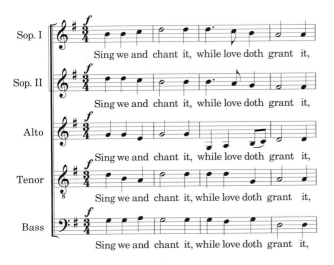

Melody and accompaniment

Texture is crucial when setting words for a solo melody with instrumental accompaniment. If the piano part is too thickly chordal, or the accompanying instruments too densely orchestrated, the soloist will be difficult to hear. Composers can avoid this by creating contrasting textural patterns, and avoiding notes in the range of the solo.

▽ **Mozart's Clarinet Quintet**
In this extract, the accompanying string quartet plays a waltzlike chordal accompaniment beneath the soloist's lyrical melody.

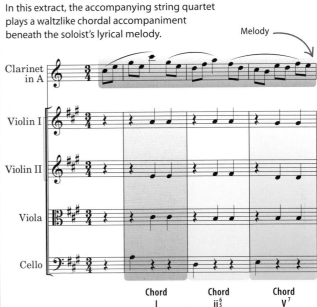

Folk, world, and roots

Every country has its own indigenous musical culture. The rise of international travel and technological advances has made all kinds of music available to us—inspiring musicians to blend traditional melodies, rhythms, and instruments to create exciting new sounds.

SEE ALSO
❰ 32–33 Compound time
❰ 40–41 Syncopation and swing
❰ 80–85 Other scales
Dance music 216–219 ❱

Music of the Caribbean

The driving rhythms of African music have contributed to the development of Caribbean music, including Cuban salsa, Jamaican reggae, and the calypso of Trinidad and Tobago. Often associated with celebrations, it is heavily syncopated, with prominent percussion, engaging vocals, guitars, trumpets, and saxophones.

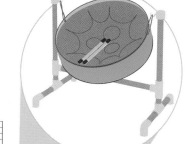

◁ **Steel pans**
Originally made from oilcans, steel pans have circular dents in their heads that play different pitches when struck.

△ **Calypso rhythm**
Often played by steel pans in a carnival, the calypso uses a distinctive, syncopated rhythm pattern—short-long-short-long-long—over four beats in a measure.

African music (sub-Saharan)

Clapping, singing, and dancing are part of everyday life in Africa. Improvised African music features syncopation, cross-rhythms, call-and-response, plentiful percussion, and varied singing styles. It is a highly influential genre and one that has been passed on by oral tradition.

▷ **Djembe**
This West African goblet-shaped drum is played with the hands. The body is carved from a hollowed trunk and is covered with goat skin.

Celtic rock

Celtic rock is a fusion of rock music and Celtic folk music, usually from Ireland, Scotland, Wales, or Brittany. Simple folklike tunes and dance rhythms are incorporated into the music, while instruments including the fiddle, drums, flutes/whistles (particularly the tin whistle), and bagpipes add distinctive colors to the electric guitars and drum kit of a rock setup.

◁ **Tin whistle**
The tin whistle sounds like a recorder. It is a popular, affordable, and durable instrument in the traditional folk music of Ireland and Scotland.

Indian music

Indian classical music has a noble tradition, passed on over centuries from master to student. It is built on melodic patterns (raga) and rhythms (tala) over a drone (a long, sustained low note). Virtuoso performers on the plucked sitar or bowed sarangi improvise complex melodies that usually start quiet, low, and slow, and end louder, higher, and faster.

◁ **Tabla**
The tabla consists of a pair of small drums that are placed on the floor in front of the player. Played with the hands, it provides the underlying rhythms in most Indian music.

When the **improvisation** becomes **really exciting**, an **Indian concert** can go on **all night**.

Gamelan

Found mainly in Java and Bali, gamelan is the name for a traditional Indonesian orchestra, which is usually heard in celebrations and religious ceremonies. Taught by listening in the "oral" tradition, it consists of beautifully decorated tuned percussion instruments—metallaphones and gongs—that are struck with beaters.

A **Javanese gamelan** consisting of **four large gongs** was reputedly **first used** in CE **347**.

▷ **Saron**
Consisting of bronze bars in a frame, the saron is an important gamelan metallophone played with wooden beaters by a seated player.

Classical music

The term "classical music" is used to describe all of Western art music, even though the music belongs only to the classical period of *c.*1750–1820. Mainly heard in concert halls, churches, and opera houses, it can be performed anywhere.

SEE ALSO

❮ **184–185** The orchestra

The Classical period **212–213** ❯

Concerts

Public concerts became popular in the 19th century. Before that, music was mainly heard in churches and courts at which musicians were employed to compose and perform music for worship or entertainment. Now, a typical orchestral program might open with a short work, followed by a concerto, ending with a symphony. A recital program, often played in a smaller hall, might include a solo sonata and several shorter pieces.

The rear balcony is closer to the ceiling than it is to the stage.

There are 837 seats across the two balcony levels.

Each level wraps around the stage.

The first and second tiers are made up of boxes each containing eight seats.

▷ **Carnegie Hall, New York**
Opened in 1891, New York's legendary Carnegie Hall has three performance spaces. The Stern Auditorium/Perelman Stage accommodates 2,804 people in six different seating zones.

- Rear balcony
- Front balcony
- Dress circle
- Second tier
- First tier
- Parquet
- Stage

Period performance

"Period" or "historically informed" performance is a way of performing Western music and theater. In this approach, performers play instruments that are copies of those that would have been in use at the time the work was composed. These "original" instruments allow us to hear music as the composer intended: quieter sounds, clearer textures, and at a pitch considerably lower than is used in modern performances.

▷ **Oboe da caccia**
Johann Sebastian Bach occasionally wrote for the curved "hunting" oboe. The cor anglais is its nearest modern equivalent, sounding deeper, richer notes than the oboe.

In October 2014, a huge **orchestra** of **1,000 performers** assembled in Sacramento to play part of **Beethoven's ninth symphony**.

Orchestral music

Music written for an orchestra is the heart of classical repertoire, and most major composers have made their mark with their orchestral works. Symphonies by Haydn, Mozart, Beethoven, Schubert, Brahms, Tchaikovsky, Mahler, and Shostakovich; tone poems by Richard Strauss, Ravel, and Debussy; and concertos by Mendelssohn and Bruch are favorites with audiences worldwide.

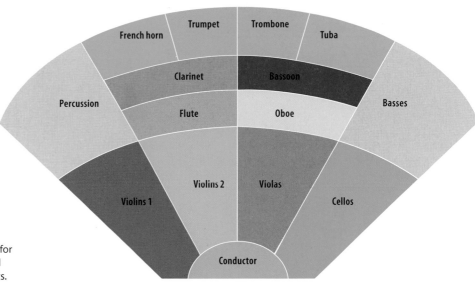

▷ **Orchestra**
Since the 18th century, composers have relished the infinite possibilities of writing for the orchestra, which offers an unparalleled range of colors, textures, and special effects.

Choirs

Church choirs are traditionally arranged in two separate groups—*Decani* (Dean's side) and *Cantoris* (Cantor's side)—on two sides of the chancel. Outside a church, choral music is also performed in halls by choirs or choruses grouped according to voice.

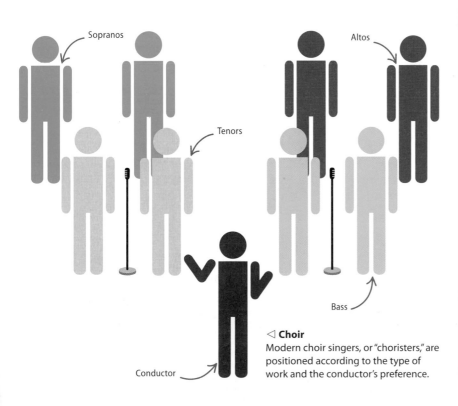

◁ **Choir**
Modern choir singers, or "choristers," are positioned according to the type of work and the conductor's preference.

REAL WORLD

Thomas Tallis (*c.*1505–1585)

One of the greatest composers of choral music, Tallis held musical posts in English churches and the Royal Court. The 40 individual voices in his 1570 motet, *Spem in alium* (Hope in Another), create a stunning effect as they reverberate around a performance space.

Chamber music

Music played in a small space, rather than a concert hall, is called chamber music. Unlike an orchestra, a chamber ensemble has no conductor and each player has an individual part to play. The most frequently heard chamber ensemble is a string quartet—two violins, a viola, and a cello— while the most popular wind group is a quintet of flute, oboe, clarinet, bassoon, and the French horn.

Wind octet
Pairs of oboes, clarinets, horns, and bassoons form a wind octet, also known as "Harmonie"—a favorite grouping for 18th-century chamber music.

Bassoons play bass line and harmony

Oboes and clarinets play upper notes, mainly melody

French horns provide harmony

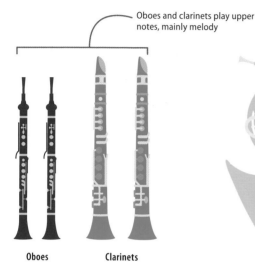

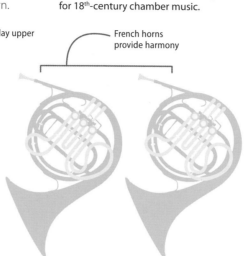

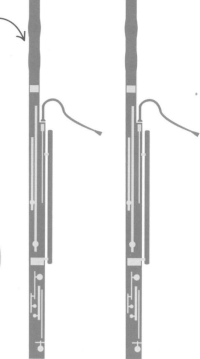

Oboes   Clarinets

French horns

Bassoons

Opera

Dating from the 1600s, opera is a dramatic musical entertainment, with a plot, arias (songs), spoken or sung dialogue, ensembles, choruses, and instrumental numbers. Depending on the date of the opera, plots, characters, sets, and musical styles vary, but performances are known for their excitement, emotional drama, and musical virtuosity.

▽ **Sydney Opera House**
Most capital cities now have an opera house. Sydney's iconic opera house has various halls and hosts more than 1,500 performances each year.

Distinctive shell-shaped "sails"

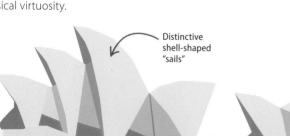

The building contains the opera house, two theaters, a concert hall, and studios.

Ballet

Ballet began in the Renaissance courts as a dance entertainment with musical accompaniment. Until the mid-19th century, music for ballet was not as important as the dance itself. Tchaikovsky (1840–93) elevated ballet music to an art form by writing ballet scores based on a story. His most famous examples are *The Nutcracker* and *Swan Lake*.

Song

From earliest times, people have sung songs for entertainment, while at work, and even to soothe babies. "Folk" songs, many ancient in origin, are often performed unaccompanied, while "art" songs may be accompanied by piano or guitar to help bring out the underlying meaning of the words.

Ja - ne - ta   ount a - ni - rem - gar - dar

Ja - ne - ta   ount a - ni - rem - gar - dar

△ **French mélodie**
Ravel's "*Chanson Française*" is a mélodie (art song) based on a popular French song. The pleasing tune in triple time has a simple, largely chordal piano accompaniment.

Schubert and Heine

Composers generally enjoy setting words that are descriptive and expressive. In the German poet Heinrich Heine's (1797–1856) poetry, Franz Schubert (1797–1828) found a rich source of inspiration and texts for many of his 630 songs *Lieder* songs.

Music for film and television

Music for the screen sets the atmosphere, time, and place, and moves the action forward. It can also describe a character, add drama, and provide continuity. Most of this is "background" music, underlining what happens on the screen. Music contained within the action—for example, someone singing—is known as "diegetic."

△ **Recording studio**
Operated from a single desk, a range of interconnected technologies can be manipulated by a skilled engineer to create remarkable results.

Modern listening

Recording began in the 1860s. It has since grown into a huge industry and has transformed the way we listen—bringing music on record or disk to the masses, without the need for live performance. Thanks to new technologies, we can now listen to any music we choose, at any time, anywhere.

△ **Going it alone**
The recent phenomenon of "solo" listening would surprise audiences of earlier centuries, accustomed to the collective experience of attending a concert.

The Baroque period

The Baroque period saw the birth of opera, the development of the orchestra, the rise of the keyboard, and the establishment of key structures. Counterpoint was the predominant texture, and musical structures were based on contrast.

SEE ALSO
❮ **174–175** Strings
❮ **180–181** Keyboards
❮ **206–207** Classical music 2

Birth of opera

Intellectuals in Florence, Italy, around 1600 sought new ways of dramatizing stories from ancient Greek and Roman times. Thus, opera was born—a series of songs (arias), sung or spoken narrative (recitative), instrumental items, and choruses, all linked to form a musical drama. In the 1600s and 1700s opera spread and flourished. Operatic works by George Frideric Handel were particularly popular.

Theorbo body

▷ **Theorbo**
This large lute has "sympathetic" strings, which resonate when others are plucked, the theorbo played "continuo" in recitative, giving a strong bass line and harmonies.

"I should be **sorry** if I only **entertained them,** I wish to **make them better.**"
George Frideric Handel

REAL WORLD

Opera scores

It was customary for the covers and title pages of opera scores, programs, and posters advertising performances to be highly decorative—almost works of art in their own right. Usually engraved, they conveyed an aspect of the story, or hinted at the particular production that awaited the eager audience. They were an important tool for promoting both the work and the profile of the composer.

Rise of instrumental music

"Concerto grosso" (large concert) was one of the favorite forms for string ensembles. It had three movements in which a small group of soloists (concertino) was contrasted with full orchestra (tutti or ripieno), in the "concertante" style.

First movement	Second movement	Third movement
Quick	Slow and lyrical	Lively and cheerful

△ **Concerto movements**
The first and second movements were often followed by a lively finale, with plenty of repeats of the main tune (ritornelli).

Keyboards to the fore

During the Baroque period, keyboard instruments—mainly harpsichord and clavichord—started to be adopted as solo instruments for the home. Many collections of keyboard music were produced, including Bach's famous two-volume *The Well-Tempered Clavier* (48 Preludes and Fugues).

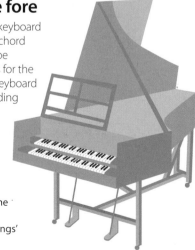

▷ **Harpsichord**
A Baroque harpsichord had one or more manuals (keyboards), and pedals that varied the strings' sound when pressed down.

Basso continuo

Baroque musical performances were held together by the "continuo." This was an accompaniment played by a keyboard instrument and bass instrument, such as a cello. Instead of a written-out part, the notation was simply a bass line with chord indications below. The bass line was played by the cello, while the keyboard player interpreted the chord indications.

▷ **Playing continuo**
The keyboard player chooses chords according to the numbers below the bass line. These showed the intervals needed to produce the correct chords.

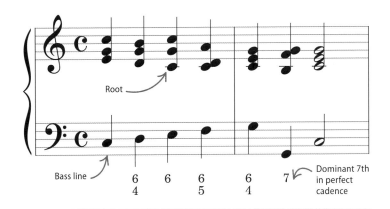

Obbligato

A contrasting (counter) melody played against the main tune is known as an obbligato. It is a familiar counterpoint in Baroque sacred music, usually played by a solo instrument in a duet with a singer, over an accompanying string ensemble. The violin, oboe, and flute were the favored instruments for playing obbligato.

△ **"Quia respexit" from Bach's** *Magnificat*
In this aria, the melancholy sound of the oboe d'amore—slightly larger version of a standard oboe—is pitted against a solo soprano.

Dancing rhythms

Courtly dances provided the rhythmic basis for many Baroque instrumental works. Sarabandes, gavottes, menuets, bourrées, and gigues (jigs) were grouped together and presented as a varied "Suite," or used as a single movement in another work.

▽ **Bach's** *French Suites*
The slow sarabande is in triple time, with emphasis on the second beat. So is the graceful minuet, while the sprightly gavotte starts, unusually, on the third of four beats.

Johann Sebastian Bach

The German composer, J. S. Bach (1685–1750) was a celebrated master of counterpoint. He composed organ and keyboard works, instrumental music, and religious choral works, including motets, cantatas, Passions, and a Mass in B minor.

Sarabande from Suite no. 6

Menuet from Suite no. 3

Gavotte from Suite no. 5

The Classical period

Influenced by the rational thinking of the Enlightenment, music in the Classical period (*c*.1750–1820) rejected polyphony and counterpoint in favor of shorter, simpler melodies with accompaniment.

SEE ALSO

❮ **130–131** Chord types
❮ **180–181** Keyboards
❮ **204–207** Classical music

Classical balance

After 1750, the impact of the Enlightenment principles of clarity, balance, and restraint were increasingly felt. A new simplicity infused the music, replacing Baroque complexity and showy ornamentation with musical ideas and structures that a listener could follow with ease.

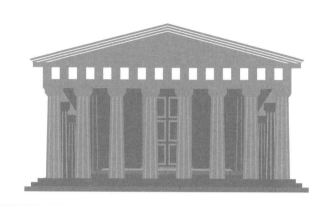

▷ **Architectural influence**
The proportions of classical buildings like the Parthenon in Athens, Greece, inspired the new fashion for simplicity and balance.

Keyboard music

During the Classical period, the pianoforte (literally meaning soft-loud) gradually replaced the harpsichord as the most popular keyboard instrument. It was favored because pressing the pedal moved the dampers away from the strings so they continued to sound. This allowed pianists to play smooth melodies with expressive phrasing.

◁ **Square piano**
More compact than the "grand," the square piano became a popular home instrument that was more suited in size and shape to the domestic room.

Alberti bass

The Alberti bass is a useful device found widely in Classical keyboard music. Consisting of repeated broken chords in the left hand, it provides a gentle, continuous, harmonic underpinning to a graceful tune that is being played by the right hand. Devised by composer Domenico Alberti (1710–1740), it was widely copied by later composers.

Broken chord of the tonic (C major)

Broken chord of dominant 7th

△ **Mozart's Sonata in C, K. 545**
Mozart's Sonata in C major uses an Alberti bass as a simple broken-chordal accompaniment to a charming melody.

Chamber music

As its name suggests, chamber music was played for enjoyment in private homes. Before public concerts were established in the 19th century, evenings of playing and listening to music were a popular form of entertainment for the wealthy.

Players	Instruments
3	Piano trios—1 violin, 1 cello, 1 piano—eg Schubert
4	String quartet—2 violins, 1 viola, 1 cello—eg Haydn
5	String quintet—2 violins, 2 violas, 1 cello—eg Mozart
6	String sextet—2 violins, violas, cellos—eg Boccherini
7	Septet—1 each violin, viola, cello, double bass, clarinet, bassoon, French horn—eg Beethoven
8	Octet—2 each oboes, clarinets, bassoons, French horns—eg Mozart
9	Nonet—1 each of violin, viola, cello, double bass, flute, oboe, clarinet, bassoon, French horn—eg Louis Spohr

▷ **Chamber music combinations**
In addition to the solo or duo sonata (keyboard alone or with another instrument), the string quartet was a favorite kind of chamber music.

Orchestral music

Four-movement symphonies and three-movement concertos for piano and violin were the most popular orchestral pieces. Balance and order were important, so that a coherent, pleasing musical whole could be created for the listener to enjoy.

Composer	Symphonies composed
Ludwig van Beethoven (1770–1827)	9
Wolfgang Amadeus Mozart (1756–91)	41
Johann Stamitz (1717–57)	58
Joseph Haydn (1732–1809)	106
Franz Xaver Pokorny (1729–94)	More than 140

△ **Symphonies**
In the late 1700s, the German Court of Mannheim valued music highly—employing renowned players and composers. It became regarded as the "home" of the symphony and the center of excellent orchestral playing.

Wolfgang Amadeus Mozart (1756–91)

Often regarded as the supreme composer of the Classical period, Mozart was one of the first "freelance" composers. For most of his working life, he did not hold a court or church position, relying for income on public concerts and commissions—requests for new compositions—from individual patrons.

Opera and oratorio

During the Classical period, opera flourished across Europe. Opera houses opened, offering a favorite social pastime for the wealthy. With arias, choruses, and instrumental items, oratorio was musically similar to opera, but was based on religious themes and was performed without action, sets, or costumes.

△ **Haydn's *The Creation***
Haydn's oratorio *The Creation* depicts the creation of the world. The lilting aria "With verdure clad" describes the serene countryside.

The Romantic period

During the period (1820–1900), composers became more concerned with expressing emotion in their music. Non-professionals began to learn instruments themselves, music publishing flourished, and public concerts became increasingly popular.

SEE ALSO

❮ **176–177** Woodwind

❮ **178–179** Brass

❮ **196–197** Words and music

❮ **204–205** Classical music

Literary inspiration

Classical themes, human relationships, and man's struggle against adversity inspired composers of the period. Goethe's *Faust* and the works of Dante and were strong influences, while contemporary German poetry provided the lyrics for songs by composers, notably Schubert, Schumann, and Brahms.

▽ *Fingal's Cave*
Mendelssohn's *Fingal's Cave* overture is an example of program music, which tells a story. The swirling opening theme suggests waves breaking at the mouth of the Hebridean cave.

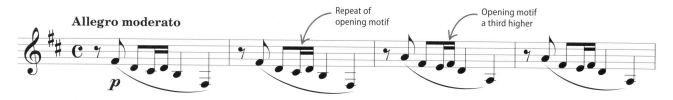

Allegro moderato

p

Repeat of opening motif

Opening motif a third higher

New instruments, new colors

Technological developments made woodwind and brass instruments easier to play and more versatile in different keys. Mass production made them more affordable, so music-making at home became popular. Different sizes of standard woodwind and brass instruments were developed and new ones were invented, adding even more exciting colors and effects to the orchestra.

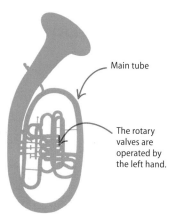

Main tube

The rotary valves are operated by the left hand.

△ **Wagner tuba**
This brass instrument was invented for use in Wagner's operas. Resembling a small tuba, it is often played by French horn players.

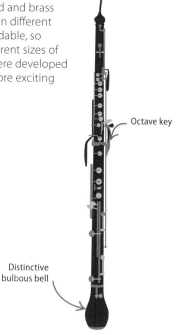

Octave key

Distinctive bulbous bell

△ **Cor anglais**
Sounding a fifth lower than the oboe, the cor anglais produces a darker, mellower sound, suitable for solos.

Music publishing

As printing became more efficient and cheaper, music was widely available to the public. The piano was a favorite home instrument for amateurs, so publishers arranged orchestral works for the piano, allowing people to get to know works they may not be able to hear in performance.

Walzer
für
Klavier zu 2 Händen
von
JOHANNES BRAHMS
Opus 39

LEIPZIG
C. F. PETERS

Virtuosity

The Romantic period saw the rise of the virtuoso soloist who played in private salons and in newly built concert halls. Traveling around Europe, they would be greeted by crowds of fans. Among these, the most famous soloists were Italian violinist Niccolò Paganini and Hungarian pianist Franz Liszt.

△ **Violin quadruple stopping**
Also a composer, Paganini created many special violin effects, including quadruple stopping where the performer plays all four strings together as a chord.

Nationalism

Political upheaval and conflict in Europe encouraged nations to rediscover their individual cultural heritage. In music, this meant using folk tunes as inspiration for music, and imitating the special sonorities of folk instruments.

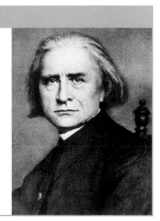

Key for left-hand little finger

Keywork based on saxophone

▷ **Tárogató**
Resembling a wooden soprano saxophone, the tárogató is a popular folk instrument in Hungary, though its ancient origins are in the Turkish double-reed shawm.

Opera

Romantic opera was dominated by Giuseppe Verdi and Richard Wagner. Verdi's Italian operas have arias, ensembles, recitatives, choruses, and dramatic stories. On the other hand, Wagner's German operas are longer and "through composed," with no distinct break between arias, recitative, ensembles, and instrumental interludes.

Melisma on "dorate" (gilded)

Va,   pen - sie - ro,   sul-l'a - li   do - ra - - te,   va,   ti

△ **"Va', pensiero" by Verdi**
"Va', pensiero" (Chorus of the Hebrew Slaves), from the 1841 opera *Nabucco*, became famous in Italy as a nationalist anthem. Its popularity was the equivalent of a modern pop hit.

Melody based on C major chord

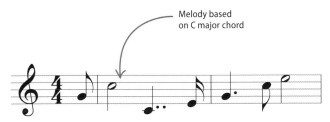

△ **Wagner's motifs**
Wagner used special tunes, or leitmotifs, to represent characters, places, or ideas, weaving them into the musical texture to add another dimension to the stage drama.

REAL WORLD

Franz Liszt (1811–86)

Franz Liszt was a Romantic musical legend. Born in Hungary, he was an exceptionally gifted pianist, writer, and composer who enjoyed fame across Europe. His virtuosic performances of outstanding technical skill were greeted with the kind of frenzy reserved for modern pop stars, in a phenomenon known as "Lisztomania."

Modern period

With the disintegration of the harmonic certainties of the 19th century, composers struggled to create new approaches for their writing. As a result, many different directions were taken, some of enduring influence, some short-lived.

SEE ALSO

❰ 40–41 Syncopation and swing
❰ 108–109 Analyzing melodies
❰ 122–123 Diatonic and chromatic harmony
Popular music   222–223 ❱

Serialism

Devised by Arnold Schönberg (1874–1951), the expressionist technique of serialism uses each of an octave's 12 notes in a particular order, forming a "whole step row series." Melodies and chords are then created from this whole step row.

▽ **Schönberg's Variations for Orchestra**
Schönberg varies his original whole step row by inverting it (turning it upside down), using it backward (retrograde), or both (inverted retrograde).

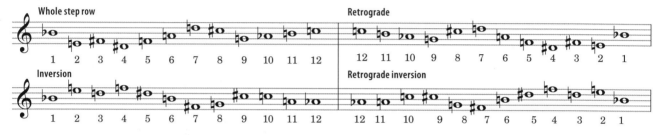

Minimalism

A hypnotic-sounding musical style, minimalism is based on repetitive structures that change gradually. It was pioneered in San Francisco in the 1960s by composers including Steve Reich and John Adams.

▷ **Ostinati**
These rhythmic, melodic, or harmonic patterns are repeated, then fragmented, interlocked, or gradually changed.

▷ **Syncopation and disrupted rhythm**
Syncopation disrupts the rhythm by shifting the emphasis from the main beat to a subordinate beat.

▷ **Broken chord**
When repeated over a long period, the broken chord, or arpeggio, device is effective in creating a rippling, trance-like effect.

▷ **Note addition and interlockings**
Texture can be varied by adding an extra note to a pattern, or by changing the way in which different patterns interlock.

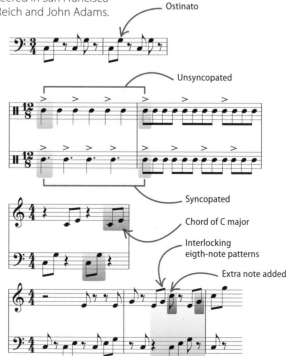

Ostinato

Unsyncopated

Syncopated

Chord of C major

Interlocking eigth-note patterns

Extra note added

Musical theater

Musical theater combines catchy songs and choruses, dance, spoken dialogue, and instrumental interludes. Also known as "musicals," these are often premiered and performed on New York's Broadway or London's West End. With simple but dramatic plots (stories), magnificent costumes, and spectacular sets, they have become a popular form of theatrical entertainment.

▽ **West Side Story**
Based on Shakespeare's *Romeo and Juliet*, Leonard Bernstein's 1957 musical, *West Side Story*, portrays the rivalry between two New York gangs, the Jets and Sharks, and the doomed love affair of Maria and Tony. The illustration below shows how the musical is structured.

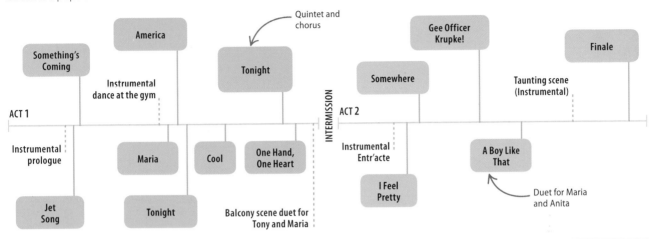

Quintet and chorus

Something's Coming

America

Tonight

Gee Officer Krupke!

Finale

Somewhere

Taunting scene (Instrumental)

Instrumental dance at the gym

ACT 1

INTERMISSION

ACT 2

Instrumental prologue

Maria

Cool

One Hand, One Heart

Instrumental Entr'acte

A Boy Like That

Duet for Maria and Anita

Jet Song

Tonight

I Feel Pretty

Balcony scene duet for Tony and Maria

New age of technology

Though recording music began in the 19th century, recent developments in technology mean that classical music can be heard by anyone, anytime, and anywhere. Anyone can create and share their work. MIDI (Musical Instrument Digital Interface) allows devices to communicate with each other, sharing digital information for musical sounds.

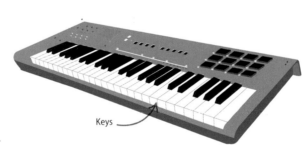

Keys

◁ **MIDI controller keyboard**
An important part of a composer's setup, keyboards such as this allow sounds to be generated and organized automatically, with mixes, delays, fades, filters, and cutoffs.

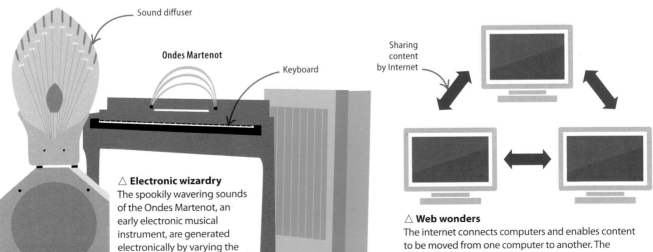

Sound diffuser

Ondes Martenot

Keyboard

△ **Electronic wizardry**
The spookily wavering sounds of the Ondes Martenot, an early electronic musical instrument, are generated electronically by varying the frequency of oscillation in its vacuum tubes.

Sharing content by Internet

△ **Web wonders**
The internet connects computers and enables content to be moved from one computer to another. The worldwide web has transformed music by allowing content to be generated, contributed to, and shared.

Dance music

Dance has long been part of celebration. Originally improvised, it is now mostly for groups, pairs, or individuals. Group dance is based on ancient folk traditions, while pair dancing is a recent evolution developed from courtly dances of the 16th century onward.

SEE ALSO

❰ 182–183 Percussion
❰ 188–189 Ensembles
❰ 202–203 Folk, world, and roots

Bhangra

Bhangra originated in Punjab, India, as a harvest celebration, accompanied with singing and drumming. It is now fused with Western music to produce a highly energetic form of celebratory dance and song for festivities and weddings.

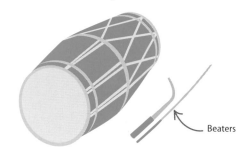
Beaters

△ **Dhol**
The large, loud dhol drum is played with cane beaters in bhangra. Sometimes European instruments, such as electric guitars, provide simple harmony.

△ **Bhangra dance**
Bhangra is performed in circles or lines, using swords or sticks. The songs are based on traditional poems, "boli," usually about love and relationships.

Irish and Scottish dance

Celtic countries, particularly Scotland and Ireland, have a long history of traditional dance tunes and songs. Among the most popular dances are reels and hornpipes, which use similar steps. The music is usually quick, with two or four beats in a measure, simple harmonies, and folk-like melodies, which are often based on modes rather than conventional scales.

▽ **Reel**
"St Kilda Wedding" is a traditional Scottish reel which are tune, often played on a fiddle. It features a characteristic "snap," or quick syncopation.

◁ **Jig**
The jig is usually in 6/8 and danced with jumping steps. The tune may be played in unison by fiddles, whistles, Uilleann (Irish) pipes, and the Irish bodhran drum.

Waltz

With origins in 18th-century Austria and Germany, the waltz has three beats in a measure and is danced by couples. Elegant and graceful with lyrical melodies, it became an important musical form beyond the ballroom for composers like Chopin and Tchaikovsky.

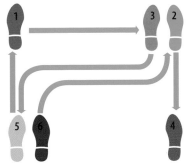

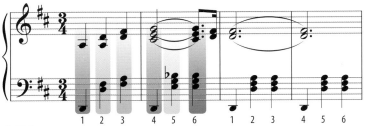

△ **Waltz steps**
Waltz steps allow the dancers to turn in circles while progressing around the floor. The first two measures on the staff show the steps for the dance moves illustrated above.

△ **Waltz dance**
The waltz can be danced at different speeds. Normally fairly slow and restrained, in Vienna it is traditionally danced more energetically, with an almost skipping step.

Tango

Emerging from Argentina in the 1880s, the tango is a powerful, highly-charged pair dance. The steps resemble different ways of walking—swaying, sweeping, and sensual. Tango features sudden contrasts of loud and soft. When there are vocals, they are usually wistful or nostalgic.

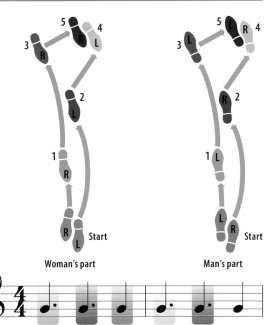

Woman's part   Man's part

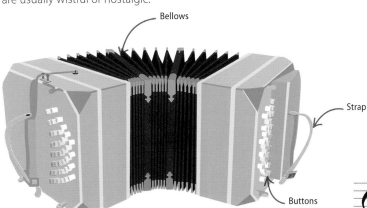

△ **Bandoneon**
Tango is often accompanied by a sextet comprising violins, bass, piano, and bandoneons—a type of concertina with a particularly melancholic sound.

△ **Tango steps**
The tango has four beats in a measure with a characteristic repetitive offbeat syncopation; however, there are many variations on the basic tango step.

»

Line dance

Mixed lines of men and women (not pairs) face the same wall and move together in a series of simple steps. The music has eight eight-beat phrases, totaling 64 beats. This is called a "basic sequence." The music is recorded, often featuring a guitar, fiddle, and banjo.

▽ **Line dancing steps**
Led by a caller, the lines of dancers make quarter- or half-turns to face another wall. This sequence is repeated until they have made one complete turn.

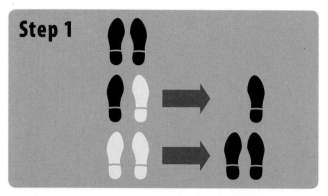

Step 1

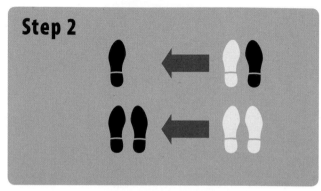

Step 2

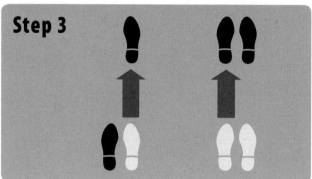

Step 3

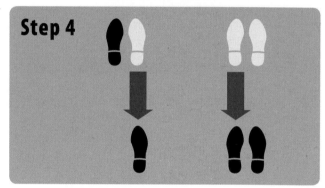

Step 4

Salsa

Inspired by Cuban and Puerto Rican music, this pair dance has four beats in a measure, two-measure phrases, and repeated syncopation. A salsa band features a piano, saxophones, trumpets, and Latin percussion—claves, bongos, congas, timbales, and cowbells.

The timbale's metal body produces a clean, crisp effect.

△ **Timbales**
A pair of shallow, high-pitched metal drums with skin heads, timbales are played with sticks, which strike the head or rim, or perform impressive rolls.

◁ **Claves**
These simple wooden sticks, when clashed together, provide the driving rhythm that underpins the lively salsa.

◁ **Salsa rhythm**
The syncopated rhythm of the salsa gives a sensual, swaying effect.

Disco

Originating in the USA during the early 1970s, disco music has its roots in Soul and Funk. It is a fast, energetic dance music, usually with four beats in a measure. This genre of music is characterized by a driving guitar and drum rhythms, and a syncopated bass line; it can also be lavishly orchestrated. The vocals are structured with verse and chorus, often delivered with reverb.

▽ **Break dancing**
This form of dance is characterized by athletic moves involving spinning during the instrumental sections (breaks).

Balancing on the head

Balancing on one arm

Both legs in the air

Feet return to the floor

Step 1 Step 2 Step 3 Step 4

Club music

Also called Electronic Dance Music (EDM), club music is generated by DJs using MIDI technology to create new musical effects by blending digitally produced sounds. These sounds can be looped (repeated) and mixed with other tracks, with effects such as delay, reverb, and panning (moving the sound around), adding to the atmosphere.

△ **DJ**
In charge of a battery of electronica, the DJ (disc jockey) can create an astonishing range of musical effects to excite dancers to more energetic moves.

Jive

The emergence of rock 'n' roll in the 1950s saw a revival of interest in jive dancing—a fast and lively Latin dance from the USA. This pair dance, with a basic six-step pattern of movement, can be adapted to include showy moves, such as the male twirling his partner around, or bending her backward toward the floor.

Blues and jazz

Jazz emerged from the USA around 1900, and it has its origins in blues and gospel music. Mostly improvised, it features distinctive syncopations (shifted accents), "swung" rhythms, and virtuosic solos.

SEE ALSO
❬ **40–41** Syncopation and swing
❬ **130–131** Chord types
❬ **178–179** Brass
❬ **190–191** Rock bands
❬ **192–193** Voices

Jazz chords

Most jazz chords are triads comprising the root (tonic), 3rd, and 5th, with an added 7th. The 3rd and 7th intervals may be flattened ("bent") to create a distinctively spicy sound. Occasionally some chords may be omitted. Jazz music is rarely notated in full. Instead, chord symbols are used to indicate which notes should be played, and the player improvises.

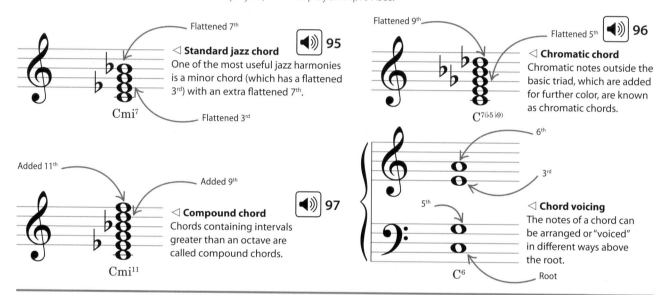

Flattened 7th

◁ **Standard jazz chord**
One of the most useful jazz harmonies is a minor chord (which has a flattened 3rd) with an extra flattened 7th.

Flattened 3rd

Cmi⁷ — Cmi^7

🔊 **95**

Flattened 9th

Flattened 5th

◁ **Chromatic chord**
Chromatic notes outside the basic triad, which are added for further color, are known as chromatic chords.

$C^{7(\flat5\,\flat9)}$

🔊 **96**

Added 11th

Added 9th

◁ **Compound chord**
Chords containing intervals greater than an octave are called compound chords.

Cmi^{11}

🔊 **97**

6th

3rd

5th

◁ **Chord voicing**
The notes of a chord can be arranged or "voiced" in different ways above the root.

C^6

Root

12-bar blues

One of the most important chord progressions in jazz is the 12-bar (or 12-measure) blues. It is a pattern based on just three chords arranged in a particular sequence: I (tonic), IV (sub-dominant), and V (dominant). Arranged normally in three four-bar (or four-measure) phrases, it is the harmonic basis for many blues songs.

▷ **Progression in the key of C major**
With chord I predominating, chord IV appears in three bars (measures). Chord V appears only in bar (measure) nine.

Bar 1	Bar 2	Bar 3	Bar 4
C	C	C	C
I	I	I	I
Bar 5	**Bar 6**	**Bar 7**	**Bar 8**
F	F	C	C
IV	IV	I	I
Bar 9	**Bar 10**	**Bar 11**	**Bar 12**
G	F	C	C
V	IV	I	I

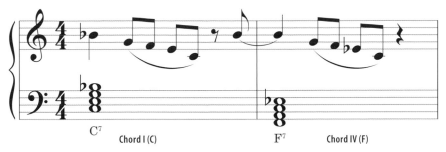

C⁷   Chord I (C)   F⁷   Chord IV (F)

◁ **Typical melodic fragment in 12-bar blues**
A typical blues melody over the 12-bar blues pattern is based on the notes of the chord. In blues songs, chromatic ("blue") notes and melisma—singing more than one note to a single syllable—are used to heighten the sense of pain or sadness in the lyrics.

Syncopation

Jazz uses off-beat rhythms known as syncopation. When written, these can look very complicated, but jazz musicians perform these complex syncopations instinctively as they improvise, putting the emphasis on an unexpected part of the beat.

▽ **Syncopation**
Syncopation adds rhythmic confusion, which can disorientate the listener's ear, by shifting the emphasis from the main part of a beat to a subordinate part.

Stress on last beat   Stress on last half beat

Swing

A form of medium-fast jazz developed in the USA in the 1930s, swing has four beats in a measure, and a characteristically "lilting" rhythm. A swing band normally includes trumpets, trombones, saxophones, clarinets, occasionally a violin and guitar, and a strong rhythm section to anchor the beat.

▽ **Swing rhythm**
Though the swing beat is normally notated as two eighth notes, the first eighth note of the pair is played longer and more accented than the latter.

Written as

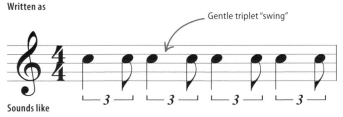

Gentle triplet "swing"

Sounds like

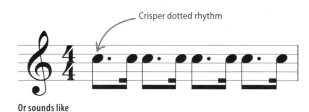

Crisper dotted rhythm

Or sounds like

Miles Davis (1926–91)

American trumpeter, bandleader, composer, and improviser, Miles Davis was one of the most influential jazz musicians of all time. He was at the forefront of various new forms, including more relaxed "cool" jazz, and "modal" jazz, which was based on modes rather than chords.

Popular music

Pop has its roots in rock 'n' roll and rhythm 'n' blues. Rock music evolved from jazz, blues, and gospel music. Its insistent beat and emotional lyrics helped transform popular music.

SEE ALSO
❮ **146–147** Bass
❮ **166–167** Ostinati, loops, and riffs
❮ **190–191** Rock bands

Gospel and soul music

Gospel originates from African-American religious songs called spirituals. Sung by groups, gospel music blends harmonies of European hymn tunes, syncopated rhythms and call-and-response patterns from West African music, and the "blue" notes of rhythm 'n' blues melodies. In soul music, the lyrics are generally about human relationships, love, and heartbreak, but the vocal style is similar to gospel music.

▽ **Call-and-response**
The spiritual song "Swing Low, Sweet Chariot" uses a call-and-response structure between the first and second phrases.

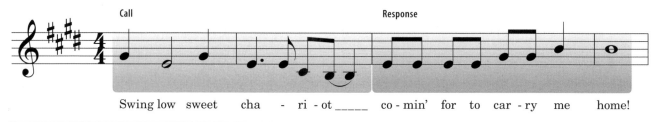

Pop song characteristics

The lineup for 1960s' pop songs—such as those by The Beatles— was generally guitars, drums, a lead singer, and backing vocals. Most songs had four beats in a measure, simple melodies, and a repeated harmonic sequence, based mainly on chords I, IV, and V.

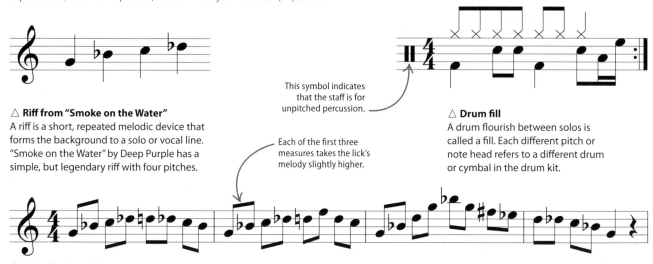

This symbol indicates that the staff is for unpitched percussion.

Each of the first three measures takes the lick's melody slightly higher.

△ **Riff from "Smoke on the Water"**
A riff is a short, repeated melodic device that forms the background to a solo or vocal line. "Smoke on the Water" by Deep Purple has a simple, but legendary riff with four pitches.

△ **Drum fill**
A drum flourish between solos is called a fill. Each different pitch or note head refers to a different drum or cymbal in the drum kit.

△ **Typical guitar lick**
A lick is a stylish solo phrase, often for a guitar, that follows a vocal phrase. This chromatic four-measure riff reaches its climax in the third measure.

Pop song structure

Many simple pop songs are arranged into four sections. The first two sections and the last section all use the same melody, usually called "A." The third section has a different melody, usually different words, and can be in a different key. The "B" section is sometimes called the "middle eight," or "chorus".

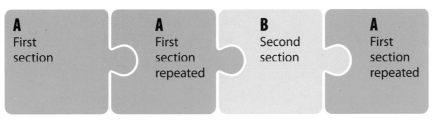

| **A** First section | **A** First section repeated | **B** Second section | **A** First section repeated |

△ **Basic structure**
The most common pop song structure features two repetitions of "A," followed by one "B" section, returning to "A" to conclude.

> **Bing Crosby's** 1942 hit single, **"White Christmas,"** still tops the **best-seller single charts,** with more than **50 million copies sold.**

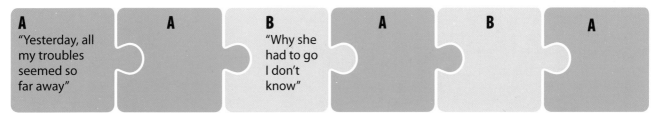

| **A** "Yesterday, all my troubles seemed so far away" | **A** | **B** "Why she had to go I don't know" | **A** | **B** | **A** |

△ **Compound AABA form 1st line**
"Yesterday" by The Beatles has two contrasting types of musical material, "A" and "B," arranged to make a longer song in a compound form.

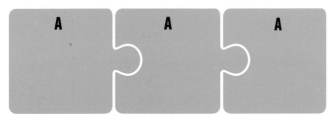

| **A** | **A** | **A** |

△ **Strophic ballad**
Pop ballads are often strophic, which means that their verses are repeated with the same tune, "A," but with different words each time. They are usually slow and sentimental.

REAL WORLD
Rock 'n' roll

Rock 'n' roll became a teenage craze in the 1950s. It is a fusion of two popular music styles: rhythm 'n' blues and country music. Loud and fast, with driving syncopated rhythms and lyrics, this genre challenged adult authority and establishment views. Elvis Presley was one of its most celebrated performers.

Reference

Note values and rest values

Note values

Note values show how many beats, or fractions of a beat, a note lasts for. Dotting a note makes its value one-and-a-half times longer. The tables below show the most common note values.

Note	Name	Value
𝆷	double whole note	8 beats
𝅝	whole note	4 beats
𝅗𝅥	half note	2 beats
𝅘𝅥	quarter note	1 beat
𝅘𝅥𝅮	eighth note	$\frac{1}{2}$ beat
𝅘𝅥𝅯	sixteenth note	$\frac{1}{4}$ beat
𝅘𝅥𝅰	thirty-second note	$\frac{1}{8}$ beat
𝅘𝅥𝅱	sixty-fourth note	$\frac{1}{16}$ beat

Note	Name	Value
𝅝.	dotted whole note	6 beats
𝅗𝅥.	dotted half note	3 beats
𝅘𝅥.	dotted quarter note	1 $\frac{1}{2}$ beats
𝅘𝅥𝅮.	dotted eighth note	$\frac{3}{4}$ beat

Rest values

Rests are used to notate and give a time value to silences within the music. Note values have corresponding rest values, as shown in the tables below.

Note	Name	Value
▬	double whole rest	8 beats
▬	whole rest	4 beats
▬	half rest	2 beats
𝄽	quarter rest	1 beat
𝄾	eighth rest	$\frac{1}{2}$ beat
𝄿	sixteenth rest	$\frac{1}{4}$ beat
𝅀	thirty-second rest	$\frac{1}{8}$ beat
𝅁	sixty-fourth rest	$\frac{1}{16}$ beat

Note	Name	Value
▬.	dotted whole rest	6 beats
▬.	dotted half rest	3 beats
𝄽.	dotted quarter rest	1 $\frac{1}{2}$ beats
𝄾.	dotted eighth rest	$\frac{3}{4}$ beat

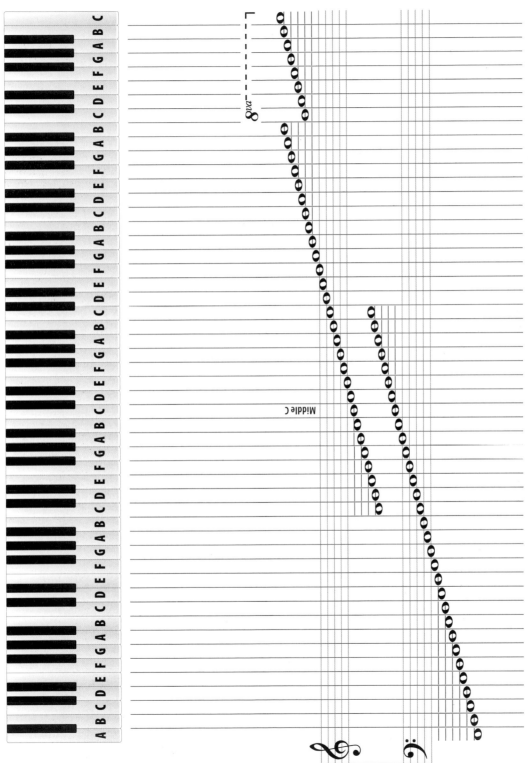

△ **Grand staff**

In piano music, the grand staff consists of a treble clef and bass clef staff, joined together by a brace (or bracket) at the left-hand side. Shown here are all the white keys of a piano and how they are written on the grand staff, with ledger lines for notes above or below the range of the staff.

Time signatures

How time signatures work

Time signatures show the number and note value of beats in a measure. The top number of the time signature shows the number of beats, and the bottom number shows the note value of each beat.

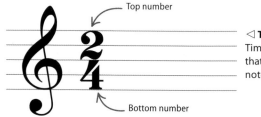

Top number

Bottom number

◁ **Time signature**
Time signature 2/4 indicates that there are two quarter-note beats in a measure.

Bottom number	Note value	Note value written out
2	Half note	
4	Quarter note	
8	Eighth note	
16	Sixteenth note	

Simple time signatures

With simple time signatures, the beat is not a dotted note and is subdivided into two. Shown below are some of the most common simple time signatures.

2/4 time signature

3/4 time signature

4/4 time signature (also called common time)

2/2 time signature (also called cut time)

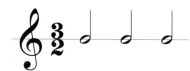

3/2 time signature

4/2 time signature

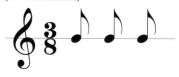

3/8 time signature

3/16 time signature

Compound time signatures

In compound time signatures, the beat is subdivided into three rather than two, and is therefore always a dotted note. For example, the time signature 3/4 and 6/8 both contain six eighth notes in a measure, but 3/4 denotes three quarter notes, while 6/8 denotes two dotted quarter notes. Shown below are more such compound time signatures.

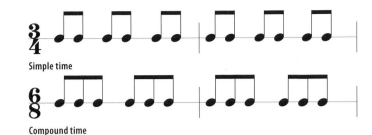

Simple time

Compound time

  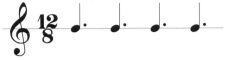

6/8 time signature   **9/8 time signature**   **12/8 time signature**

6/4 time signature   **9/4 time signature**   **12/4 time signature**

6/16 time signature   **9/16 time signature**   **12/16 time signature**

Irregular time signatures

Time signatures do not always have two, three, or four beats in a measure. Shown here are examples of some unusual or irregular time signatures. If the beat is a eighth or sixteenth note, the notes can be grouped to show where the strong beats are.

△ **Calypso rhythm**

In a calypso rhythm, the time signature is 4/4, but the beat is subdivided in an unusual way: 3 + 3 + 2. This rhythm is common in calypso, folk, and popular music.

5/2 time signature   **7/4 time signature**

11/8 time signature   **13/16 time signature**

Keys and key signatures

Major and minor key signatures

Key signatures show the sharps or flats that are needed for a particular key. Major key signatures have the same sharps or flats as the key's major scale, while minor key signatures have the same sharps or flats as the key's natural minor scale.

E major

E major key signature

G minor

G minor key signature

How key signatures are written

The sharps or flats of a key signature are written immediately after the clef, at the beginning of each line of music. Sharps and flats are always written in the same order, as shown below.

◁ **Sharps in a key signature**
The sharps in a key signature are always written in this order: F♯, then C♯, followed by G♯, D♯, A♯, E♯, and finally B♯.

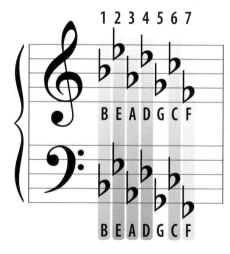

◁ **Flats in a key signature**
The flats in a key signature are always written in this order: B♭, followed by E♭, then A♭, D♭, G♭, C♭, and finally F♭.

Relative major and relative minor

All major keys have a relative minor key. The relative major and relative minor share the same key signature. The keynote of the relative minor is a minor third below the keynote of its relative major.

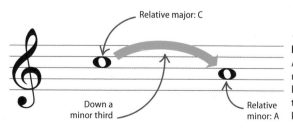

Relative major: C

Down a minor third

Relative minor: A

◁ **Relative minor keynote**
A minor is the relative minor of C major. Its keynote, A, is a minor third below C, the keynote of C major.

Table of keys and key signatures

Shown here are the key signatures for all the different major keys and their relative minors, in the treble, bass, alto, and tenor clefs.

Major key	Relative minor key	Number of sharps or flats	Key signature—treble clef	Key signature—bass clef	Key signature—alto clef	Key signature—tenor clef
C major	A minor	0				
G major	E minor	1 sharp				
D major	B minor	2 sharps				
A major	F♯ minor	3 sharps				
E major	C♯ minor	4 sharps				
B major	G♯ minor	5 sharps				
F♯ major	D♯ minor	6 sharps				
C♯ major	A♯ minor	7 sharps				
F major	D minor	1 flat				
B♭ major	G minor	2 flats				
E♭ major	C minor	3 flats				
A♭ major	F minor	4 flats				
D♭ major	B♭ minor	5 flats				
G♭ major	E♭ minor	6 flats				
C♭ major	A♭ minor	7 flats				

Enharmonic equivalents

Two keys whose scales consist of the same notes, but where the notes are given different names, are called enharmonic equivalents. The table below lists such pairs of keys.

Major keys	Minor keys
B major and C♭ major	G♯ minor and A♭ minor
F♯ major and G♭ major	D♯ minor and E♭ minor
C♯ major and D♭ major	A♯ minor and B♭ minor

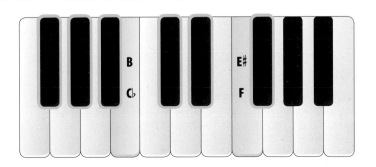

Chords

Triads, sixth, and seventh chords

Shown here—in root position—are the major, minor, diminished, and augmented triads, and the most common sixth and seventh chords.

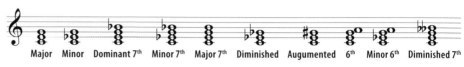

Major | Minor | Dominant 7th | Minor 7th | Major 7th | Diminished | Augmented | 6th | Minor 6th | Diminished 7th

Major | Minor | Dominant 7th | Minor 7th | Major 7th | Diminished | Augumented | 6th | Minor 6th | Diminished 7th

Major | Minor | Dominant 7th | Minor 7th | Major 7th | Diminished | Augmented | 6th | Minor 6th | Diminished 7th

Major | Minor | Dominant 7th | Minor 7th | Major 7th | Diminished | Augmented | 6th | Minor 6th | Diminished 7th

Major | Minor | Dominant 7th | Minor 7th | Major 7th | Diminished | Augmented | 6th | Minor 6th | Diminished 7th

Major | Minor | Dominant 7th | Minor 7th | Major 7th | Diminished | Augmented | 6th | Minor 6th | Diminished 7th

Major Minor Dominant 7th Minor 7th Major 7th Diminished Augumented 6th Minor 6th Diminished 7th

Major Minor Dominant 7th Minor 7th Major 7th Diminished Augumented 6th Minor 6th Diminished 7th

Major Minor Dominant 7th Minor 7th Major 7th Diminished Augumented 6th Minor 6th Diminished 7th

Major Minor Dominant 7th Minor 7th Major 7th Diminished Augumented 6th Minor 6th Diminished 7th

Major Minor Dominant 7th Minor 7th Major 7th Diminished Augumented 6th Minor 6th Diminished 7th

Major Minor Dominant 7th Minor 7th Major 7th Diminished Augumented 6th Minor 6th Diminished 7th

Major Minor Dominant 7th Minor 7th Major 7th Diminished Augumented 6th Minor 6th Diminished 7th

Scales

Major scales

All major scales are broken down into the same pattern of whole steps and half steps as the C major scale. To maintain this pattern, major scales that start on a note other than C must include sharps or flats. The scales with sharps are shown first, followed by the scales with flats. Major scales include the same sharps or flats as their corresponding major key signatures.

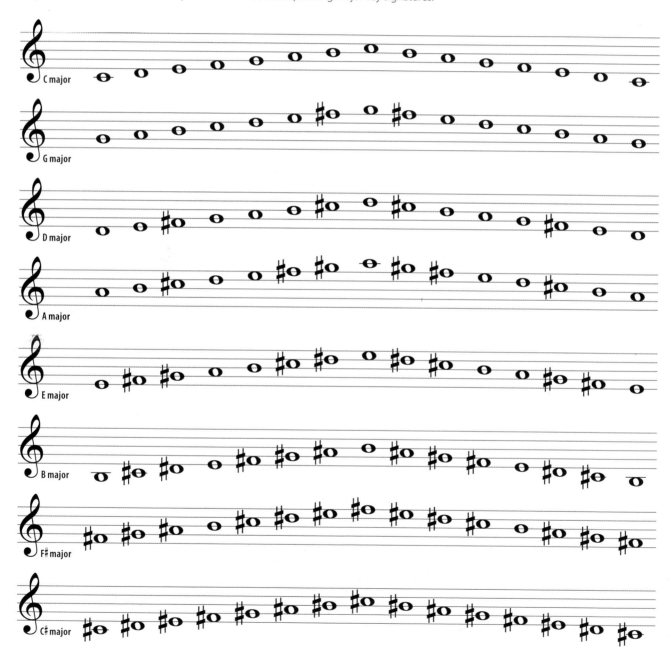

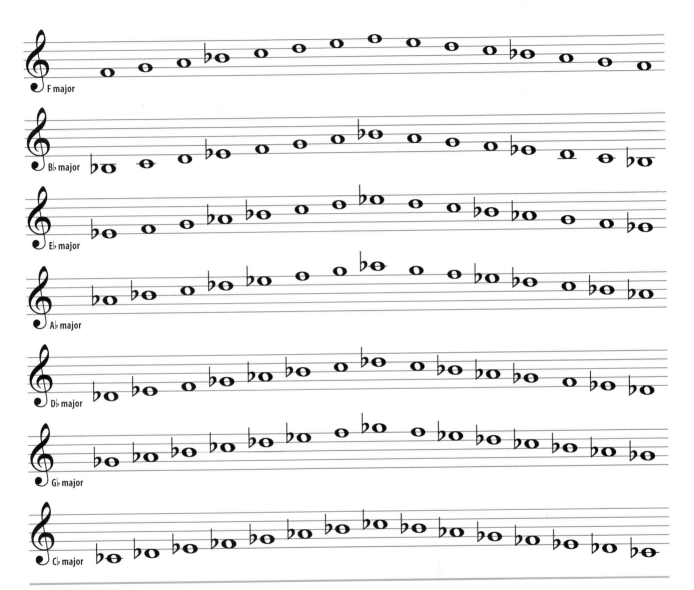

F major

B♭ major

E♭ major

A♭ major

D♭ major

G♭ major

C♭ major

Enharmonic equivalents

Two scales that use exactly the same notes on the keyboard, but give all their notes different names, are known as enharmonic equivalents. The pairs of major scales that are enharmonic equivalents are F♯ major and G♭ major (shown here), B major and C♭ major, and C♯ major and D♭ major.

◁ **On the keyboard**
The F♯ major and G♭ major scales use the same notes, but give their notes different names.

Natural minor scales

The natural minor scales follow the same pattern of whole steps. They have the same sharps or flats as the key signature of their relative major key.

A natural minor

E natural minor

B natural minor

F# natural minor

C# natural minor

G# natural minor

D# natural minor

A# natural minor

D natural minor

G natural minor

C natural minor

F natural minor

Bb natural minor

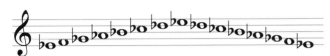

Eb natural minor

Ab natural minor

Harmonic minor scales

The harmonic minor scales follow the same pattern of intervals. All harmonic minor scales have an augmented second between their sixth and seventh notes, and some harmonic minor scales have double sharps.

A harmonic minor

E harmonic minor

B harmonic minor

F# harmonic minor

C# harmonic minor

G# harmonic minor

D# harmonic minor

A# harmonic minor

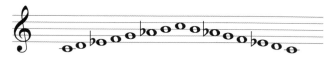

D harmonic minor

G harmonic minor

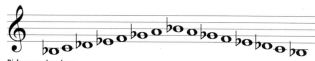

C harmonic minor

F harmonic minor

B♭ harmonic minor

E♭ harmonic minor

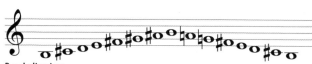

A♭ harmonic minor

Melodic minor scales

The melodic minor scales follow the same pattern of whole steps and half steps. The sixth and seventh notes of melodic minor scales are a half step lower going down the scale than they are going up the scale.

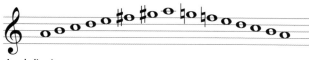

A melodic minor

E melodic minor

B melodic minor

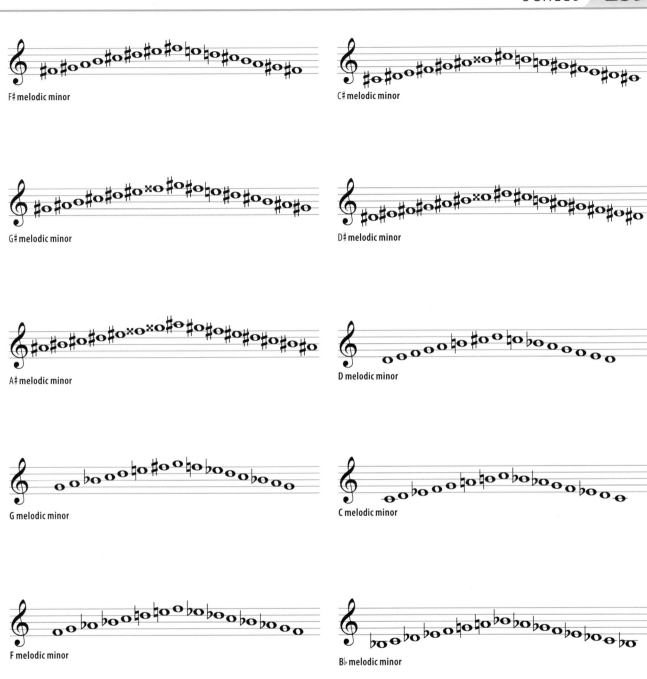

F# melodic minor

C# melodic minor

G# melodic minor

D# melodic minor

A# melodic minor

D melodic minor

G melodic minor

C melodic minor

F melodic minor

B♭ melodic minor

E♭ melodic minor

A♭ melodic minor

Musical terms

Musical term	Meaning
accelerando, accel.	gradually increasing tempo
adagietto	slow, but faster than adagio
adagio	slow—a tempo between andante and largo
ad libitum, ad lib.	at choice—passage may be played loosely improvised, or part can be left out
affettuoso	tenderly
agitato	agitated
alla marcia	in the style of a march
allargando	broadening—getting slower and louder
allegretto	quick, but not as quick as allegro
allegro	quick
amabile	amiable, pleasant
andante	at a walking pace
andantino	slightly faster than andante
animando	more lively
animato, animé	animated, lively
a piacere	at pleasure—no need to follow rhythm strictly
appassionato	with passion
arco	bow of a string instrument, used if players have previously been asked to play pizzacato
a tempo	in time—return to the original speed
attacca	go straight on to the next section without a break
bravura	skill, brilliance (con bravura: in a brilliant style)
brio	vigor, animation
calmato	calm, tranquil
cantabile	in a singing style
capriccioso, capricieux	unpredictable, volatile
colla parte	keep with the soloist (for accompanist)
colla voce	keep with the singer (for accompanist)
col legno	with the wood (of a string instrument)—the player should play with the wood of the bow
come prima	as before (not necessarily as at the beginning)
come sopra	as above
comodo	convenient (tempo comodo: at a comfortable speed)
crescendo, cresc, cres.	gradually getting louder
da capo, D.C.	from the head—from the beginning

Musical term	Meaning
dal segno, D.S.	from the sign
deciso	decisively
decrescendo, decresc.	gradually getting softer
détaché	act of playing notes separately
diminuendo, dimin.	dwindling—with gradually decreasing volume
divisi, div.	divided—for orchestral players (usually strings) to divide into groups
dolce	sweetly (dolcissimo: as sweetly as possible)
douce, doux, doucement	softly, sweetly
energico	energetic
en retenant	slowing slightly, holding back
espressione	expression
espressivo, espress.	expressive
fin, fine	end
Flatterzunge, Flzg.	flutter-tonguing (for wind instruments)
forte, f	loud
fortepiano, fp	loud then immediately soft
fortissimo, ff, fff	very loud
forza	force (forzando, forzato, fz: forcing, accenting)
furioso	furious, frenzied
giocoso	playful, humorous
giusto	exact, proper (tempo giusto: in strict time)
glissando, gliss.	slide (for piano or harp)—sweeping finger along the keys or strings
G.P.	general pause—all performers silent
grandioso	grandly
grave	very slow, solemn
grazioso	graceful
joyeux	joyful
lacrimoso, lagrimando, lagrimoso	sad
lamentoso	lamenting
langsam	slow
largamente	broadly
larghetto	slow, but a little faster than largo
largo	slow
legato	smooth, with no break between notes

Musical term	Meaning
légèrement, leggiero	light, nimble
leichtlent, lento	slow (lentement: slowly)
liberamente, librement	freely
l'istesso	the same (l'istesso tempo: at the same speed)
loco	at the normal pitch
lunga	long
maestoso	majestic
main	hand (main gauche, m.g.: left hand; main droite, m.d.: right hand)
mano	hand (mano sinistra, m.s.: left hand; mano destra, m.d.: right hand)
marcato, marc	accented
martelé, martellato	strongly accented
mesto	sad
mezza, mezzo	half, moderately (mezzo forte, mf: moderately loud; mezza voce: in an undertone)
misterioso	mysteriously
misura	measure (alla misura: in strict time; senza misura: in free time)
moderato, modéré	at a moderate speed
morendo	fading away
mosso	with motion, animated
moto, movimento	movement, motion
mouvement, mouvt	movement, motion (au movement: in time; premier mouvement: original tempo)
naturale, nat.	naturally, in the usual way
nobilmente	nobly
nuovo	new (di nuovo: again)
obbligato	obligatory—indicating an instrument's important role
ossia	or, alternatively—shows an alternative, simpler version of a passage
ostinato	persistant (basso ostinato: a bass line with a repeated rhythm or melodic figure)
ottava, ott.	octave (ottava bassa: octave lower; ottava alta: octave higher)
parlando	like speech, pronounced clearly
pausa	rest
pesante	heavy, ponderous
piacevole	pleasant
piano, p	played or sung softly (pianissimo, pp: very quiet)

Musical term	Meaning
pizzicato, pizz	pinched, plucked
ponticello	on the bridge, in string playing, an indication to bow or to pluck very near to the bridge
portamento	carrying, slide
presto	very quickly, fast
ralentir	slowing
rallentando, rall.	broadening of the tempo, progressively slower
retenu	hold back
rigoroso	strict
ritardando, ritard, rit.	slowing down, decelerating
ritenuto, riten., rit.	suddenly slower, held back
ritmico	rhythmical
rubato, tempo rubato	robbed, flexible in tempo
scherzando, scherzoso	playful, humorous
schnell	fast
sec, secco	dry—staccato, without resonance
segue	carry on to the next section without a pause
sforzando, sforzato, sfz, sf	made loud, a sudden strong accent
sordino, sord.	mute
sostenuto, sost.	sustained, lengthened
sotto voce	in an undertone, quietly
sourdine	mute
spiccato	distinct, separated
spiritoso	spiritedly
staccato, stacc.	making each note brief and detached
stretto	tight, narrow
stringendo	gradually getting faster
tacet	silent, do not play
tenuto, ten.	held
tranquillo	calmly, peacefully
tremolando, tremolo, trem.	shaking
tutti	all, all together
unisono, unis.	in unison
veloce	to be played rapidly
vibrato	vibrating
vigoroso	vigorously
vite	fast
vivace, vivement, vivo	lively, brisk

Musical periods

Music styles through history

From the earliest times humans have made music, first with the voice, then by adding simple instruments. In the early medieval period, music took on a more formal structure as plainchant came into use in churches and multiple voices singing at once marked the beginning of harmony. From the late Middle Ages onward, the history of music is divided into distinct periods, each with its own musical style.

RENAISSANCE 1400–1600

Feature	Explanation	Key composers/works
Polyphony, meaning many voices, is the most important form of sacred choral music.	Vocal lines imitate one another, weaving a complex musical tapestry of sound, heard at its best in the vast spaces of a church.	Thomas Tallis, *Spem in alium*; William Byrd, *Mass for five voices*; Giovanni Pierluigi di Palestrina, *Missa Papae Marcelli*
The madrigal, an unaccompanied part song for several voices, becomes popular in Italy and England.	Written for two to eight solo voices, madrigals often use texts based on love and death, or pastoral topics.	Carlo Gesualdo, "Moro, lasso, al mio duolo"; Thomas Morley, "It was a lover and his lass"; Orlando Gibbons, "The Silver Swan"
The lute becomes a favorite instrument for solos, and as a vocal accompaniment.	The quietly expressive lute gained popularity throughout Europe. The lute song was a successful English creation.	John Dowland, "Flow my tears"; Thomas Campion, *Books of Ayres*

BAROQUE 1600–1750

Feature	Explanation	Key composers/works
Opera is born in Italy and catches on quickly, especially in France and, later, England.	Emerging from Florence around 1600, opera is the result of adding music to make stories more dramatic.	Claudio Monteverdi, *Orfeo*; Henry Purcell, *Dido and Aeneas*; George Frideric Handel, *Xerxes*
Rise of instrumental works, as interest in instrument manufacture increases.	Development of three-movement trio sonata (quick-slow-lively), featuring solo instrument and continuos.	Arcangelo Corelli, *Concerto Grossi*; Antonio Vivaldi, *The Four Seasons*; George Frideric Handel, *Water Music*
Continuo binds together musical ensembles.	A bass instrument and keyboard play chords indicated by "shorthand" figures.	Continuo is heard in instrumental and vocal ensembles throughout the period.
Early orchestra takes shape.	Typical ensemble includes strings, oboes, bassoons, and continuo.	Johann Sebastian Bach, *Orchestral suites*
Keys and key signatures become established.	Composers use harmony as a structural element of works.	Johann Sebastian Bach, *48 Preludes and Fugues*

CLASSICAL 1750–1820

Feature	Explanation	Key composers/works
Sonata principle (forms) established as a useful structure.	Three-part sonata form consists of exposition, development, and recapitulation.	Features widely as basis for first movements of sonatas, symphonies, and concertos.
Symphony becomes the favorite form for orchestral music.	Four-movement structure is established: fast-slow-dance-lively.	Josef Haydn, *Symphony no 100*; Wolfgang Amadeus Mozart, *Symphony no 41*
Development of the orchestra—notably at Mannheim, which has a famously musical Court.	The modern symphony orchestra emerges with strings, flutes, oboes, clarinets, bassoons, horns, trumpets, and drums.	Johann Stamitz, *Symphony in E♭ major*
Instruments are made simpler to play in every key.	Composers can write music of greater technical difficulty in more extreme keys.	Wolfgang Amadeus Mozart, *Horn Concerto no 3*; Ludwig van Beethoven, "Spring" violin sonata
Chamber music, especially the string quartet, features prominently.	Most famous composers, notably Haydn and Mozart, played quartets with friends.	Josef Haydn, *Quartets op 76*; Ludwig van Beethoven, *Quartet op 131*; Franz Schubert, *Piano trio no 1*

ROMANTICISM 1820–1900

Feature	Explanation	Key composers/works
Composers prize originality in their quest to express emotion and tell stories in music.	Literary works inspire opera and song, and new forms of program music, such as the tone poem.	Carl Maria von Weber, *Der Freischütz*; Robert Schumann, *Kinderszenen*; Richard Strauss, *Don Quixote*
Though still used, traditional forms such as symphony become less important.	Rise of freer forms of concert overture, tone poem, and suite.	Hector Berlioz, *Symphonie fantastique*; Franz Liszt, *Hamlet*; Peter Ilych Tchaikovsky, *Romeo and Juliet*
Opera becomes concerned with the emotions of characters and relationships.	Italian opera features dazzling singing, while German opera explores myth and symbolism.	Gioachino Rossini, *The Barber of Seville*; Giuseppe Verdi, *La Traviata*; Richard Wagner, *Tristan and Isolde*
Orchestra grows further to include harps, and extra wind, brass, and percussion.	New instruments offer vivid musical colors and special effects.	Hector Berlioz, *Harold in Italy*; Richard Strauss, *Ein Heldenleben*
Piano music moves center stage as the public recital becomes popular and virtuosity flourishes.	The expressive piano attracts major composers, dazzling performers, and enthusiastic audiences.	Frédéric Chopin, *Preludes*; Felix Mendelssohn, *Songs without Words*; Franz Liszt, *Sonata in B minor*

1900 AND BEYOND

Feature	Explanation	Key composers/works
Music takes off in different directions.	Many composers try to break with the past.	Composers develop individual "voices."
Orchestral music takes many different forms as the symphony declines in popularity.	Some composers write for standard orchestra; others invent their own combinations.	Richard Strauss, *Don Juan*; Igor Stravinsky, *The Rite of Spring*; Dmitri Shostakovich, symphonies
Neoclassicism is adopted by a few composers in some of their works.	Neoclassical composers look back to old musical styles for inspiration.	Igor Stravinsky, *Pulcinella*; Maurice Ravel, *Le Tombeau de Couperin*
Jazz flourishes as a form in its own right.	Its influence is heard in music by mainstream composers.	Igor Stravinsky, *Ebony Concerto*; George Gershwin, *Rhapsody in Blue*
Serialism is Arnold Schoenberg's response to the breakdown of tonality (key structures).	Based on the 12 whole steps of a scale, it was further developed by Alban Berg and Anton Webern.	Arnold Schoenberg, *Five Orchestral Pieces*; Alban Berg, *Violin Concerto*; Anton Webern, *Variations for Orchestra*
Minimalism uses deliberately limited material.	Material is comprehensively repeated, developed, and transformed.	Steve Reich, *Clapping Music*; John Adams, *Short Ride in a Fast Machine*
Musical theater becomes popular in the USA and later in Europe.	Similar to 19th-century light opera, music theater is a popular entertainment form.	Leonard Bernstein, *West Side Story*; Andrew Lloyd Webber, *Cats*
Technology is transforming the way music is created, performed, and shared.	Composing and performing music is no longer confined to professionals.	Karlheinz Stockhausen, *Stimmung*

Instrument families

Family groups

Instruments are grouped in families according to how they make sound. Orchestral instruments (shown here inside the circles) form each family's heart. Related instruments (outside the circles) are heard in modern popular music, jazz, and folk.

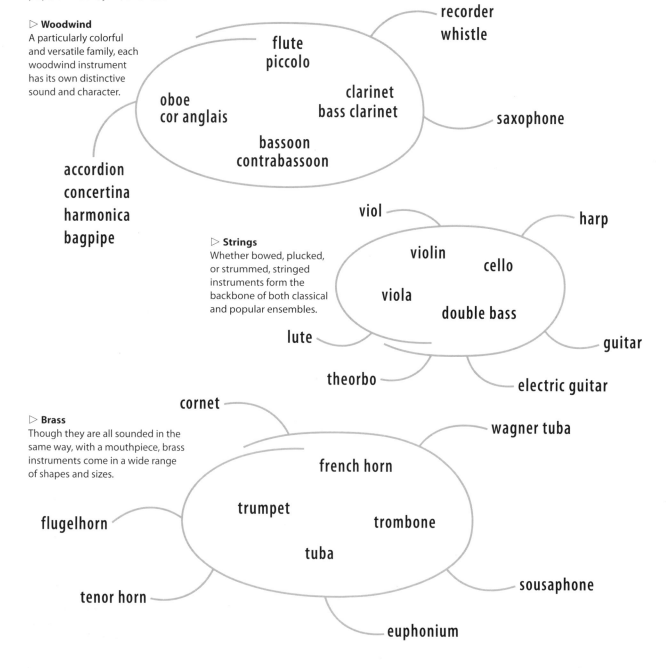

▷ **Woodwind**
A particularly colorful and versatile family, each woodwind instrument has its own distinctive sound and character.

recorder
whistle

flute
piccolo

clarinet
bass clarinet

oboe
cor anglais

saxophone

bassoon
contrabassoon

accordion
concertina
harmonica
bagpipe

viol

harp

violin

cello

▷ **Strings**
Whether bowed, plucked, or strummed, stringed instruments form the backbone of both classical and popular ensembles.

viola

double bass

lute

guitar

theorbo

electric guitar

cornet

wagner tuba

▷ **Brass**
Though they are all sounded in the same way, with a mouthpiece, brass instruments come in a wide range of shapes and sizes.

french horn

trumpet

trombone

flugelhorn

tuba

sousaphone

tenor horn

euphonium

▽ Keyboards
One of music's most useful devices, a keyboard allows a single player to produce a large range of notes and effects.

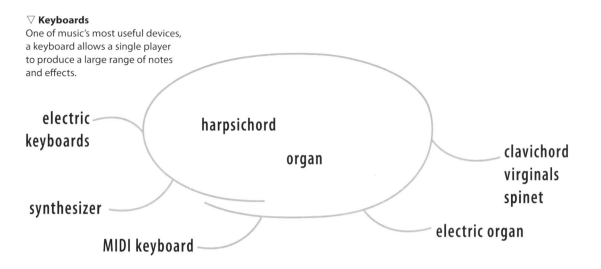

electric keyboards

harpsichord

organ

clavichord
virginals
spinet

synthesizer

MIDI keyboard

electric organ

▽ Percussion
Music's largest and most diverse family, percussion instruments are found on every continent, and in most musical ensembles.

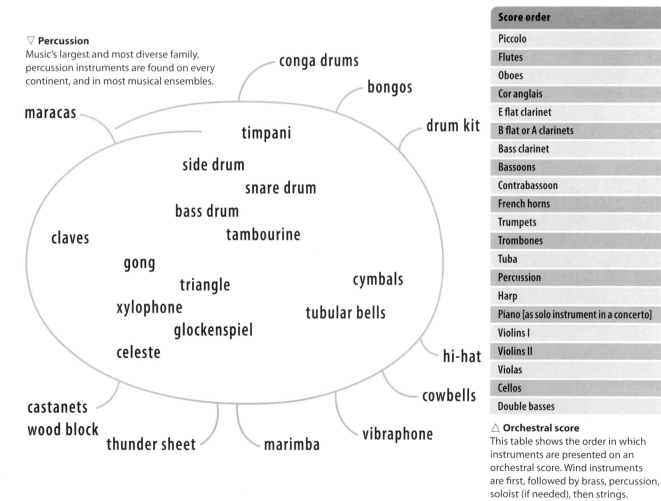

conga drums

bongos

maracas

drum kit

timpani

side drum

snare drum

bass drum

tambourine

claves

gong

triangle

cymbals

xylophone

tubular bells

glockenspiel

celeste

hi-hat

castanets
wood block

cowbells

thunder sheet

marimba

vibraphone

Score order
Piccolo
Flutes
Oboes
Cor anglais
E flat clarinet
B flat or A clarinets
Bass clarinet
Bassoons
Contrabassoon
French horns
Trumpets
Trombones
Tuba
Percussion
Harp
Piano [as solo instrument in a concerto]
Violins I
Violins II
Violas
Cellos
Double basses

△ **Orchestral score**
This table shows the order in which instruments are presented on an orchestral score. Wind instruments are first, followed by brass, percussion, soloist (if needed), then strings.

Glossary

a cappella
Unaccompanied vocal performance.

accent
A stress on a particular note or beat.

accompaniment
A musical part that supports the lead instrument or vocal part.

acoustic
An instrument that does not use electrical amplification, or the music such an instrument produces.

alto
The highest of the broken male voices and lowest of the female voices. An instrument lower in pitch than a treble instrument.

aria
A solo vocal piece in an opera or an oratorio.

arpeggio
A chord in which the notes are played separately.

arrangement
The adaptation of a piece of music for different instruments or voices.

articulation
The technique used by a musician to affect the length a note is sounded for, or the transition between notes.

atonal
Describes music without a recognizable key.

badinerie
In 18th-century music, a light instrumental piece.

bar
A segment of time containing a fixed number of beats. Also called a measure.

baritone
The male voice between tenor and bass. An instrument sounding within this range.

Baroque
The period between 1600 and 1750.

bass
The lowest of the male voices. The lowest part of a chord or piece of music.

basso continuo
See continuo

beat
The basic unit of time from which a rhythm is built.

blue note
A flattened note—usually the third, fifth, or seventh—in a scale, often used by blues and jazz musicians.

bow
A long, thin piece of wood with horsehair stretched along it, used to play string instruments. Used as a verb, it means to play with a bow.

break
A short, improvised or sharply contrasting passage or pause in a piece of music..

bridge
In a piece of music, a passage that makes a transition from one section to another. On a string instrument, the upright piece of wood over which the strings are stretched.

broken chord
A chord in which the notes are each played in turn.

cadence
The closing sequence of a musical phrase or composition.

cadenza
A passage within a concerto designed to show off the soloist's skill. Usually unaccompanied.

caesura
A pause in a piece of music.

call-and-response
A musical phrase in which the first part is answered by a second part, often played or sung by a different musician.

canon
A piece in which separate voices or instruments enter one by one, repeating the same melody.

cantata
A piece of music for solo voices, choir, and orchestra, usually in several movements.

cantor
The leader of a choir.

chamber music
Music for small groups of two or more instruments, such as duets, trios, and quartets.

chanson
Medieval or Renaissance French part-song. Later came to refer to any song to French lyrics.

chord
Any simultaneous combination of notes.

chorus
A group of singers. A piece of choral music. Part of a song that follows the verse.

chromatic
Based on the scale of all 12 half steps in an octave.

Classical
The period between 1750 and 1820. Also used (with a lower case c: classical) as a general term

meaning Western music intended for a formal context, as opposed to popular music.

clavier
An old-fashioned word meaning keyboard instrument.

clef
A sign placed at the beginning of a musical staff to indicate the pitch of the notes on the staff.

coda
A final section of a piece, often distinct from the overall structure.

concertante
A 17th- or 18th-century piece with parts for solo instruments.

concerto
A large-scale piece for a solo instrument and an orchestra.

consonance
A chord or interval that sounds pleasing to the ear.

continuo
An accompaniment used in Baroque music, played on a keyboard and other bass instruments. Also called basso continuo.

contrabass
Any member of an instrument family that is lower in pitch than the bass instrument of the same type—for example, contrabass clarinet.

contralto
Another word for alto, but only used for female singers.

contrapuntal
Music that uses counterpoint.

counter melody
A secondary but subordinate melody that is played at the same time as a lead melody.

counterpoint
The simultaneous playing or singing of two or more equally important melodic lines.

damper
A device that deadens the vibrations of strings to reduce the volume of a note. In a piano it is a pad that deadens each note as the corresponding key is released.

descant
A melody or counterpoint that accompanies a melody and is higher in pitch. An instrument of higher than normal pitch.

diatonic
Based on a scale of seven natural degrees—five whole steps and two half steps.

dissonance
A combination of notes that clash with one another.

distortion (clipping)
The effect produced by overloading an amplifier so that the sound is distorted. Most commonly associated with the electric guitar.

duet
A composition written for two instruments or voices.

duple meter
A meter with two, or a multiple of two, beats in a measure.

dynamics
Differences in volume of a piece or section of music. Also the notation system used to indicate these differences.

enharmonic note
These are notes that have the same pitch as each other but different names; for example, C♯ and D♭ are enharmonic notes.

ensemble
A group of musicians.

exposition
The part of a composition where the principal musical themes are first introduced.

falsetto
A technique used by male singers to extend the top of their range.

fantasia
A loosely structured, usually instrumental, composition.

fermata
A symbol used in musical notation over a note, chord, or rest to indicate that it should be sustained for longer than its value indicates. Also called a pause.

figure
A recurring sequence of notes that acts as a musical motif.

figured bass
A bass part with numbers specifying the harmonies to be played above it.

fill
A short passage that runs between the main sections of a melody. Common in pop music.

finale
The last movement of a Classical composition.

finger-picking
A style of guitar-playing in which the right thumb plays the bass strings and the index and middle fingers pick out a melody on the treble strings.

flat
A note that has been lowered by a half step. Also describes an instrument or voice that is out of tune by being lower than the intended pitch.

fugato
A passage written in the manner of a fugue.

fugue
A complex contrapuntal piece in two or more parts.

galant
An elegant musical style of the 18th century.

ground bass
A repeated pattern in the bass part of a musical composition.

half step
Also known as a semitone, this is the smallest musical interval in diatonic harmony

harmonic
A harmonic series consists of the note played and an ascending progression of overtones, which determine the individual timbre of an instrument.

harmony
The grouping of notes to form chords.

homophonic
A style in which a melody line is supported by chordal harmony and a solid bass.

hornpipe
A fast dance tune, often instrumental, originating from 16th-century sailors' dances.

hymn
A religious song that uses the same melody for successive verses and choruses, designed to be sung by a congregation during Christian worship.

improvisation
The art of composing while performing, without the use of written music.

instrumentation
The scoring of music for particular instruments.

interlude
A short piece of music to be played between main sections of a composition.

interval
The difference in pitch between two notes.

intonation
The pitching of a voice or instrument, or the musician's skill at sounding notes in tune.

inversion
Changing the order of the notes in an interval or chord.

jig
A lively dance associated with Celtic music, which is the origin of the gigue that often closes Baroque dance suites.

key
The tonal center of a piece of music, based on the first note (tonic) of the scale.

key signature
A group of sharps or flats at the beginning of a staff that indicates which key a piece of music is played in.

keynote
The first note of a scale, also called the tonic.

leading note
The seventh note of a scale, a half step below the tonic.

leitmotif
A recurring musical phrase that relates to a character, emotion, or object.

libretto
The text of an opera.

lick
In jazz and popular music, a short pattern or phrase that is usually a single melodic line.

lyrics
The words to a song.

major
This term can be applied to a key signature or any chord, triad, or scale in a major key. Music in a major key is often described as sounding happy or bright. Major intervals are a half step larger than minor intervals.

Mass
Main service of the Roman Catholic Church.

measure
A segment of time containing a fixed number of beats. Also called a bar.

medley
An arrangement of several different compositions run together as one piece.

melody
A series of notes that create a tune or theme.

meter
A recurring, rhythmic pattern of stressed and unstressed beats.

mezzo-soprano
The lowest soprano voice.

minimalism
A modern musical style based on repeated short patterns.

minor
The term minor can be applied to a key signature, or chord, triad, or scale in a minor key. Music in a minor key is said to sound dark or sad. Minor intervals are a half step smaller than major intervals.

minuet and trio
A graceful dance in 3/4 time, normally in three sections.

modes
Seven-note scales, commonly used in the Middle Ages and in folk music.

modulation
A shift from one key to another.

monody
A single, unaccompanied melodic line.

mordent
An ornament similar to a trill.

motet
A highly varied choral composition usually without instrumental accompaniment.

motif
A recurring figure, often used to refer to a character or idea.

movement
A self-contained section of a larger work.

musicology
The academic study of music.

mute
A device that reduces the volume or changes the tone of an instrument.

natural
A note that is not sharp or flat. The symbol that cancels sharps and flats.

notation
The symbols used to represent a piece of music visually.

note values
The duration of a note—how long it should be played.

octave
The interval between one pitch and another with double or half its frequency—for example, between the notes C and C on a keyboard.

octet
A group of eight singers or musicians.

ondes martenot
An early electronic keyboard instrument.

opera
Drama in which the characters sing, usually written for full orchestra, soloists, and chorus.

operetta
A light opera, often including some spoken dialogue.

opus
A Latin word meaning "work," often abbreviated "op." and used with a number to catalog a composer's pieces.

oratorio
A sacred work for voices and instrumental accompaniment.

orchestra
A large ensemble, with players divided into strings, woodwind, brass, and percussion.

orchestration
The art of writing for an orchestra.

ornament
An embellishment of a note or chord.

overtone
Part of the harmonic series of a single note.

overture
An instrumental introduction to an opera or ballet.

part-song
An unaccompanied song for two or more voices.

passage
Any section of a piece of music.

Passion music
A musical setting of the suffering of Jesus from the Last Supper to the Crucifixion.

pedal bass
A held note in the bass.

pentatonic scale
A scale of five notes.

phrase
A group of notes that form a unit of music.

pitch
The position of a sound in relation to the whole range of tonal sounds.

pizzicato
A style of playing stringed instruments that are usually played with a bow, by plucking the strings with the fingers.

plainsong
Medieval church music, also known as plainchant.

polyphony
A style of writing in classical music in which all parts are of equal importance.

prelude
An introductory piece of music.

principal
The lead musician in a section of the orchestra, responsible for leading the group and playing any solos.

program music
Music written to tell a story, or describe a scene using sound.

progression
The transition from one note to the next.

quartet
A group of four instruments or voices.

quodlibet
The combination of two or more folk tunes in counterpoint.

range
The range of an instrument or voice is the distance from the lowest to the highest pitch it can play or sing.

recital
A performance of classical music by a soloist or small group.

recitative
Style of singing in opera and oratorio that uses the rhythm of ordinary speech and is used for dialogue.

reed
A thin piece of wood, metal, or plastic that is attached to the mouthpiece of a woodwind instrument and vibrates to produce a sound.

reel
A fast-paced dance tune common in Irish and Scottish folk music.

refrain
The line or lines that are repeated in a piece of music, for example the chorus of a song.

Renaissance
The period between 1400 and 1600.

repertoire
The range of works an individual or group is able to perform, or the range of works in a genre.

Requiem
A piece of music written as a memorial, or a musical setting of a Requiem Mass celebrating the dead.

rest
A gap in the music, when the player or singer does not produce any sound. As with note values, there are symbols that indicate how long a rest should be held.

rhythm
The pattern of relative durations and stresses on the notes of a piece of music, commonly organized into measures.

rhythm section
In popular and jazz music, instruments that focus on the rhythm and accompaniment rather than the melody.

riff
A short, repeated series of notes, that forms part of the melody.

Romantic
The period between 1820 and 1900.

rondo
A musical form in which the first section recurs several times.

sample
A short extract from an existing recording that is used in a new recording.

scale
A series of notes that define the key of a piece.

score
A musical composition in written or printed form showing all the parts on separate staves.

serenade
A love song or a calm, light piece of music.

serialism
A system of atonal composition that uses fixed sequences of the 12 notes of the chromatic scale.

sharp
A note that has been raised by a half step. Also describes an instrument that is out of tune by being higher than the intended pitch.

slur
To perform a series of notes smoothly, without breaks between each note.

solo
A piece or section of a piece performed by an individual instrument or voice.

sonata
An instrumental piece in several movements for one or more players.

song
Text set to music for vocal performance.

sonority
The quality of sounding deep and rich.

soprano
The highest of the four standard singing voices.

staccato
A performance technique whereby each note is very short and clipped.

staff
The grid of five horizontal lines on which music is written.

string quartet
An ensemble of four musicians playing stringed instruments, usually a first and second violin, a viola, and a cello.

suite
A work, usually instrumental, made up of several movements. In Baroque music, these are typically contrasting dance movements all in the same key.

suspension
A note that is held, often creating a dissonance, before being resolved by falling to the next note down.

symphony
A large-scale work for full orchestra, usually in three or more movements.

syncopation
Accentuation of a subordinate beat rather than the main beat.

tango
Argentinian dance form and music with its roots in African dance and rhythms.

tempo
The pace of a work, usually indicated in beats per minute.

tenor
The second highest adult male voice after alto, or an instrument that sounds in this range.

tessitura
The range that occurs most often within a piece of music.

theme
A simple melody used as a motif.

tie
A curved line used in musical notation that connects the heads of two notes of the same pitch and indicates that they should be played as a single note.

timbre
The particular quality of a sound that allows a listener to distinguish one instrument or voice from another.

time signature
The numbers that indicate the number and note value of beats in a measure.

tonality
The system of major and minor scales and keys that forms the basis of Western music.

tone
The quality or timbre of a pitch sounded.

tonic
The first note of any diatonic scale. Also called the keynote.

transcription
Writing music down.

transposition
The setting of a melody into a different key.

treble
The highest unbroken male voice. The highest instrument or part in a piece of music. The treble clef indicates the notes above Middle C on the piano.

tremolo
The rapid repetition of a single note to create a trembling effect.

triad
A chord of three notes, which can be broken down into two intervals of a third.

trill
An ornament involving the rapid alternation of two adjacent notes.

trio
A group of three musicians or voices. The second section of a piece in minuet and trio form.

whole step
An interval that consists of two half steps.

Visual index of symbols

Symbol	Action/Description
	staff
	ledger lines
	treble clef
	bass clef
	alto clef or C clef
	tenor clef or C clef
	bar lines
	double bar lines (for a key change or new section)
	double bar lines (for the end of the piece or movement)
	bracket
	brace
	whole note (4 beats)
	half note (2 beats)
	quarter note (1 beat)
	eighth note ($^1/_2$ beat)
	sixteenth note ($^1/_4$ beat)

Symbol	Action/Description
	beamed notes
	dotted half note (3 beats)
	dotted quarter note (1$^1/_2$ beats)
	dotted eighth note ($^3/_4$ beat)
	time signature
	common time (4/4)
	cut time (2/2)
	whole rest
	half rest
	quarter rest
	eighth rest
	sixteenth rest
	dotted half rest
	dotted quarter rest
	dotted eighth rest
	tie
	slur

Symbol	Action/Description
(triplet notation, 3)	triplet
(6/8 duplet notation, 2)	duplet
♯	sharp
♭	flat
♮	natural
♭♭	double flat
×	double sharp
tr	trill
∽	turn
∾	inverted turn
↝	mordent
↯	inverted mordent
(grace note)	acciaccatura
(grace note)	appoggiatura
(slanted line)	glissando
p	piano
pp	pianissimo
mp	mezzo-piano
f	forte
ff	fortissimo

Symbol	Action/Description
mf	mezzo-forte
fp	forte-piano
sfz	sforzando
<	crescendo
>	diminuendo
𝄐	fermata (pause)
(staccato dot)	staccato
(tenuto line)	tenuto
>	accent
(arpeggiated chord)	arpeggiated chord
‖	repeat marks
Ped.	use sustaining pedal
✳	release sustaining pedal
D.S.	dal segno
𝄋	segno
D.C.	da capo
⊕	coda
♩ = 60	metronome mark
(treble clef with key signature)	key signature

Index

Acknowledgments

DORLING KINDERSLEY would like to thank: Jeremy Hughes for his advice and for checking all music examples; Ruth O'Rourke for proofreading; and John Noble for the index.

Anne-Marie Stanley would like to thank Kevin Murray for checking the music examples on her pages.

The publisher would like to thank the following for their kind permission to reproduce their photographs:

(Key: a-above; b-below/bottom; c-center; f-far; l-left; r-right; t-top)

11 Dreamstime.com: Thomas Perkins (br). **18** Dreamstime.com: Michal Janošek (bc). **25** Dreamstime.com: Shannon Fagan (bl). **31** Corbis: Leemage (br). **33** Dreamstime.com: Trak (cra). **64** Dreamstime.com: Georgios Kollidas (cr). **75** Dreamstime.com: Georgios Kollidas (bc). **76** Dreamstime.com: Denys Kuvaiev (bl). **81** Getty Images: De Agostini / G. Dagli Orti (tc). **84** 123RF.com: svglass (bc). **86** Corbis: Hulton-Deutsch Collection (cr). **95** Getty Images: Slaven Vlasic (tr). **97** Corbis: Bettmann (bc). **103** Dreamstime.com: Jackq (bc). **110** Getty Images: David Redfern (cra). **115** Corbis: Amanaimages / Miyako (cr). **119** Dreamstime.com: Mozzyb (br). **120** Alamy Images: Chronicle (crb). **131** Corbis: Neal Preston (bc). **133** Dreamstime.com: Skif55 (bc). **134** Getty Images: Michael Putland (bc). **135** Getty Images: ChinaFotoPress (br). **137** Getty Images: Jeff Kravitz (cra). **140** Dreamstime.com: 1000words (bc). **142** Getty Images: Frans Schellekens (crb). **143** Corbis: Alinari Archives / Luciano Pedicini (bc). **149** Getty Images: Hulton Archive (bc). **150** Corbis: Leemage (br). **165** Getty Images: Gerti Deutsch (bc). **167** Dreamstime.com: Simon Peare (bl). **169** Corbis: (bl). **174** Dorling Kindersley: Barnabas Kindersley (bc). **179** Dreamstime.com: Albanili (br). **180** Dorling Kindersley: Richard Leeney (bl). **189** Dreamstime.com: Igor Dolgov (bc). **191** Getty Images: CBS Photo Archive (cra). **205** Alamy Images: Heritage Image Partnership Ltd (br). **207** 123RF.com: Georgios Kollidas (cra). **208** Getty Images: Culture Club (cr). **209** Dreamstime.com: Georgios Kollidas (br). **210** Getty Images: Dea Picture Library (br). **211** Dreamstime.com: Georgios Kollidas (br). **213** Corbis: Austrian Archives (crb). **219** Dreamstime.com: Ivan Sinayko (br). **221** Corbis: Michael Ochs Archives (crb). **223** Corbis: Sunset Boulevard (br)

All other images © Dorling Kindersley
For further information see: **www.dkimages.com**